The Ranch on the Cariboo

The Ranch on the Cariboo

ALAN FRY

TouchWood Editions Ltd.
Victoria, BC
www.touchwoodeditions.com

This book is distributed by The Heritage Group, #108-17665 66A Avenue, Surrey, BC, Canada, V3S 2A7.

Cover and book design by Retta Moorman; book layout by Katherine Hale and Darlene Nickull.

TouchWood Editions acknowledges the financial support for our publishing program from The Canada Council for the Arts, the Government of Canada through the Book Publishing Industry Development Program (BPDIP) and the Province of British Columbia through the British Columbia Arts Council.

This book is set in Goudy.

Printed and bound in Canada by Friesens, Altona, Manitoba.

National Library of Canada Cataloguing in Publication Data

Fry, Alan, 1931-
    The ranch on the Cariboo / Alan Fry.
    ISBN 1-894898-02-8

    1. Fry, Alan, 1931-   2. Ranch life—British Columbia—Cariboo Region. 3. Cariboo Region (B.C.)—Biography. I. Title.
FC3845.C3Z49 2002   971.1'7503'092   C2002-911163-3
F1089.C3F79 2002

BRITISH
COLUMBIA
ARTS COUNCIL
We acknowledge the support of the Province of British Columbia
through the British Columbia Arts Council

The Canada Council | Le Conseil des Arts
for the Arts | du Canada

DEDICATION

To the Old Man

Alan Fry and his father Julian are seen here atop Johnny in the early 1930s.

CONTENTS

FOREWORD

This book by Alan Fry is probably the best ever written on ranch life in the Cariboo. His account of everyday events is so perceptive and so true to the mark that all we country types yearn to re-experience the joys and miseries of this way of life. And the miseries are many. In the winter, there is the biting cold experienced in long cattle drives, when only intermittent dismounting from the saddle horse and walking averts frozen feet. Then there is the agony of biting insects in the summer; the mosquitos, no-see-ums, black flies, horseflies, deer flies and gnats swarm in clouds and leave welts over all exposed flesh. During all months of the year, hard, monotonous work seems never-ending. In the summer there is the cutting and curing of hay, and in the cold of winter the same hay must be spread out on the snow for the hungry cattle.

Alan brings out well the joys that make all the miseries bearable. There is a heady, exhilarating sense of freedom. A freedom to run one's horse at breakneck speed through unspoiled woods, freedom to give chase and tree a marauding bear, freedom to ride with brother Roger, on a moment's notice, over miles of wilderness trail to visit two old bachelor friends eking out a hard-scrabble living on a lonely homestead.

Alan finds a further richness in the isolated Cariboo country: the friendship formed between himself and the families on neighbouring ranches. There are the earthy Hallers with their common-sense approach to life, the entrepreneurs Buster and Millie Hamilton on their Spout Lake Guest Ranch, the old stock ranchers the Bert Wright family, and the Felkers, descendants of German pioneers. Through the years these friends gave love, advice and support to the Fry family, particularly to Alan. And while they weren't close geographically, they were always there to give wise counsel and practical teaching to the somewhat innocent Fry family.

Noteworthy is the love and respect shown to Alan's venerable father, Julian, a product of a prominent English family and English public schools, whose presence brought a sense of civility to a rather rude environment. His father, when greatly exasperated, reverted to his upbringing and cursed mightily in French.

The Ranch on the Cariboo covers a number of years in Alan's life, and the lifestyle exacts a penalty: while his youth was attended with much freedom, there was also a good deal of isolation. This made it difficult for him to relate to the outside world and resulted in a number of tumultuous and unsettled years. It also led to an ineptness at pressing his suit with his chosen member of the fair sex; however, true love overcame these disadvantages.

The isolation and hardships of frontier life grind away at relationships: any weakness is exposed, and the vessels of the potter are shattered. This is evidenced by the marital difficulties of his parents and their eventual divorce, and the severing of ties between Rex and Tom, who had tried to make a success of an isolated cattle ranch. In the end, the ranch on the Cariboo failed too, and was disbanded and the family scattered.

The Frys learned two traditional pearls of Cariboo wisdom. The first is that cattle cannot be sustained through a winter on wild hay without heavy losses and, from this, that once a cow goes down on a winter feedlot, she will never rise again. The second is that no cattle ranch depending on wild hay can succeed. These truths were reaffirmed on the ranch in the Cariboo, and the consequences spelled disaster for the Frys' ranching venture.

The Ranch on the Cariboo is a good book, and while it may not make a pretty sight to the tractor jockeys, by damn it is authentic. I should know, because I was raised on a similar ranch just 18 miles north.

Eldon Lee

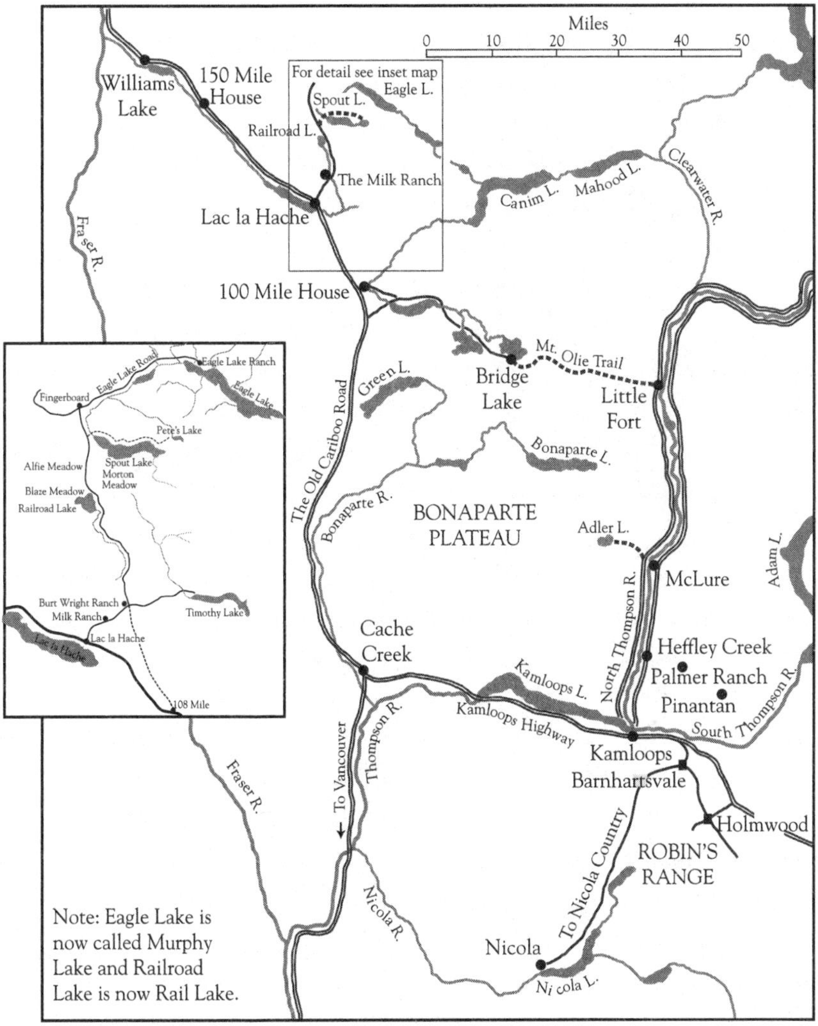
Miles
0
10
20
30
40
50
For detail see inset map
Williams Lake
150 Mile House
Spout L.
Eagle L.
Railroad L.
The Milk Ranch
Lac la Hache
Canim L.
Mahood L.
Clearwater R.
Fraser R.
100 Mile House
Mt. Olie Trail
Bridge Lake
Little Fort
Green L.
The Old Cariboo Road
Bonaparte L.
Bonaparte R.
BONAPARTE PLATEAU
Adler L.
McLure
Adam L.
North Thompson R.
Cache Creek
Heffley Creek
Palmer Ranch
Pinantan
Kamloops L.
Kamloops Highway
South Thompson R.
Thompson R.
To Vancouver
Kamloops
Barnhartsvale
Holmwood
Fraser R.
ROBIN'S RANGE
To Nicola Country
Nicola R.
Nicola
Nicola L.
Eagle Lake Ranch
Fingerboard
Eagle Lake Road
Eagle Lake
Pete's Lake
Alfie Meadow
Spout Lake
Morton Meadow
Blaze Meadow
Railroad Lake
Burt Wright Ranch
Milk Ranch
Timothy Lake
Lac la Hache
Lac la Hache
108 Mile
Note: Eagle Lake is now called Murphy Lake and Railroad Lake is now Rail Lake.

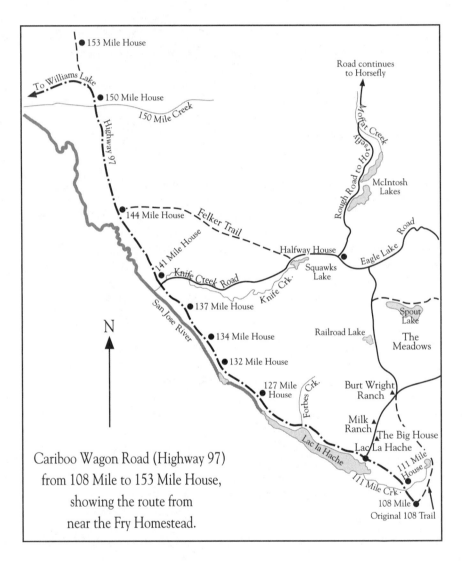

● 153 Mile House

To Williams Lake

● 150 Mile House

150 Mile Creek

Highway 97

Road continues
to Horsefly

Moffat Creek

Rough Road to Horsefly

● 144 Mile House

Felker Trail

McIntosh
Lakes

● 141 Mile House

Halfway House

Eagle Lake Road

Knife Creek Road

Knife Crk.

Squawks
Lake

Spout
Lake

● 137 Mile House

San Jose River

Railroad Lake

The
Meadows

N

● 134 Mile House

● 132 Mile House

127 Mile
House

Forbes Crk.

Burt Wright
Ranch

Milk
Ranch

The Big House

Lac la Hache

Lac La Hache

Cariboo Wagon Road (Highway 97)
from 108 Mile to 153 Mile House,
showing the route from
near the Fry Homestead.

111 Mile Crk.

111 Mile
House

108 Mile
Original 108 Trail

BEAR

I t was the summer I was twelve and had to become a man. Halfway around the world the labour force of the nation fought an alien war, the few men behind went into heavy industry, and mainly children gathered the harvest for the country's larder.

It was Gussy Haller's job to teach me. The son of a Pennsylvania Dutchman of gold-rush days and a Fraser River Native woman, Gussy was a fine man, raised in hard days, and he'd had a pitchfork in and out of his hands for fifty years. Life itself to him was hay and horses and hard, unrelenting work in broiling heat or bitter cold. I could have no better master.

His wife, Maggie, cooked for the crew, while Maize, fifteen, and Marvin, thirteen, worked in the field. Verne, too young to hay, helped his mother about camp. Roger, my brother, also thirteen, and Johnny Hamilton, another old-timer like Gussy, made up the rest of the Old Man's crew.

It was the beginning of the haying season and we were at the Milk Ranch, in the Cariboo country of central British Columbia, the home place of the Old Man's cow outfit. We had no truck with milch cows — the name — lay in history. When one Isaac Ogden, son of a Hudson's Bay Company factor, ran a store and fur trading business on the Cariboo road around the turn of the century and before, he found there was a market for milk products, mostly butter, in the stagecoach trade. He owned these fields and here he

1

kept an ill-bred bunch of cows from which, somehow, he extracted milk. The Old Man had bought from Isaac's son, Percy, who still owned the store and traded for fur but had no use for milkers.

The Milk Ranch sat astraddle the Eagle Lake road, a track which left the highway at Lac la Hache, winding through the timber into the heart of the great wilderness beyond us, becoming no more than a wagon trail between the trees.

Fifteen miles out on the Eagle Lake road from the Milk Ranch and on the points of a triangle several miles from each other lay the wild hay meadows, which gave us the rest of the feed we needed to winter a hundred and thirty head of cattle carrying the J over E brand and seventy-odd horses. These meadows were known as the Blaze, the Alfie, and the Morton respectively, each after the man who first had taken it up, built a cabin, scrounged a few cows, and tried to start a ranch in the wilderness. Morton had them all when the Old Man bought from him. They were no more than great glorified bogs, lakes of mud overlain by a sedge root sod, light green patches in a darker green forest. Still, the best of the three, the Morton, was good for a hundred tons of feed in a decent season.

Running this ranch meant two complete circuits a year, the first in the summer with a haying crew to cut and stack the feed while the cattle were out on the summer range, the second in the winter with a team, a sleigh, and the cow herd, pitching it all out again, keeping the cows alive. The horses rustled till they couldn't stand it any longer, then came on the feed ground with the cows. We were now, therefore, at the beginning of the first circuit, the haying circuit.

We used an ingenious derrick system to raise the hay, still used in the Cariboo today. Two long poles are the basis of it. These need to be fifty to sixty feet long, strong and dry. They are raised in a pair, tied at the peak, their butts apart by the width of the stack, guy lines fore and aft holding them up and letting them swing the needed distance. A cable and pulley system, attached to them before they are raised, draws up the hay.

Raising the poles gave the Old Man his most trying moments. There was the poor fellow sweating away with a pair of pliers, trying to make a satisfactory tie at the peak of the raising frame, an inverted V of two lighter poles propped under the fore guy line to give the main poles a lift when the best team of horses on the ranch would begin the all-important pull.

It was nearly noon and the poles had failed to go up twice already. The perspiration poured down over his glasses and he could hardly see. He had not had a pipe all morning and he loved his pipe. The mosquitoes were so thick they would have had to be smaller if you were going to pack any more in, and every once in a while he'd throw down his pliers, curse mightily, and slap blindly at the tormenting insects.

Those of us in with the first loads of hay were standing around waiting for a derrick to raise them with. We had all kinds of advice to offer, advice the Old Man needed the way he needed the mosquitoes. The old hands had some advice too, but they kept it to themselves, all the while the payroll going on, nothing being accomplished.

Maybe the Old Man would reach the swearing-in-French stage. An Englishman, he'd been in France as a boy. He may have forgotten whatever else he'd learned, but he kept alive the art of a foreign profanity in resounding Gaulish syllables. If a boy hadn't the brains to get the devil out of the way when he heard it coming, he soon found out he ought to have. When the raising of the stacking poles came by such bad times as to be accompanied by swearing in French, there could easily be some ructions.

Yet if raising the stacking poles had its trying moments, running a crew of children was every bit as difficult. Theoretically, we needn't work nor the Old Man make us do so. But in fact what choice was there? The hay had to go up or the cattle starve come winter. And what twelve-year-old boy, offered a place on the crew, wouldn't take it ahead of child's games around the cookhouse?

Still, there is more to being a man than wishing it were so. One morning the rains began and put an end for the time to our haying.

3

The Old Man told Gussy, Johnny, and Roger to bring axes, Marvin, to harness a team for the big wagon. He reckoned as long as it was raining and he had a crew on he might as well build some fence.

He turned to me. "You and Maize stay with Mrs. Haller and help with the washing." We had an agitating washtub operated by a lever, a jolly modern piece of equipment for that neck of the woods, I can tell you. The lever, in turn, was handily operated by a small boy or girl.

The disappointment was too much. To do woman's work after bearing so much in the field to do man's work was a letdown beyond anything the Old Man might have anticipated. Right there in front of the crew I cried, oblivious to the disgusting scene I created.

The Old Man relented, wisely or not I cannot say. "All right, get old King and harness him. You'll skid rails, but you remember this: if it's too much for you, don't you fuss to me about it."

So I went with the men, but my shame to have cried was worse than had I done woman's work and learned what any self-respecting backwoods ranch hand discovers before he's done: cooking and washing can be anybody's chore and he is a poor man who can't take his turn when need be.

And I skidded rails, gathering them in bundles where the men had split them into fifteen-foot lengths out of jack pine, wrapping the heavy logging chain around the end of the bundle, scrambling up and down from old King's back, pinching my legs under the backband when the tugs tightened, banging my teeth on the hames when I had to duck to avoid a branch. But I kept my hardships to myself for I knew I'd work a long time with my mouth shut tight before the burning inner shame for what I'd done would leave me.

We built a fair chunk of fence, at that. It was Russell fence, an ingenious stake-and-rail structure held together by heavy wire and named, I'm told, after the man who invented it; the panels thirteen feet long, five rails to the panel and of course a set of stakes every thirteen feet to hold the rails in place. Many a man in the Cariboo who hadn't his own outfit made much of his living contracting to build fence at anything from two hundred and fifty to four hundred dollars a mile, depending on many things, from how good the man was to what price the rancher got for beef the fall before.

Yet for all that hard work, there was play to make it lighter. In the corral there were horses. Around the ranch were the semi-open hills of the Lac la Hache valley, full of wildlife, full of adventure.

A boy would say to his companions, the teams brushed down and turned out after the evening meal: "Reckon we ought to saddle us some horseflesh and go up the big lease."

"Yeah, I s'pose so," would be the considered reply, and in a scramble that would leave the Old Man wondering how much work he really was receiving from his half-mast crew, Marvin, Roger, and I would be polishing saddle leather with the seats of our pants, heading for any hellery we could find.

Once, riding at a brisk pace across a big open, the fresh evening breeze billowing out our shirts, cooling us, repairing us after our labour, we spotted a mule deer three hundred yards away at the edge of the bush.

Marvin struck his horse, plunging into the chase. In the instant we were with him. I leaned down, my face against the flying wisps of mane, speaking to my mare, feeling the thrust of her muscles beneath me, responding.

The deer fled but we bolted into the light brush in pursuit, the branches slapping us, the horses lurching to dodge the aspen trees.

For me, confusion followed. Marvin turned right, I behind him. Roger went to the left.

"Wolf!" Marvin cried, and spurred his horse into the thickets, all but tearing himself from the saddle. I stayed behind him, pressing my mare, fighting to ward off the tangle.

Then he pulled up. "He's gone. 'Sno use. We can't keep up. Didja see him? Criminy, he was big!"

We stopped, quieting our horses, listening for Roger, not knowing what had become of him.

"Bear! Bear! I've got a bear!" It was Roger, screaming from a clearing away to the left.

We bolted again and broke into the clearing to find Roger sparring with a black bear and two cubs. She was facing him, standing on her hind legs, her cubs back of her. He was fighting his horse to retain his ground, wondering, I guess, what the blazes you do next.

Marvin saw his indecision. He rushed in at the bear. She gave ground. Suddenly she rushed him and he gave ground. She would not follow far for concern for her cubs, and when she faltered, Marvin grabbed the offensive for another charge.

Then one of the cubs climbed a small sapling, about twenty feet off the ground. Marvin drew back and we waited.

The bear hesitated at the foot of the sapling. Then, hoping the cub was safe, she moved off into the timber with the other. We closed in on the sapling to hold the hostage cub, knowing without it the old sow wouldn't go far.

There was little doubt what must be done. We wanted black hides on the saddles, knowing well the havoc done from time to time on the Old Man's calf crop by marauding bears in the spring and early summer.

Marvin took command. "Al, you got the fastest horse. Fetch Dad and his .30-30 fast as you can."

It was a good two miles to the ranch house. I turned to go, not a moment to waste. Marvin stopped me for one more instruction. "Don't say nothing about that wolf. Nobody going to believe us, so no use them thinking we're making up stories."

I must have been an odd sight, riding up to the house, my horse in a lather, all but jumping up and down in the saddle. Gussy had seen me coming and was waiting on the step.

"Gussy, you got to get your gun and come with me!" I cried. "Marvin and Roger got a bear and a couple of cubs up in the bush!" I was breathless and excited. Gussy looked at me with no more urgency than if I'd said we'd found a nest full of robin's eggs.

"You put the bear up a tree?" he asked.

"That's right. Gee, c'mon! That old bear's gonna chew those guys up." How impatient I was and how he ignored my impatience!

"Not if she's up a tree she won't."

He went back in the house, coming out with his carbine, then saddled his horse with no more nor less urgency than he'd ever done it. Soon we were riding at a good but hardly hurried pace to kill us a batch of bear. How painfully I wanted to push him on; how well I knew better than to try.

Everything was the way I had left it. Roger begged to shoot the lone cub and Gussy consented. He coached my brother and with one shot, at close range, of course, the cub tumbled out of the sapling. Roger burst with excitement; Gussy spoke sharply to him and he was as quickly subdued. Then we tied our horses in the clearing, entering the timber on foot in search of the old sow and her other cub.

We came to a big tree, a short way into the timber. Gussy inspected the bark, looking for the telltale claw marks.

"Here she is," he announced matter-of-factly. This divination struck me as darn well uncanny, but of course I know now that since it was the only large tree in the vicinity she would naturally make use of it.

The light was failing. Though it was early July and the evenings were long around the solstice, a great deal had taken place, leaving little time for shooting. Gussy walked about the tree, searching the heavy branches above him. Then he stopped, raised the rifle, and, without a rest, fired.

My fingernails cut the flesh of my palms. I fought the swelling of fear in my breast. I'd have gone for my horse had I not a greater fear of shame. Mind you, I had faith in this old cuss of a man, but I also saw that bear flying down out of the tree, clawing for my hide, settling a score or two in the last seconds of her life.

Gussy waited a moment, then stepped back. In a limp mass, what had been a bear landed with a thump precisely where he had been standing.

We were skinning her out, after bringing down the second cub, when I discovered a fist-sized lump of matter lying on the ground by the carcass. I poked it with my knife.

"What's this?" I queried.

"Her brains," Gussy replied. I believed in his musketry then and never doubted it again.

We rode home in the moonlight, the reek of the bears spooking our horses. The trials of one's days were forgotten. A boy was brave inside, stirred by the manhood that life, in such a moment, promised him so short a way ahead.

My Just Heritage

We cut and stacked perhaps ninety tons of hay at the Milk Ranch altogether: sixty of good timothy and thirty of wild meadow hay good — feed if put up well, fair bedding otherwise. It was not long then before we moved to the Blaze meadow and this I greeted with sheer joy. The Milk Ranch was home base and the meadows were the outposts. As to any boy, the wilderness was best to me, though living conditions anywhere on the ranch were seldom more than camping.

But at the Milk Ranch the house was of lumber and two-storeyed; at the Blaze there was only a log cabin. With a crew our size, canvas was a matter of necessity and for months we might live under it.

Mrs. Haller was the best hand in camp at moving time. She fed us a breakfast no less than any other she'd made, packed everything she'd conceivably need at the meadow to run a cookhouse, helped load it on the wagon and then climbed on with it, rode to the meadow, cleaned the cabin on arrival there, finally putting on a meal not noticeably different from any other she'd ever served. Somewhere in the day's work, too, had been the time to make sandwiches for the whole crew, spread out as it was from the Milk Ranch to the meadow cabin.

It was some caravan heading up the Eagle Lake road that day. The pickup truck took the lead, followed by a mower with the cutter bar raised up, out of gear. Next came a wagon with a hay rake loaded lengthways and innumerable items of equipment tucked in every which way, slings and cable, pulleys and ropes, plus an assortment of small, essential tools that are part of any proper haying outfit.

Horses that were needed but had nothing to draw on the move were tied behind the wagons. One might pull back, breaking a halter or tearing a tail gate from a wagon, but this was all part of the day.

Next to the end came the camp outfit, everything with which to cook, eat, sleep and live, including the cat stowed in a gunny sack. This was a big wagonload and the Old Man drove it himself with four horses hitched up in the old fashion you rarely see these days.

Last came two milch cows, two calves, and two boys on horseback, Marvin and me, whose task it was to deliver the cows so the calves might be taken from them in time in the evening to save adequate milk for a milking the following morning.

And we got into a bundle of grief. The first eight miles went well enough, but then we took the saddle horse shortcut along Railroad Lake, a body of water one came to before the meadow. Much of the way the trail went into the lake and one rode in the shallow water by the shore until it rose again on the bank.

The cows objected to wading. They came where the trail dropped into the water, then stood, impassively, occasionally lowering their heads and blowing through their nostrils at the water. Their calves, like all calves on indecisive occasions, stuck by their dams.

We pushed our horses up against them to force them into the water. At this point the bank was steep and once in they wouldn't stand much chance of coming out.

"Once their feet'r wet," I said, "they'll be no trouble. HI, HI, there you damn ole cow, take to that water!"

Well, they took, and it seemed to me we were doing fine. In fact we looked at the sun and we guessed it was maybe four o'clock and since we'd left the Milk Ranch in midmorning, we were doing fine, standing a good chance of supper at the meadow cabin by six.

I rode next the shore in only enough water to keep from being pressed against the overhanging brush. Marvin splashed along on my left in water to his stirrups.

Maybe if I'd seen it in time I could have stopped her and then again maybe I couldn't. Anyway around a bend we came suddenly on an extensive bog that bordered the lake. A low dyke-like ridge lay betwixt mud and water, and the inside cow flopped her left ear twice while she made up her mind. Before I could sock the spurs to my horse to head her, she was over to the mud. Equally quickly, the other followed with both the calves.

I put my horse to the shore and up we lunged, then down, over into the bog. I leaned back on the downward movement, instinctively bracing my legs to take my own weight when the horse would level out at the bottom.

Then the mud was coming at me and in a queer, half-real instant, I knew I had been stupid, that my horse was miring and that I couldn't keep the saddle, suppose there'd been any sense in doing so.

I heard Marvin's voice, heeding it in the same instant. "Get away from 'im, Al! Get away from 'im!" On my hands and knees I crawled, my heavy chaps a curse, the treacherous mud slowing me, even as bits of it from the flailing hooves of the panicky horse landed on my back.

With a last lunge I threw myself across a half-sunken log, then struggled to my feet, turning to see how bad was the lot of my mount. He had stopped lunging and now was sunk to his belly, all four legs clean out of sight. I drew a sigh of relief but gasped the next breath in fear again.

"Marvin! He's going to lie over sideways! He'll break his legs!" I'd never seen it happen but I'd heard it was a prime danger with a heavy horse bogged down in the mud and this gelding was no pony. Now, clearly, if the animal's weight went too far sideways for him to recover and there wasn't enough give in the mud, he'd break a leg, sure.

Already Marvin was rolling down his lariat. I caught the end he threw me and took the chance I had to: of going in the mud up to that horse again to where my inexperienced hand could put a loop on his neck. As luck had it, he had turned in his lunging to face the lake at an angle which would enable Marvin to take a straight pull.

I slipped the running noose over his head onto his neck with no trouble for he had given up completely to the mud. Then Marvin took wraps on the saddle horn and began backing his horse, screwing the bit on his jaw when he hesitated.

The rope tightened and the big horse began to choke. His eyes swelled from his skull, he sucked breath past the rope in ever weaker, rattling gasps. Still he wasn't moving.

"Harder, Marvin! Harder!" Marvin was doing all he could. Riding a single rig, he had the saddle standing on the pommel with the strain and still the gelding wouldn't start to fight. I watched him let the rope take all his weight, relax almost it seemed, and lean sideways. I couldn't see him breathing. I stood terrified and angry, angry that this stupid thing was happening and nothing I could do was going to change it.

Then it happened as it always happens. Suddenly, shorn of breath, in a violent panic greater than the mud could incite, the big horse reared in a fantastic surge of sheer power. Marvin, with the innate capacity he always had for doing the right thing in a bad spot, lifted his own horse backward by the poor beast's very jawbone.

The gelding flew forward and before his forelegs could sink he leaped again, reaching the solid ground of the raised bank. Weak with relief I stumbled through the mud to the bank too, and sat down, shaking uncontrollably.

Marvin brought his horse to the shore and dismounted, the makings of a grin on his well-built face. At thirteen he was years ahead of me in experience and whenever we'd get into a tight spot together, he'd make me laugh afterwards. It was good medicine. Soon we were giggling like girls and allowing as how we'd maybe not tell the Old Man about that little mishap.

But there was still the problem of the cows. These beasts were standing placidly a couple of hundred feet away, in the mud for which their feet are built and in which they seem to be quite at home and where a horse daren't trod. I watched them flicking their tails at the flies and chewing at the sedges that grew in the swamp.

"Marvin," I declared, "I'd leave 'em in this swamp if they was mine. I don't care if I never drink milk again."

"I don't reckon your dad'd take it too good."

"Don't s'pose he would."

There was only one way to chase cows in the mud, so with no further ado we went about it, lunging and cursing through the swamp on foot, tormented by mosquitoes and flies, frustrated by the ease with which two cows could turn back to the depths of the swamp every time we had them on the verge of going into the lake.

Finally in desperation we drove them along the edge of the lake in the mud and on the raised bank where the brush would permit it, taking turns leading the horses up in the water. This was slow, but it was progress, and at long last we came to steep ground which forced the cows to take the water route again.

Then in a while the trail went out of the lake and we were into the timber, nothing between us and the meadow cabin but another hour of riding, now on solid ground.

Hours late, we came at last to the cabin where we corralled the cows, turned our horses into the big yard and, making apologies to Mrs. Haller, wrapped ourselves around the biggest heap of meat and potatoes she could muster up, no mean supply by a long ways.

It was dark by the time we hunted up our bedrolls and found some unoccupied ground in a tent by the shore of Railroad Lake. An owl landed in a nearby tree, setting up a frightful screeching. The last sound on my ears that night was of Marvin screeching back at the owl which, astounded, fled into the darkness of the forest.

The day following saw haying begin at once. The stillness of the vast pine wood, in which this wild sedge meadow was merely a splash of light colour against the dark of the endless trees, was feebly broken now by the chatter of the mower knives.

Always the best teams went on the mowers. It took the pace of a fast walking horse to keep the wheel-driven pitman rod driving back and forth, creating the reciprocating action of the knife in the cutting bar, an action so fast the knife was a blur to the eye as it advanced into the standing hay. The mower was a good place to break in new horses or take the nonsense out of old ones that liked to run away in the harness. If you could keep them in the cut for the first round or two you had them, so heavy was the draw in a thick stand of hay.

After two mowers had a supply of hay ahead and some had dried enough to gather, one team came onto the rake. At the same time the rest of the crew kept busy fixing sloops.

These were simple rigs for hauling hay and, like everything else about our outfit back in the outpost meadows, were made almost entirely of jack pine wood. There were several at every meadow so that on arrival each year one had only to replace any worn-out poles and the rig was ready to go.

Two jack pine runners, to polish on the stubble and run as slick as sleigh runners, lay beneath the hayrack. The rack itself was of light poles laid lengthways, three sturdy cross members between deck and runners. Eight feet wide and maybe fourteen long, enough hay could be hauled on it to strain the collars on a good-sized team. Ordinarily there was no more to it than the flat deck, but in deference to the youngsters on the crew that year the men put a front and back on the deck that made a virtual hay basket out of it. There was no chance then of a badly built load skidding off the back end on the way to the stackyard.

Then of course the poles had to be raised and wood cut for the cook at the cabin. Tents, put up hurriedly the day of arrival, might now be straightened, and the moment there was hay dry enough to serve the purpose, enough would be put under the bedrolls to separate a boy or man from the cold hard ground.

But hay dry enough to sleep on was dry enough to stack, and nothing counted then but to hay again, ten long hours under the sun, pitching out of the raked-up bunches onto the sloops, hauling sloop load after sloop load alongside the derrick poles, watching the Old Man working higher and higher above us as the stack crept toward the peak of the fifty-five footers we'd found for derrick poles.

Inevitably, too, we young sprats grew more proficient at our tasks and the men, though they daren't let on, grew daily more pleased with us. Once my team bogged down in the mud when I tried to reach a bunch near a soft place in the meadow. The whole meadow was a raft of sod on a sea of mud and to avoid going through the treacherous places was part of a teamster's task.

Gussy came to help me out. We unhitched the horses and unsnapped the crosslines, separating them. One horse then fought his way out but the other sulked, refusing to move. Therefore we fetched some rope and pulled the second horse out with the first, much the way Marvin had done with my saddle horse.

Finally we used the rope to take a long hitch from solid ground back to the sloop, bringing it safely to better footing where I could hook up again. All done, I thanked Gussy, apologizing for the trouble.

"That's all right," he replied. "Anyone can get stuck in the mud. But now I'll tell you what you do. When you see your horses starting to break the sod, you get 'em to hell outa there in a hurry. Rush 'em up. Get 'em moving. Then they might get over the soft place."

It wasn't two loads later, and Gussy was pitching my load with me, that I had to go near soft ground, for two or three bunches. I saw the danger when the right-hand horse began breaking through and sawing on the bit from side to side. Pulling the team sharply to the left, I virtually attacked them with the handle end of my pitchfork.

"Git, you knotheads! Git!" I screamed, plunging along beside them. Mud flying everywhere, we soon came to good footing and stopped, the horses heaving and blowing, me triumphant as only a twelve-year-old boy could be.

"That what you mean?" I asked.

Gussy, grinning and chuckling, caught up, walking with the swinging limp left him by too many bad broncs in his early days.

"By God, boy, you're agoin' to be a teamster yet. You bet you boots that's what I mean!" So for that brief moment, inexplicably, I was let into the company of men and though I knew better than to expect to be allowed to stay, I would never again need feel entirely remote from it.

Thus the days went on and with them evenings of play, for boys are boys, a man's job notwithstanding. We slipped halters on the saddle horses and wrestled each other bareback, ducking and pulling, running away and charging, clinging with legs and hands to our mounts, joyous when we might throw an adversary to the ground.

Roger had a mare, a fine little animal but skittish, and we dared him to take her on the meadow, to let us put a flank rope on her. Only his anxiety to be thought a horseman overcame his fear of a dumping and soon the little mare was crow-hopping around on the soft sod, making the best of a bad situation. Of course she threw him, but Roger was a fleshy lad and his collision with the sedge sod was like a marshmallow landing on a hotcake, a pretty well absorbed impact.

And I was happy, the hardest of the beginning behind me. I was proud too, to learn my father's work, to feel I was part of his cow outfit, to begin to earn my place in the round of tasks that made up the running of the ranch. The ranch after all was the established order as I knew it in my short life. The fields, the animals, the cabins and barns and tools and good, true men: these were all my world. To join in this now was a rich reward and, I believed, unquestionably my just heritage.

But there was another world, not one of my choosing, to which I was also subject: the world of school, of books and stuffy classrooms, of teachers dull and uninspiring against the colour and glory of a Gussy Haller, of boys who taunted the awkward ways of a country lad. We moved but once more, to the Morton meadow, and then, after a few more weeks of haying, that world demanded us again, taking us boys away from the free life of hard work and open air.

Williams Lake, forty-five miles northwest of Lac la Hache on the Cariboo road, was not then more than you would call a one-horse town. A busy place economically and one of the high volume beef-shipping points in North America, the handful of houses and stores a mile up from the stockyards wouldn't have let on as much.

Cattle poured in every fall from the millions of acres of range land around the town, from hundreds of miles in every direction and, following the only payday of the year they experienced, the ranchers, big and small, laid in vast quantities of supplies and paid their bills.

When Roger and I left the ranch to stay with Mother and go to school there in the fall of 1942, the population of the town was possibly six hundred souls. I think there were a hundred children in school in all grades from one to twelve. A formidable crowd; I had not before known half that number of children.

The first morning in that alien place I felt close to tears. Seated near a panel of windows, I could see on a distant hill a little clear knoll with a fir tree in the opening. This bit of landscape somehow symbolized the vast outdoor life of the ranch. Visible from the strange interior of a classroom which housed three times as many desks as there had been enrolment in the log schoolhouse at Lac la Hache, it served not to ease the pains of academic bondage but to magnify them.

I found it impossible to make friends with the other boys in town my age. I made the terrible error of saying, in talk of some activity, that we used to do it this way or that at Lac la Hache, bringing groans of derision from these sophisticated town dwellers.

I expect I should have learned but I did not. Daily my naive ways brought me to shame. Had I been athletic I might have redeemed myself on the playing field but, all thumbs, my attempts to be a ballplayer made matters worse, not better.

Accustomed to being picked last when two sides were drawn up for games, I could detect an expression of positive relief on the part of the captain who managed to avoid my presence on his team.

Looking back, I know how fortunate I was that my own times were so much fuller than theirs and how many more resources I have had with which to deal with life because of the demands the ranch made on me as a boy. Nevertheless in those dark days I could only feel inferior to the youngsters in town, and every day I was obliged to be there made every hour on the ranch a precious, savoured bit of happiness. It is little wonder now that my memory is full of the intervals of ranch life and devoid of what happened in those interminable ages of servitude in school.

It was little easier to go back the second fall than to begin the first.

Cow Drive

The first snow of winter came early that year. Harsh blasts of arctic air ushered in November. The hot days of harvest were forgotten. The cattle came in from the summer range in early October, mostly by themselves, but with riding for the last stragglers. The Old Man turned the herd into the hayfields to feed on the aftermath, the short growth that takes place in the remainder of the season after the crop is cut. The beef he separated from the rest and took to the shipping yards on the Pacific Great Eastern railway, five miles away around the end of Lac la Hache. The ponds froze over, the last stubborn leaves drifted down from the aspen trees, and it was winter.

The Old Man sent word he would bring us from town for the long weekend of Remembrance Day, to move the cattle from the Milk Ranch to the Morton meadow for the start of winter feeding. It would be my first real drive, and Roger and I were to do it by ourselves.

Leaving Williams Lake after school was out, we were on the ranch for a big supper of mulligan, a hefty stew the Old Man built out of turnips, carrots, potatoes and moose meat, all cooked together in large chunks in the same pot. There was no more Maggie now, the Hallers having moved back to their own home after the haying.

We got our orders between bites of moose meat. "All the cattle are in the Milk Ranch field so you won't have to go into the big

19

lease. It shouldn't take you long to find them. Your horses are in the corral and you can go down after supper and put them in the barn. Take some oats with you and put plenty of hay down."

"We gonna take 'em out by ourselves, huh? You're gonna take the truck and the camp outfit?"

"I'll 'gonna' you if you don't learn to talk English. Yes, you're going to be on your own tomorrow and you'd better look sharp. I don't want every cow we own tangled up in the jack pines from here to the Morton meadow. Pass the stew, please."

I passed the stew, but I guess I was a little excited at the prospect of tomorrow. I spilled some gravy on the oilcloth.

"Look out, you ass!" Oh, the Old Man must have been glad to have his boys around again, no doubt about that.

We rose before daylight for a feast of porridge and eggs. But for sandwiches, this might have to last us far into the night. We therefore stuffed our stomachs with all they could hold, a staggering heap of victuals. Then we went to the barn and by the light of the coal-oil lantern saddled our horses. It was bitter cold. I had butterflies down deep and wished I hadn't eaten so much.

Gradually, almost reluctantly, a grey light broke down through the mist. We took our horses from the barn and mounted up, the chill air cutting our nostrils. The saddle leather was cold, even through denims and long underwear. The Old Man must have sensed that I was tense. He stood by my horse while he gave us last instructions and slapped the knee of my chaps when we turned to go.

"Good luck, old chap," he said, and I loved him dearly.

The first snows had gone again. The lasting snow that would persevere had yet to come but it could suddenly cover the fields any day now. The grass, frozen and coated white, rustled with a strange new sound as the horses hurried through it, impatient and spooky in the frost.

We separated. Roger went beyond the irrigation dam to ride the bush beyond it, next the upper fence. I turned left to climb a high knoll from the top of which I could see much of the Milk Ranch field below me.

Fog lay in the low ground, in patchy blobs of white. The irrigation dam was white with hoarfrost on new ice. Nowhere was there a cow to be seen, not one beast. Still bedded, they were out of sight.

Roger, small in the distance, rode at a steady jog toward the bush beyond the open field, slipping from sight when he reached it. His fading figure was in some odd way unreal, so far away below and half hidden by the swirling mist even before the wood swallowed him up. I forgot the cattle for the moment and thought of my brother, poor old kindly Roger, to whom the summer had hardly been kind, to whom much of life was hardly kind and even then I sensed, half understanding, as boys so often do, what was wrong.

He'd always had an exquisite sense of justice and little by little reality was letting him down. When we were small, away back in the first faint flicks of my memory, his greatest pain was me getting a licking he didn't think was due and he had no doubts about the justness of a licking if a boy'd been bad.

He had an odd good sense for a young 'un, but he nevertheless lacked the quick, competitive alertness that keeps a fellow ahead in the often cruel society of boys at school. This was doubly a setback because it never occurred to him that he should take advantage of anyone: he had no fire to fight fire. I have a picture of him yet in an agony of indignation confronting the teacher in the log schoolhouse of our first years with an inequitable decision she had been led to make through the shrewdness of the other boy in Roger's grade.

I've forgotten the substance of course, but how clearly I see him, on the verge of tears, protesting: "But that's not fair!"

She, seeing her own error, could only silence him and let it pass. But it wasn't that *he* had been wronged that hurt, it was that a wrong had occurred.

How much more he suffered, then, in the hard school of the hayfield and the cow camp where only performance counted, where sincere intentions unaccompanied by tangible, useful results served no more purpose than snowballs on an empty feed ground in a hungry winter.

The Old Man had always admired him for his efforts, and Heaven knows he was a tryer, but this made matters only harder when in that first summer he was plunged into the crew to sink or swim on the hay he could pitch and the horses he could drive, where *no* boy's best was good enough and you hadn't begun until you'd been growled at and scowled at, scorned and ridiculed, reduced to a shameful confession of your own utter uselessness.

Roger would not be so reduced. Stubbornly he fought the school of hard knocks because essentially, practical though it might very well have been, it was not just. But to Johnny and Gussy it was part of life as they knew it, *they* had had their turn once long ago, and the reward for being masters in their work was that they should hand it back again in full to succeeding generations of greenhorn hands.

If he drove too close to the bunch, crowding the rack against the hay, they growled; if he wasn't close enough, they heaved audible sighs of weariness. Suppose he rested his team on the haul to the stack, letting them blow a bit, they wondered what kept him so long getting rid of his load; suppose he hurried, they remarked in significant tones how a horse wouldn't last long if it hadn't a chance to rest in a hard pull.

No, Roger would not be reduced. He stood it, he ignored it, he fought back and he would not be reduced, and it was tough times for him thereby. After a bunch is pitched onto the load, a few wisps of hay lie on the stubble. Not to be wasted, these are gathered into a heap in dexterous twirling of the fork tines and then the heap is thrown aboard. Two men working together can both twirl onto the same heap and then one may throw it aboard or each may make his own heap — it matters little.

Now, chiefly the men, Gussy and Johnny, did the pitching while we youngsters drove our teams and built our loads. Nonetheless, while one man finished off one youngster's load, the other would begin the next. Until both men reached your sloop, you helped pitch. For some reason, while thus pitching with one of the men, Roger had cause to wonder whose was a heap of hay that was being gathered between them.

"That your heap?" he queried.

Innocent enough, perhaps. But thereafter whenever Gussy and Johnny were finishing up Roger's load there'd be a time when a middling sized heap would grow between them. Then they'd both stop work, eyeing the thing, scrutinizing it carefully.

"That your heap?" Johnny would ask.

Gussy would rest his hands on his fork and give this serious matter his complete attention. "Well, now," he'd say thoughtfully, "I thought sure it was your heap."

"'Sfunny. Thought it was yours. Oh well, no matter." Then he'd shrug, catching the heap with his fork, tossing it up on the load.

So it went. Roger couldn't win because it all made him mad as old billy-ho and it made him mad because it was so unfair. He was doing his level best every hour of the day and if Gussy and Johnny couldn't see that, then the devil with them. He either couldn't see or couldn't bear to take the easy way out, to humble himself, justly or not, and then start struggling slowly and hopefully up the ladder to acceptance.

Cruelly, we all began playing the heap of hay game and I cannot but think it was a terribly lonely summer for Roger. I think he was glad now it was over and once again there was just the Old Man and us two boys and if we could somehow make the Morton meadow with these cattle before dark, all would be well in our world.

I came out of my thoughts at the sound of a cow bawling for her calf. Then I heard another, and another, until soon the familiar, incessant bawling of an entire herd began to build up in the air, a sound audible for miles on a still day.

Then here and there out of the bush, across the rolling flat below, down the draws and gulleys came a trickle of red shapes in the mist. The trickles became a stream of movement, the bawling loud and persistent. Soon Roger appeared, hazing a bunch of reluctant yearlings toward the cows and calves. I could see now he had come across the whole herd, bedded down together in one piece of wood, and we were saved a lengthy search in every comer of the field for scattered bands of cattle.

We pushed the herd westward to the gate that would let us out of the Milk Ranch field onto the Eagle Lake road, where we would make a count. Eager to travel, the first few head rushed through the opening as soon as they saw it. We closed in from either side, forcing the remainder to go one at a time, each of us counting quietly. All through, we compared, finding we both had the same figure and it agreed with what the Old Man said we should have. We closed the gate behind us, pushing the stragglers to catch up with the leaders that by now were half a mile up the road.

Driving cattle in the open plains of Alberta or the semi-open country of south central British Columbia is one thing, while in the bush country of the Cariboo it is quite another. To be a good cowpuncher in bush country, you must give up the notion that a horse is meant to be ridden in an upright position in the saddle; instead, be prepared to hang tooth and nail to his hide anywhere you might have to, to dodge the oncoming brush and stay aboard. A good cow horse will get the cow, while the cowboy looks after himself.

When you see a horse coming out of the bush bringing back a straying beef and you do not immediately see a rider, you should wait a moment before you go to look for him. If he is a good hand he should soon reappear, crawling up from the other side where he has been clutching the rigging for his life while his dedicated cayuse took him under some big jack pine limbs with maybe three inches of clearance over the saddle horn. These skills we boys must develop, I could see that.

Our first trouble, the Old Man had warned us, was only a mile up the road. There a trail took away to the right, short-cutting back to the big lease, beyond the Milk Ranch field. It was spring calving pasture and not a cow in the outfit wouldn't try to head in there.

And so we barely had the tag end up to the main herd before we could see the makings of a dead run ahead of us, the leaders clean out of sight around not one but at least two bends in the road. The bush on both sides was thicker than hair on a horse's mane and we were in grief.

24

Roger had been on more cow driving with the Old Man than I had. "What are we gonna do?" I asked him, eyeing the bush with a fair idea of what he would have in mind.

"You stay on the road. I'm goin' through the bush to the trail and hit it ahead of 'em and push 'em back." With that he plunged into the woods and I was alone with a stream of red backs moving just a mite too fast for comfort.

The leaders must have been a long way up the trail before Roger got there because the unhappy result of his efforts was not to head them but to run into them on the flank and disperse them into the timber on all sides. He then did the only thing he could: he rode up the trail far enough to be sure he was beyond the last of them and began laboriously gathering cattle all over again.

Back on the road, I moved along behind the drag, pushing the odd late-born calf that grew reluctant to keep up, and generally wondered what the blazes was happening. Then I came around the corner that let me see where the trail turned off to discover not a cow beast on the road beyond that point. The whole herd was taking the trail and taking it on the dead run.

I turned off the road to my right, plunging into the sticks. A branch slapped my face, a tree caught my knee and I cursed. The thickets looked impassable, but if I went back to go on the road and then down the trail I would only drive cattle ahead of me in the wrong direction.

My horse had stopped, sensing my own indecision. Then I knew if I was going to call myself a cowboy there was only one thing for it. I drove my spurs into that poor cayuse's hide so hard he grunted and the next thing I knew the brush was going by to beat sixty, the old horse picking his way through the best of it at a dead run, me hanging and dodging, scared white but too busy to notice it.

I hit the trail maybe three hundred yards in from the road. There were a few cattle standing about, sorting out calves and shifting off again but not in any specific direction. Then I heard Roger crashing around ahead of me and suddenly a big roan cow popped out of the sticks, coming straight for me, him hard behind her.

25

"They're scattered all through here, Al. C'mon!" For a moment, but only a moment, I thought of protesting that it was hopeless, that we should go for help. Then I pushed off into the tangle to start gathering cows, for if there was one self-evident truth about ranch work it was that you don't go for help because there's no damn help to go for.

There were cows, calves, and yearlings everywhere. As soon as you pushed one little bunch in the right direction, you found another making off in the wrong direction. But we stayed at it, riding furiously, shouting and cussing, striving to be heard above the constant bawling of cows seeking their own young ones in all that mix-up.

Then gradually the herd began to take shape again. Almost as if they wanted to, the strays attached themselves to the new stream of movement going our way now and we were making progress back toward the road.

"You suppose," I asked Roger, "they'll turn down the road again when they hit it and go back to the Milk Ranch?"

"Yep," he replied and with that he was off, heading across to the road now on the same errand as before: to try to intercept the leaders before they got too far in the wrong direction. I groaned in exasperation to myself. I had a picture of spending the next interval of my life going back and forth from road to trail, never reaching the Morton meadow at all.

But then, maybe unaccountably or maybe because we'd fought them hard enough to win the fight, those red and white beef makers just turned up the road as nice as you please and we were on the way, everything so quiet we had time to tell each other how we reckoned if we had to we could handle twice that many cows. In a little while Roger went ahead through some open timber till he caught the lead, then let the herd go by him, taking a rough count that assured us we had the lot.

The cattle moved well then. We passed Burt Wright's ranch house, the last ranch headquarters beyond us on the Eagle Lake road, and went on well until we hit a piece of partly open country about halfway to the Morton meadow turnoff, roughly six miles from the Milk Ranch. There we put in a bad hour with the cattle trying hard to break, but we held them because the open nature of the terrain gave us a better than average command of the situation: we could watch more cows and ride much faster.

That over, we took a last rough count, knowing we'd be in timber again and wouldn't have another chance. At the time of that count we still had all the cattle.

We hit the timber and hell came calling. The stubborn grew more stubborn. Tired of the drive, they began looking for a way out. The bush at its worst, any time a cow wanted to quit all she had to do was walk into the next good thicket she saw. If she was lucky both of us would be busy with the last cow that had done the same thing and she'd be well into the bush before anyone came to bring her out.

You must go farther than the cow each time, for you have to go around her to head her back. With one or two it's annoying, with thirty of them at it all at once it's a downright furious business. Your head's down half the time dodging the stinging branches and up the rest of the time to see where in tarnation the cow went to. I'd heard of a cowboy so angry at a cow he roped her, tied her down, and rubbed dirt in her eyes. When he let her up she had to rely on her sense of smell and she daren't leave the herd.

We weren't prepared to go to this extent. Had we been, we lacked the skill with a lariat to down a full-grown cow. We could only go on riding hard, pushing the cattle back on the road as fast as they strayed from it, our mounts in a white lather, our backsides tender from the continual jolt of a horse going fast in several directions at once.

The Old Man came by in midafternoon. He eased the truck along behind us for a while, long enough to see what a dickens of a time we were having, and concluded that since he couldn't help us he'd be just as well off to push on through on his way to get the cabin ready and let us get back to our swearing good and proper. We had a remnant of inhibitions in front of our venerable parent.

27

He eased the truck into the herd then, passed a couple of rough sandwiches out the window, waved his hand in the funny way he did with his fingers stuck out, and was gone. We wolfed down the sandwiches on the dead run, business as usual.

We lost all idea of what went on in the lead. We could only hope for the best, completely occupied as we were on the drag end where fully half the herd was hanging out, looking for a chance to break. It was two riders trying to prevent sixty head of cattle from scattering out and disappearing in the bush in every direction, the rest of the herd left to its own devices. At times, two hours made only a mile. Daylight running out, we had three hard miles yet to go.

We were learning, nonetheless, and I imagine this was why the Old Man had us out there alone with every confounded cow he owned in the toughest tangle of jack pine I ever expect to see. We pushed our horses harder, impossible though that seemed. With so many beasts to be kept on the road there was little time for each of them.

We discovered a new truth about herding cows on a tough drive. We didn't merely go after a cow and bring her back, we persecuted the devil out of her till her one desire was to lose herself in the milling, bawling herd. One didn't chase a cow any longer, one charged her, horse full out, spurs ready to thrust him into a furious collision at catching her, throw her off her balance, send her stumbling in panic back where she belonged.

"Looka' that," I'd say to Roger, after half crippling an unfortunate cow. "I'm cowboy enough for any crittur!"

"Oh, maybe," he'd reply, sceptically, giving me a dubious look and a dusty grin as he went off into the bush after a victim of his own.

But the light we needed was gone before we reached the meadow. We grew exhausted, the long day catching up with our young bodies. We had constantly to fight the breakers and also watch for cattle that might have slid away from the lead to wait in the bush till we were by, then drift back toward the Milk Ranch. Tired eyes and failing light soon reduced this task to futility.

At long last we broke onto the meadow, barely enough light left to make the count that told us what we already dreaded: we were short eleven head. An inspection of the herd soon told us that among the missing was a new shorthorn bull the Old Man had bought to cross on his Hereford cows.

It was hard not to be despondent. We said little. To have tried so hard and to have failed left us each with our own silent disappointment. We agreed it was useless to go back on our tracks.

"Let's go, Al. The Old Man'll want us to help around the cabin."

I sat a moment, still looking at the cattle, strung out now, feeding on hay the Old Man had scattered for them to eat on their arrival. "I'm going back," I said at last. "Just a short way. I know it's no use, but I'd like to ride a bit and maybe bump into them."

It was strangely quiet there in that forest alone, the din of the bawling cattle out of earshot at last, the darkness of the night fast shutting out all but the stretch of trail on which one rode. Above, the treetops silhouetted against the night sky and somewhere far off an owl hooted.

I stopped my horse to quiet even the clop of his shod hooves on the frozen earth and, palms crossed on the saddle horn, rested myself forward, listening to the stillness. I felt strangely very old, very old indeed for a boy who still had to grow some if his chaps were to quit dragging on the ground when he wasn't on his horse.

The old gelding stamped impatiently and tried to turn back. He'd been at the Morton meadow enough to know where hay and barn were and his day was over, that much he knew.

"Well, away you go, you old reprobate," I chuckled, feeling very kindly to this beast who was my sole company for this moment on a weary night, and let him have his way. I slumped in the saddle, tired, hoping the Old Man had one of his stews going in the camp across the meadow.

Arriving at the barn, I found Roger putting out hay for some horses the Old Man had brought in earlier in the week. There was a light in the cabin and Roger said the Old Man was trying to put together some new stovepipe so we could get a fire going. I finished with my horse, leaving the saddle on but loosening the cinch till he would cool down in an hour or two.

"I'll go help the Old Man," I said. "You can put out this hay by yourself. Okay?"

"Fine by me. He's having trouble with the stovepipe, I think."

The Old Man always had trouble with stovepipe. He hated the stuff. It is especially designed so that each piece fits tightly into the next. In their enthusiasm to have it do so, however, the manufacturers have ensured that it is damned well next to impossible to put it together at all.

This vexed the Old Man badly at the best of times, but on a cold November night by lamplight, with no fire in a cold cabin and nothing to eat since breakfast but a rough sandwich, it was sheer havoc what it did to his nerves.

Not only had he reached the swearing-in-French stage before I came, he had been there for the past half-hour at least. The stovepipe had been cussed inside and out, about four times, and the manufacturers had had their licks. Now we were halfway through giving the wholesalers and retailers their share for having taken part in a diabolical scheme to prevent the Old Man from lighting the fire to cook his supper.

I had to try to help. There was no way out. Had I realized the nature of the situation I would have stayed the devil out of that cabin till there was smoke in the air, but I was in before I was fully aware.

"Well don't stand there, man, hold this pipe!" He indicated two lengths he had finally fitted together, onto which he was attempting to fix a third.

I grasped the lengths while he shoved and poked with the third piece, uselessly. With three lengths and an elbow to go, I could see where we would be jolly hungry before supper was cooked.

"Don't wiggle the thing, hold it still!"

"I ain't wigglin' it. You shovin' at it like that, I can't keep it still!"

"Here, give me the thing! And don't say ain't." He banged the pipe down onto the receiver on the stove to help to keep it rigid. "Now hold it."

I took it once more and he started all over again, with excruciating impatience.

So I laughed at him. I was scared silly at the prospect of doing so, but I was only a boy and sometimes a boy has to laugh whether he figures it's safe or not.

"I *don't* see what there is to laugh at!"

"I can't help it."

"It may be a jolly joke to you, but when I think of those bastards who made this stovepipe, I could wring somebody's neck."

Mine, perhaps?

Well, we finally put it together though how the Old Man was so forbearing I'll never know. I mean if I'd been him, I would have wrung my neck, snickering away like a ninny in all that confusion.

Before long we had hot food and over it we discussed the day, particularly the missing cattle. The Old Man said not to be concerned. He had a man coming in to feed cattle for him and as soon as the man arrived, he could go himself for the missing animals.

"You boys did well," he assured us. "You had a pretty good bunch of cattle to drive for only two of you and you don't have to be ashamed of a few doubling back in the bush."

That was nice of him, especially after all that stovepipe business.

Then we did the chores, piled some fresh hay on the floor in a corner of the cabin, threw our bedrolls on it, and climbed in for a rest we really needed.

WOLVES

We returned to the Morton in December for the Christmas holiday. The new hired man was there, Bill Wilson by name, an immigrant Englishman and not a top hand by any means, which even I could tell, but fond of animals and conscientious, a combination of qualities pretty useful in a ranch hand.

He loved to talk and he loved to read so, given magazines or company, he was equipped for life in a meadow cabin where the long winter nights can be mighty troublesome for those who won't settle for simple entertainments.

While he talked we learned about him. He'd come from a poor family in England — genuinely poor. His feet gave him trouble that he attributed to inadequate shoes as a child. Then he'd served a hitch in the regulars when the British Army still laid claim to a mounted regiment or two.

I was never sure, though Heaven knows he must have mentioned it, how long he'd been out from the old country but clearly it was some years. He told us about attending a sort of school for emigrants in England where an attempt was made to prepare men for life in the colonies. They'd taught him to use an axe but the way poor Bill's axe got dull on him they hadn't shown him how to sharpen it.

Now he owned a little meadow in the Bridge lake country, sixty miles or so southeast of Lac la Hache, fondly hoping that he might make enough of a ranch out of it to scrounge a living for himself.

He might save enough, working for the Old Man, to buy a few tools and a wagon and maybe another horse. But by the sound of it he was going to be pretty busy looking after his little homestead: it wasn't big enough that it would ever look after him.

He had a chunky roan saddle mare and never a day went by that he didn't take a few minutes to scratch her back of the ears and tell her what a devil of a fine friend she was. Then he'd tease her a bit, tickling her ribs. She'd lay back her ears, taking a harmless nip at him, which he'd counter with a slap on her big thick neck, and then he'd go fetch her some oats.

The Old Man had come by a collie bitch late that fall, a friendly, intelligent beast whose purposes, he intended, would be largely functional, like keeping breachy horses to hell out of the garden and chasing in the milk cow. The first thing she did at the Morton meadow was produce a litter of pups, a whole two thirds of a dozen blind, squirming, squeaky little pups.

Well, the old bitch and Bill had been fast friends from the moment he arrived: they had adopted each other on the spot. So when these pups arrived there was a great to-do between them. The old girl fussed around showing Bill what a fine miracle she'd wrought; he fussed around with some hay and a few pieces of jack pine to make a little enclosure for the family in one corner of the cabin. The weather had turned cold and there was just no question of that litter toughing it out in a drafty barn or any other place that wasn't right handy to where old Bill could help her with her burden of love. As the pups grew and could use it, he carefully chopped up a little moose meat every day, mixing it with milk and seeing to it they all had a good fair share.

He talked in his sleep a lot, never a night passing that he hadn't an engaging conversation with the dog or the big team he used to haul hay out to the cattle.

He also preferred to be alone at the cabin. He wasn't unsociable — indeed he loved to have a visitor. It was just a lot more convenient not to have resident company. He told me once he suspected, after the Old Man had come out from the Milk Ranch and stayed a durable while, that he'd expressed these sentiments in remarkably pithy terms nocturnally, for the following morning the Old Man announced he had urgent reasons for returning to the Milk Ranch while only the day before he'd been planning some work around the meadow.

Yes, take him all around, Bill was a good sort and getting to know him a little that Christmas vacation, I reckoned him up as a pretty fair addition to life on the ranch.

The Old Man had done some riding since we had brought the cattle to the Morton meadow, rounding up the shorthorn bull with the ten cows and calves he'd had with him. Mulling things over, however, he concluded we were still missing two heifers that hadn't been in the herd for the drive at all, in fact had never shown up from the summer range.

The only chance to find them was to scour the Milk Ranch field and the big lease, hoping they might have drifted in there in the last few weeks. The old one-room cabin was crowded, what with two men, two boys, a bitch and a litter of pups, so it made sense two ways for the Old Man and me to saddle up, striking out for the Milk Ranch in search of the heifers.

Brother, was it cold! Hanging at zero degrees Fahrenheit in the daytime, the mercury was socking down to twenty below at night, and in the still, snappy air was the promise of sixty below the following month. The evening we decided the next day we'd ride, I slipped on my jacket for a short walk down on the meadow, to catch a breath of the night.

The great northern wilderness was at its best and it stirred me the more to be native to it. A brittle moon riding in a star-filled sky spilled its chilling light onto the white reach of the meadow. Hoarfrost glittered on the snow and every few moments the boom of a dry jack pine snag splitting in the cold cut the quiet of the night.

Not far off a wolf turned to the moon and howled. Soon another answered, then another. Before long the full-throated cry of the pack rolled across the forest and somewhere perhaps a moose heard it on all sides of him, terror his companion in the night. Near me in the woods a cow bawled restlessly and her calf answered from the weaning yard. I turned back toward the yellow light of the cabin and soon the hairs on the back of my neck laid down again.

We left early in the morning. The snow squeaked under the hooves on the packed part of the trail and the long guard hairs under the horses' chins were white with frost. I rode in file behind the Old Man and long before the shortcut trail to the Eagle Lake road was half behind us, I had my feet out of the stirrups, swinging them back and forth in a futile attempt to keep them warm.

We reached the road. "You cold?" the Old Man asked.

"Froze," I declared.

"Better walk." We climbed down and after stumbling a few tentative steps began to walk along leading the horses. A brisk three quarters of a mile later my feet were warm again.

We mounted up, running the horses a few hundred yards, then held them to a walk once more. The running made an icicle out of my nose. I took off a mitt, holding my hand on my nose to warm it. Then my hand got cold so I put it back in my mitt. My nose got colder than ever.

"You cold?"

"Froze."

"We'll walk some more."

We did and it helped, but it took longer to limber up. While we walked the saddle leather grew colder than a frosty pump handle so it was like straddling a chunk of ice to mount up again. This and the creeping stiffness tended to keep us in the saddles, our chins pulled down on our chests, shoulders humped, miserable and numb. We disciplined ourselves to walk twice more but after that we merely sat there and suffered.

From Railroad Lake on down we began riding into the timber wherever we knew there was a string of wild hay meadows, too small to cut but handy for a few stray cows to scrounge feed from by pushing through the snow to get at last summer's grass. Nowhere did we find a cow or the sign of a cow.

35

Once I thought I had a track. "Got somethin' here, Dad."

The Old Man rode over and looked down on the track, not bothering to dismount that he might inspect it more closely. "Moose," he said, matter-of-factly.

"But it's rounded off," I protested.

"Yes, it is," he explained. "But while a moose sometimes has his toes rounded off, a domestic cow never has hers pointed up. That track is only round compared to a normal moose track. Compared to a cow track, it's still sharp-toed."

I could see what he meant. I had been leaning over to look at the track and so I straightened up. My horse had shifted next to a tall willow bush and I banged a twig-load of snow, getting half of it down my neck, the rest in the saddle.

"Keeripes!"

"Too bad, old chap! Can I help?"

"Don't think so." I leaned over, brushing what I could out of my shirt collar, then straightened up and stood in the stirrups, doing my best to brush out with my hand the snow under me. The best I could do left me a fair bit to soak up in the seat of my pants. My backbone was acrawl with what went under my shirt.

"You sure we *are* missing a coupla heifers?"

"Positive. More I think about it, the more sure I am."

"Well let's go see if they're at the Milk Ranch."

"All right. We'll just take a look in a few more of these sloughs on the way."

It was pitch dark and I was numb as a frozen calf by the time we put ourselves back on the road with enough of it behind us that a boy could expect to live as far as Burt Wright's ranch house.

"We'll be to Wright's pretty quick," I said.

"Yes," the Old Man agreed. "We shouldn't stop, though. It'll be just that much tougher to start out again afterwards and it's getting colder all the time."

I thought about Wright's and how it would be there, Burt and the three boys, Stanley the eldest, then Willie and David, all gathered around the heater and Mrs. Wright with the girls making a meal that could take a half-dozen visitors without notice any time.

"I think I could stand that," I said.

"Stand what?"

"Starting out again afterwards." Then to clinch it I added: "Nobody down at the Milk Ranch cooking any supper."

"You have a point there, my boy. You have a point."

We put our horses in the barn the moment we arrived and I left my chaps on till I was in the house so David could undo the snaps for me. To me that heater was a big cheery chunk of promised land and I homesteaded right next to it till supper was served.

Gussy used to say you might find neighbours as good as the Burt Wrights but you'd never find them any better. What I knew of them bore out to the letter what Gussy said.

Mind you, in a pioneering community, and this was a pioneering community in its last years in that state, good neighbouring is a matter of necessity. You are your brother's keeper if for no other reason than that you need your brother to be your keeper when the chips are down against you. But the reason the Wrights lived so successfully and effectively in such a community was that being good neighbours came straight out of the goodness of their hearts.

A stall in their barn for the horse of any man in need of rest and grub in his journey, their door was closed to none. There was room at their table for the hungry, and if you didn't soak up a hefty draught of good cheer in their company, whatever was wrong with you was keeping the best things in life out of your heart. I never walked out of that house without being measurably better for having walked in and stayed awhile.

Burt's father was an Overlander. Johnnie Wright was his name, and he had arrived on the Cariboo road in 1865 at ten years of age when the gold fields to the north were ajump with hard-cut miners and the road itself, freshly hewed out by a company of Royal Engineers committed in 1858 to making a passable trek to Barkerville, bore a daily trek of men, men afoot, men with packs, men with mules, donkeys, horses, even pushing wheelbarrows.

Johnnie came with his father, stepbrother and stepmother. Little was said of the trip that I ever heard, except it took a year and was tough, a trip with ox team and wagon in search of gold. No one seemed to know now how many wagons, but they came by way of Oregon and the Wright wagon for one forsook the gold fields for the more enduring wealth of the road and the good earth.

Johnnie's father took up land at the 137 Mile, twenty-two miles north of what was now Lac la Hache as we knew it, and with the handful of stock he'd brought, began to farm and feed his produce to the travellers. In such a way, with rare exceptions, were all the ranches built that ribbon the Cariboo trail from the Fraser Canyon north.

Times were good, really, in those first years. At least there was money enough in the Cariboo that a young man might go out to Victoria, even as often as once a year, to relieve the hardship of life on the frontier. So it happened that in Victoria in 1875, at twenty years of age, Johnnie Wright met and married one Alice Ann Rowbottom, daughter of Captain and Mrs. Rowbottom of the Royal Engineers' garrison at Esquimalt.

Now Alice Ann's parents, it seemed, had come around the Horn, arriving in the garrison just two weeks before her birth. It had been a fierce journey, storms off the Horn battering the *Thames City* about like a cork. The passengers were required to throw furniture overboard to lighten the cargo. Mrs. Rowbottom, asked to discard a stove, threw away treasured linens of an equal weight instead, with what pangs of sorrow one can only guess. But she had the only cookstove in the garrison for several years afterwards, to reward her for her foresight.

And so of these came Burt's mother. Johnnie brought his bride up on the road by stagecoach, walking once on logs fallen across the boiling Fraser where a bridge had washed away. They lived first at the 137, but Johnnie pre-empted the 134, then traded it for another place, the 127. There they built their home and their children were born, Burt among them, six sons and six daughters.

Anxious to be in business at once, Johnnie built a house big enough to live in, then promptly pitched a big blue tent for a dining room and hung out his shingle as it were. He, too, was then in the trade of the road. Later of course he expanded the house to provide dining space and lodging rooms, but even yet the Wright family was spoken of by the old-timers as being of the old blue tent.

Johnnie and his family prospered as the road and the gold towns to the north prospered. Butter became the most salable commodity they could produce and at one time Alice Ann Wright dealt with the milk of seventy cows, three days' supply always on hand, no separators, and all the skimming done by putting the milk in pans to stand. "Pans, pans, and more pans," Mrs. Burt Wright said of it. "I've gone through it with only seven cows and I know what it must have been like."

Barkerville and the gold fields were the market, apart from the roadhouse itself. One heard stories of seven hundred pounds to this customer, five hundred pounds to that one.

They hayed with scythes, gathering the hay with pitchforks of forked willows if nothing else, stacking by dragging bundles of the wild grass in a lariat loop from the saddle horn, riding the horse over the pile of hay each time, one man on top undoing the loop and spreading the hay.

It was a hard way to make a living and only the good men, men humble enough and wise enough to put their lives into the labours of the good earth, stayed at it. Burt was of such men and his own family grew about him in the same traditions, traditions which are fast giving way in the gaudy, come-quick values of our times.

Yes, though every ranch house in the Cariboo was our stopping place when we might need it, it was best when our need brought us to Burt Wright's door.

Burt was a short man, strong but not stocky, balding noticeably, and smiling in a perpetual attitude of greeting.

"Hello, Julian." Then he saw me close on the Old Man's heels. "Alan," he said, in recognition. Then back to the Old Man again. "You're riding in cold weather."

"That we are," the Old Man acknowledged, pushing his glasses down on his nose to peer over them till they'd de-fog and he could see again. Then in explanation: "I'm missing two heifers."

"Oh? No sign of them around the meadow?"

"No. I'd done a lot of riding around out there after we moved the cattle and I haven't seen a track. I thought I'd better have another look out this way, now the boys are here for a few days."

Burt was silent, thinking about the heifers the Old Man was missing, knowing what two heifers meant to a small man because he was a small man himself. Only the big men, running outfits up to a thousand head or more, could shrug off a couple of missing animals comfortably.

The Old Man was sitting in a chair now, his feet toward the heater, his hands searching around his cumbersome clothing for the place he'd last left his pipe and tobacco. He found them, began filling the bowl. "If I don't spot them around the Milk Ranch, I guess I've lost them. It's getting pretty late, unless they've found their way onto someone's feed ground."

"I was just thinking that," Burt declared. "I counted up right this fall for once, but we'll take a good look tomorrow when we feed. We've got everything together here just now."

Stanley broke in: "Willie and I looked them over this morning while they were strung out on the hay. We were pretty sure we recognized every animal there." The long shaggy winter coat obliterates a brand, so a man can easily winter his neighbour's cow and not know it till spring. But with small herds a close look will sometimes tell you you're looking at a beast you didn't feed the winter before.

The Old Man shook his head. "You'd notice these heifers if you had them here. They're from the Hance stock I bought and you know how they stand out from the rest."

I was warm now. Indeed I had to pull back a ways from the heater at the smell of scorching wool. I slumped in my chair, drowsy and especially happy, listening to the talk of men, feeling that it wasn't long until I would truly be one of them.

Burt spoke again; this time his voice was heavy, rare with him. "The wolves are getting bad again."

"I know," the Old Man replied. "They're around the meadow more than they have been for quite a while. Not just a wolf or two either: a whole damn pack."

I thought of my walk to the meadow the evening before and I longed to put in my few words. I could say casually that I'd been thinking just that myself the other night when I'd heard them howling at the moon. Seemed an unusual lot of them I could say, but I decided against saying anything.

"I think," the Old Man went on, "I'm going to put some strychnine out. I'll set out pellets on the islands after we move to the Blaze so there's no chance of a dog picking them up." The islands were the small patches of pine and spruce timber on little rises of high ground that occurred here and there in the several hundred acres of the meadow. "You chaps will want to leave your dogs behind if you ride that way."

"That'll be a good idea," Burt agreed. "Then you can go around and pick them up in the spring. You'll have an idea how many wolves you got and you won't lose a dog next summer in haying."

The talk went on of the things that interest a cowman, that worry him and take up his time, of cows and calves, of horses and hay, and whether it was likely to be a tough winter and how it was better to have some cold weather now and get it over with, rather than a long cold spring that would hold back the green grass. Then in a while we all gathered around the table to a huge meal of root vegetables and beef, roasted in a great hulking chunk that would yield slice upon slice of hot juicy meat, thick and tender and smothered in gravy.

But all too quickly the meal was over and the Old Man was saying as he pushed back his chair how he'd like to sit and have another smoke but we'd really better shove along to the Milk Ranch and get the horses in for the night, warm up the old house for ourselves.

How cold the road then: out of the warm house into the night air, air so cold you coughed at the first few breaths of it, down to the barn for the horses, Stanley going along with a coal-oil lantern to make it easier getting around in the stalls, and back in the saddle for the last leg of the day's journey.

We spurred the horses up to a canter for as long as we dared, then walked them with an occasional spell of trotting to put the last two and a half miles in its place as quickly as we could. It was going for thirty below, no two ways about that, and we neither of us had any ambition to be out in it longer than necessary. At last we came to the shortcut trail to the big lease, leaving us less than a mile to go. We dropped off the saddles to walk that last bit, both for our own warmth and to be sure we cooled the horses well after the light run we had asked of them.

The horses into the stalls and generously fed, we turned eagerly toward the house, the same thought in both minds: fire up the old airtight and see how hot we could make 'er, how fast.

"Boy," I declared, "I'm sure gonna light up that ol' stove."

"Not unless you're quicker at it than your old dad, you won't."

We bypassed the front door, going directly around to the lean-to where we always had dry wood and kindling for just such a moment. We gathered an armful each, made our way in the back door.

Somehow there is no colder place in cold weather than the inside of a house that isn't lived in. Odd smells assail your nostrils, an emptiness surrounds you, you feel all about you is alien, be it even your own place. But light a lamp and stoke a fire why, all is well again and the place is home, an old log cabin under a shake roof at the meadow, or the frame house, boasting two rooms and an attic, at the home base.

The Old Man was the first to find a lamp, mainly because he'd been the last here and knew where he'd left it, and even before he had it lit I'd found some old newspaper to put under the kindling. The Old Man was a purist about fire lighting: he'd make shavings off a kindling stick with his pocket knife, big, curly shavings that lit with a great, cracking blaze and he scorned the use of newspaper.

But on an occasion like this he was strangely able to forego his purism; he even grasped up a sheet or two of paper himself and bundled it into the heater.

One of the old airtight type, this heater had a long pipe that drew so fast only the weight of the cast-iron body prevented the heater being sucked up its own chimney hole. The blast furnace nature of these old heaters cannot be appreciated by one who does not know the tremendous fire which may be generated with dry wood and a good draft. Draft depends on a long smoke pipe, so all the smoke pipes in our cabins on the ranch towered above the roof tops.

We heaped in the kindling, then dry wood. "Here," I urged, "let's put some more on. I'm darn near froze."

"Look out, man," he rebuked me dryly, "do you want to be warm or do you want to drop a chunk of cherry-red cast through the floor?"

He only barely exaggerated. Overstoked, I've seen the entire box turn bright red. Before long we were backing away; within minutes we opened the door. How good it felt!

I tended the horses in the morning while he made a breakfast of the staples we stocked in all our places. He was washing dishes, I drying, when I chanced to look out the window, across the field to the edge of the timber, over four hundred yards away.

"Dad! Look at this!" He came to the window at once.

"Well, what do you know about that," he said slowly. "Timber wolves. Big, aren't they?" They were the first timber wolves I had ever had more than a fleeting glance at, and they looked gigantic to me, but a timber wolf is a big canine. Two of them, they gambolled about at the edge of the timber for a while, then disappeared into it. There was neither time nor range to get a shot away, suppose the carbine had been in the house instead of in the Old Man's saddle scabbard in the barn.

"Do you suppose maybe the heifers ..." I paused, wondering if what I was about to say was reasonable.

"I'm quite ready to suppose so, boy." And he went wearily back to washing dishes, bent over with the lumbago that had struck him that morning. Many things eat away at the profits in the cow business, some most literally.

We saddled up to search the Milk Ranch field, then the big lease, finding no heifers, nor signs of heifers. Not a cow beast had been there in the past two weeks, probably more. We gave it up, deciding to start for the meadow at once so we'd make it back by nightfall.

As we turned north on the road, we heard the deep voice of a wolf howling in the timber not three hundred yards away. In a moment a coyote howled near the irrigation dam. He sounded impotent and ridiculous. The wolf howled again and the Old Man and I looked at each other significantly. This time the coyote kept quiet.

CABIN TROUBLE

There wasn't much to do around the Morton meadow, especially with four of us to do it. A couple of sleigh loads of hay a day, a few water holes to chop in the ice, some wood to split, a little cooking and water to pack: these were the daily tasks. The cabin no bigger than it had to be, which wasn't very big, and with a lot of time to sit in it, trying to keep the devil out of one another's way, each of us began to see that the other three weren't such a fine bunch of cabin partners after all.

Roger's attempts to whistle a tune — he couldn't whistle for stew if he was starving to death — grew from mildly ridiculous toward outright unbearable. Bill's habit of letting his false teeth clack when he talked got so you wanted to clack 'em right out of his mouth with a chunk of firewood.

The Old Man's insistence that we eat a little of the dried fruit every day that he set to soaking every night, to which we ordinarily acceded to keep our venerable parent happy, became the unreasonable demand of a tyrant that we dine on hog slop. I for one craved oranges so badly in deference to apple rings I was sorely tempted to quit camp and ride to Ogden's store at the highway on the off chance I'd find the fruit of my desires — though gosh knows oranges fit to eat were a far-from-common sight in a Cariboo country store at that time of year.

As for my bad habits, I sharpened my pocket knife and took to whittling, making an ingenious ball-in-a-cage contraption out of a piece of jack pine stove wood. Everyone was downright unreasonable when jack pine chips started showing up in their bedrolls or their porridge.

After a while it got so the old collie bitch was the only one in the bunch fit to live with and she only remained sane from the therapeutic necessity of tending her pups.

The Old Man made a suggestion one evening. "Tell you what, boys. You know it gets pretty tough if a couple of fellows are stuck in the same cabin too long together."

Then he stopped to suck on his pipe, make sure it was going. I stared at him in dumb amazement. Couldn't he count? I looked around quickly. One, two, three and me made four. Why, my gosh, the Old Man's going daft!

"So," he went on, "I kind of thought it would be a good idea if you paid a visit to Tom and Rex at Pete's Lake. They've been stuck in there quite a while now and it's a long time till spring. You boys might be just what they need, sort of cheer 'em up for a couple of days."

Oh, well, now that was different. Not talking about our little cabin at all. "Sure thing," I agreed. "Let's go first thing in the mornin', eh Roger?"

"'Sfine with me," Roger said.

So first thing in the morning we were off to visit Tom Barton and Rex Williams, a couple of middle-aged bachelors, tillicums of long standing, who were trying to hew a ranch out of the wilderness at Pete's Lake, a pond surrounded by a limited quantity of poor hay meadow and way to heck and gone back in the spruce and jack pine, a fair day's ride in the winter time from the Morton. Why the name Pete's Lake I never knew, save that the first man who went there to build a cabin and trap for muskrats and beaver in the pond and along the creek most likely was known as Pete.

To go there we would ride north on the Eagle Lake road another four miles — there was a shortcut trail from that end of the meadow to take us to the road — to Spout Lake where Buster and Millie Hamilton had their hunting and fishing camp. We'd visit there long enough to warm up, then take a trail eastward along the north shore of the lake and beyond the lake into the next depression several miles to Rex and Tom's cabin, a distance from Buster's camp of perhaps ten miles.

That first jag went quickly and we caught Millie making bread, something she was nearly always doing and at which we knew from experience she was extremely good. Alongside the bannock at the Morton meadow cabin her bread was the food of paradise.

Buster descended from a Hudson's Bay Company Scot and an Italian immigrant with a fine dash of Native, some Cree, some Salish. An expert hunter and trapper, he was even now out on his line, harvesting the best of the upland fur.

Millie was Swiss, second generation in Canada, dark and tall, finely shaped, kind as she was beautiful, and that was a mighty heap of kindness.

They were married in the tag end of the thirties and with a team and wagon, a few pots, pans, and tools and a good tent they trekked to Spout in early summer, making camp where the creek spills out of the lake. By fall they had a cabin of logs to live in. By the winter of which I now speak, they had several cabins and a modest lodge house built and were on their way to a thriving hunting and fishing business, catering largely to American sportsmen.

The winters free, Buster trapped, sometimes alone, sometimes with his father, Moffat Hamilton. Between them they'd make more in six weeks of fur chasing than the hunting and fishing brought in all season. Later, when the bottom dropped out of the fur market, the hunting and fishing developed to take up the slack. Buster was a man so competent in his native bush, in which most men only scraped by, that he extracted a good living from it.

Roy, their first born, was a toddler then and a healthier tad you never saw. He liked to sit on the couch, to bounce against the back. His day wasn't complete if he didn't bounce. Once Buster took Millie and Roy to stay in his brother's cabin at Lac la Hache for a few weeks and there was no couch. There was one raucous to-do when Roy discovered that fact and he demanded an immediate return to Spout to bounce.

Well sir, Millie fed us hot bread and Roy bounced for us while we warmed up next the heater and if we hadn't already said we were on our way to Pete's Lake, we'd have stayed right there.

"So you're going to visit Rex and Tom, are you? I think that's a nice idea. They get along better than most partners do, stuck off by themselves like that. But it can be awfully difficult, sharing the same cabin with the same face all winter, you know." Did we know? You bet we knew. We'd just had a few days of it and we could see the hazards, never mind a whole winter.

"We thought we'd cheer 'em up," Roger explained.

"Well, you just do that. They're a fine pair of men, even if they do seem to be cut a little rough at times. We've been wondering about them. They haven't been out since they started feeding their cattle, and Buster doesn't go in that way often."

We promised we'd cheer them up no end and report back to Millie on the way home. Then we wrenched ourselves away from the warmth, taking the long, cold trail north of the lake.

The air still and brittle, a bright sun, bereft of warmth, shone icily down on the great stretch of lake, an endless whiteness coldly bejewelled by the glittering flakes of hoarfrost. Even the treetops had their coat of frost, the cold penetrating everything. The upland willow, as resilient a wood as grows, would snap clean at a twist, just as here and there it had where a moose had broken down a thick stalk to reach the high growing, tender shoots.

Roger stopped by a tree, took a foot from the stirrup, and began kicking the tree.

"You be a long time 'fore you kick that tree down," I observed, anxious to keep moving.

"If you're bored, boy, get yaself a tree. When I'm done this foot, I'm goin' to start on the other one."

It seemed like a good idea so I chose a hefty pine tree and started kicking. Before long my foot was warm and I changed over. I could see this was a good way to keep your feet from freezing after you were too stiff to want to climb down any more for walking. The day wore on. The trail, well blazed, was easy to follow. Only where a number of moose had gone by, branching off the main trail, did we have to hunt for blazes to be sure which way belonged to man and which to beast. We were careful for, though we suffered no lack of confidence in our own ability to manage, it did not escape us that we were alone, we had never come this way before, and we were one devil of a long way out in the bush if anything did go wrong.

It was with a touch of uneasiness that we watched the December shadows lengthen and the sun drop quickly out of sight behind the timbered horizon.

"You figure it can be far?" I queried.

"No. But the Old Man and I came over the trail below the lake last time. I never been this way before."

We kept riding in silence, wanting to push our mounts but not daring to, knowing any moment we should arrive and it would be a bad business to arrive with warm horses.

Then suddenly we broke into the clearing wherein lay the barn and cabin of the homestead, snug in the winter landscape. A yellow light reached out from the cabin window, defying the oncoming night.

We held a quick council and rode in silence to the very door of the cabin. Then at a signal we began in unison to shout and whoop in all manner of disrespectful swearing at the occupants we knew to be within.

I grabbed the saddle horn as my horse flew back in terror, striking Roger's mount, all but spilling him, horse and rigging, into the snow. There stood Tom, door flung open, long face hanging out, giving tongue to the most colourful string of cuss words I'd ever heard. Only a man who, like Tom, had devoted his life to unrivalled mastery in the fine art of a varied profanity, could have matched it.

It was a joyous welcome. Holed up so long as they had been, a couple of wandering boys were an exciting social experience and Tom was soon fetching a lantern to show us our way to the barn. We watered and fed our horses, then were ushered into the cabin where Rex was busy cooking up moose meat and rice.

"You fellas lost? How's your dad? He got that new Englishman workin' for him yet? He any good? I got a good story about an Englishman."

"Never mind your stories. These boys are hungry. They come all the way from the Morton meadow today. You want some rice? Have some meat? You see Buster and Millie on your way in? How's Millie? When'd you come down from Williams Lake? You stop at the store?"

So they went on, news hungry, poor devils, and it was all we could do to get around any rice and meat what with answering all their questions. After the meal the tobacco tin came down on the table and they took out papers and baccy, rolling up cigarettes.

Tom pushed the tin toward us. "Smoke? Guess your old man don't let you, huh? Well, suit yaselves. Your Old Man ain't here." So we suited ourselves and pretty soon we were smoking like chimneys, having a whale of a time.

They were an odd pair, that. Tom was a lanky, humourous bloke who must have been a plague to his parents if half the stories he told of his youth were true. He seemed eternally good-natured and more than half of what he said was in appreciation of or contributed to the funny side of life. He was a little like a circus clown might be if, his talents innate, he decided to lead an ordinarily serious life but never quite succeeded.

Rex, by contrast, was short, well built and quick moving, once a prize fighter, fast tempered but as fast to forgive, emphatic and decisive in his speech and while he appreciated humour, his contribution was the funny story well told, for the laughs didn't grow in his bone the way they did with Tom.

Their cabin was a better affair than ours at the Morton, but still it wasn't much. There was a partition, dividing off a small bedroom at the rear and the remaining area, like all cabins, was kitchen, dining, and living all rolled into one, sometimes even tackle room, especially in cold weather when you brought the bridles in to save the horses the pain of frozen steel in their mouths in the morning.

They weren't men who'd been raised to ranching, but had found their way into ranch life for bread and butter. Tom's brother-in-law was the son of an original settler in the valley and in that way Tom found himself working around cattle and hay. Rex had come by it simply as a labourer in search of hire, and years earlier he'd worked for the Old Man.

I don't know how long they'd known each other, but I do know they were both around Tom's brother-in-law's place for a few years. This is the way of course such partnerships are made. Two men, working on the same outfit, find each other congenial. Unattached by family, they team up and decide to strike out on their own, hoping that through sacrifice and small beginnings, they might someday build a cow outfit to be proud about.

Tom's brother-in-law had helped them in some way, I had the impression, but in any event their beginnings were small and if living back this far in the bush as frugally as they had to was not a sacrifice to those two men, I'm no judge of men. I didn't count their cattle — you don't make a point of seeing just how limited a man's operation is when he's struggling to make a start — but I did help Tom feed each morning and the jag of hay we loaded out was only a fraction of what would feed the Old Man's herd, and his herd wasn't big enough yet to be economical.

But they seemed happy and enthusiastic about the beginnings of their ranch. We sat around after supper for hours and when they'd done extracting news of the outside from us, they began telling us where the ranch house would be built, how many rooms it would have, how the barn had to be expanded, where the land would be cleared to grow some tame hay, and what could be done to the meadows to cut more feed from that source.

Finally it grew late and we must turn in. Roger and I had already brought our bedrolls in from the backs of the saddles where they'd

51

been tied and we asked Tom and Rex where we should lay them out. We could see there were only two narrow pine-pole bunks and we made it plain we didn't intend to cause them any rearranging of their own facilities.

"Just which part of the floor's all we need to know."

"Why then," Tom declared, "take your pick. Never let it be said that in this sumptuous hotel, the guests don't get their choice of the rooms."

We did an inspection of the floor. It was ancient shiplap, unfinished of course, and time had warped it, curling up the edges of each board, creating ridges and valleys everywhere. We decided on the bedroom as against the kitchen and not wanting to clutter up their cabin with hay or spruce boughs for the few nights we might be there, we laid only our saddle blankets and chaps beneath our bedrolls.

Well sir, I tried it all ways. Disposed to sleep on my side, I gave that up because the boards weren't wide enough to fit a hipbone between the ridges. Then I tried my back. That wasn't handy because a boy's shoulder blades aren't designed to accommodate quite that much relief between mountain top and valley bottom. Finally I settled on my front, pulling one knee up to the side, a posture I've found to be as useful as any for sleeping on a tough surface.

Tom listened to us rolling around in the dark in our futile search for comfort. His voice boomed out of the corner of the cabin: "You boys okay?"

"Oh fine," I said. "Just trying to fit the floor as best we can."

"That's good. Comfy?"

"Sure. You betcha boots."

"Well, g'night. Anything you want, you ring for the butler."

"You bet we will."

We had a wonderful visit. We set to readily, helping to feed the cattle and do the usual chores around the cabin. What was drudgery at home seemed an adventure when we did it for Tom and Rex. We even looked around for things to do without being told.

Tom was preparing to put a proper roof on the barn, which presently was flat-roofed with hay stacked on top. In the warmest part of the day, early to midafternoon, he would work at cutting rafters from the long slender poles he had hauled in from the woods nearby. Roger went to help him and they argued good-naturedly for fully an hour on how you calculate the pitch of the rafters.

While Rex did the cooking, I volunteered to straighten up the cabin. Every little while we'd sit down and chat, invading the tobacco tin.

It seemed these fellows led the ideal life. Humble though their lot might be, what they did, they did for themselves, not for some outfit where they hired at going wages. The sacrifices they made were so that they themselves would know a better day. And after all, though they experienced little material abundance, there was no cause ever to be short of food. They could grow all the vegetables they needed, and meat walked the forest for the shooting. Being so congenial and being together, they were spared the hardship that faces a man starting out alone: the struggle of the long winter by himself, feeding cattle from snowfly to break up without a day's rest or a soul to talk to. It was easy to believe in their dream, just as assuredly as they did, that someday here would be a ranch to reckon with, a cow outfit with an iron that would be known a long way from home.

Mind you, you couldn't help realizing that basically Rex didn't care for livestock. He hadn't been born a husbandman as some are: soil, crops, and stock their destiny as sure as the sun rises and the seasons pass. Cattle were the means of beef and beef the means of money. Horses were sheer necessity and the sooner they could be replaced by tractors the better. As for cowboy work, Tom could handle that.

Certainly Tom was more of a stockman. He could look at well-bred, skillfully finished steers and appreciate the accomplishment for what it was without seeing it only as so many pounds at so much a pound on the hoof. Still there wasn't quite the love in the labour of the land and the animals that will hold a man to his piece of ground and his cow herd no matter what the odds. He'd once punched a time clock in a plant of some kind, a symbol of the regimented life the rancher works twelve or more hours a day to avoid, and he saw his present way of life partly as an escape from that other, where perhaps he should have valued it more for what it was in itself.

About the third morning of our stay we happened to finish up feeding early and the men decided, since the larder was low, to go out for meat while a good carcass could still be taken, before the winter advanced too far. We would split into two parties: Tom and Roger to hunt the spruce and willow bottom along the lake, Rex and I, the upper meadow and the woods toward Bluff Lake, another small body of water to the northwestward.

Only one problem remained before setting out. Rex and Tom were caring for a Doberman pinscher, owned by a friend at the highway who was away for the winter, an uncontrollable oaf of a dog whose presence on a hunt was an almost certain preclusion of success. Nor could the dog be left behind. The barn wasn't dog tight and he'd make a mess of the cabin. He was sure to go berserk and hurt himself if he was left tied.

Rex felt his chances of success, all other things equal, were better than Tom's. He therefore felt it logical the dog should hinder Tom's hunting, not his.

"You take the dog, Tom," he said, as we paired up outside the cabin, ready to leave.

"Why should I take the dog?"

Rex took no notice of Tom's protest and began walking off. A little confused but presuming the matter was settled, I followed. The dog did too.

Rex turned suddenly on the beast. "Go back, you mutt!" he shouted, raising his rifle as he would a club. The dog took the hint, scurrying back to Tom. I saw Tom's face then as I'd never seen it before, black with fury.

"Sure! The hell with old Tom! Tom don't count. Push the goddamn dog on old Tom. Tom's an easy mark. Tom won't say nothin'!"

It was a frightening moment and suddenly I knew two things: that if anything angered Tom it was the suspicion someone was deliberately taking advantage of his good nature and also that all was not as well as it might be in the cabin at Pete's Lake.

"C'mon, Al," Rex said quietly and again we simply walked away, this time without the dog. After a time I glanced back and I could see Roger and Tom just leaving the clearing, the curse of a dog bouncing around in front of them, oblivious, obviously, to Tom's efforts to make him heel.

"Tom ain't very happy, huh?" I suggested.

"Oh, he'll get over it," Rex shrugged.

And, seemingly, he did. We all returned without meat but Tom was his same old self as far as we could tell, and never mentioned the subject again.

After another day or two we left, for we knew the Old Man would begin to wonder about us. He had no way of knowing we had arrived safely until we returned and therefore we were anxious not to overstay our visit. We saddled up early in the morning by lantern light and took the trail at daybreak, waving and shouting a rowdy goodbye until we were gone from sight, a couple of spare smokes rolled up in our shirt pockets, knowing full well there was one little game would be over as soon as we were back to the Morton and wondering how the devil we'd keep our yellow fingers hidden until the stain wore off.

I fear I left with the distinct feeling that the seeds of dissonance were sown within that cabin, all the best natures and intentions in the world notwithstanding. That's all I can say, except that even yet I hear of Tom and Rex as pals good and true. But within a year or two of the time when we visited them, they quit their piece of meadow and came out to civilization to stay. Maybe that was the price of friendship.

Wet Summer

C hristmas went and Easter came. The Old Man had saved some necessary riding so we could help him. After Easter we were out to the ranch most weekends. We left school for the summer a month early on a war measure applicable to students with farm work to go to. We joined in a roundup for branding the new calf crop and turnout onto the summer range. There were long days in the saddle and good weather to go with them.

Only days after turnout, we had bear trouble on the range about halfway to the meadow. Riding enough to watch for just such grief, the Old Man came on a calf that had been clawed by a bear but escaped, presumably when the bear turned to kill another animal in the herd. We suspected, in fact, that once a bear had become a killer he wouldn't necessarily want food to do damage but would ravage through the herd, maiming to left and right of him out of the sheer savagery of his nature.

The Old Man brought the calf to the Milk Ranch to try some doctoring. Milking a brindle with plenty to spare after providing for her own calf and ourselves, we had milk enough to give him. But the brindle's milk and the Old Man's doctoring weren't enough. The open wound, which appeared to be draining successfully at the top of the shoulder, infected badly, and soon there was a seam of putrid matter throughout the flesh below the shoulder blade. The calf grew less active and finally would only stand in a corner of the corral, head down, back humped up, the eyes lifeless. The Old Man fetched the carbine and shot him.

The losses continued, with several animals missing. It was hard to be sure of course, unless you found a carcass, that an animal had been killed, the entire herd scattered as it was over many square miles of summer range. Still the situation was critical and would remain so until later in the season when, other food more plentiful, the bears might lay off the livestock.

"What you gonna do, Dad?" I asked.

The Old Man groaned at my abuse of the language but said nothing, having long since given up. "I'm going to kill a horse for bait and offer a reward for bear."

Picking a scrubby horse out of the bunch, the kind of animal that would never bring the price of raising him no matter who you saw coming, he led him onto the infested territory and shot him. Then he passed word around that bears shot on his range were now worth ten dollars a piece and we went back to other tasks.

A couple of the local men with a yen for bear hunting went out to lie by the bait. One bear was soon shot and another wounded. This reported to the Old Man, he paid for the dead one but not the wounded, preferring to have one more attempt made to finish the beast off.

I begged to go out with the hunters on an expedition to track the wounded bear, but apart from finding a place where the brute had lain for several hours and bled, we came on no traceable spoor. Evidently he had lain still long enough for the bleeding to stop, then moved far back into the timber.

The trouble was by no means over. Several more bears were killed during the month, but the signs of damage persisted. Bordy Felker, the owner of the Lazy R ranch, the biggest outfit in the valley, reported calf-killing on his range several miles to the east.

But nothing more could be done. It was June and the spring growing weather had been good: just enough rain, plenty of sunshine. The Old Man got to walking around in the hay, trying to decide what he needed most: ten days more of growth or a ten-day head start on the harvest. His mind made up, bears were forgotten for lack of time to worry about them.

He gathered crew for which he had earlier made tentative arrangements. Olie Karlander, a hard-working, one-legged Swede who lived down the Eagle Lake road from us, came to work, his wife to cook. Her daughter by a previous marriage, Sylvia Ogden, two years older than I and as good a hand, joined the crew in the field. With Bill Wilson, that made the crew.

Olie was a good man. He'd immigrated years ago, working in the bush as a logger in other parts of Canada. He lost a leg in an industrial accident which put him out of logging, but didn't by a long ways prevent him from making a living. Fitted with a wooden limb, he took to carpentering mainly, but he'd turned his hand at many things, even hacking railroad ties with a broad axe to see himself through the depression.

A slight man but strong, not tall, quick to laugh, he was strongly principled. Conscientious, he was the sort of man who would work extra time at the end of the day to make up if you gave him coffee in the middle of the morning. And a jug was a yug and a "yug was a damn good ting" but it never interfered with getting on with the job come Monday morning.

Gussy Haller, his family for crew, contracted, taking the Blaze and the Alfie meadows. "It's no use you working under me," the Old Man told him. "You know more about this haying business than I do. Two separate crews running, we'll be through quicker."

Contracting was Gussy's meat, bone and sinew. He was one of that breed of men who are thoroughly competent and hard working in the day to day business of getting the job done. No man, given the same equipment, could get more hay up in a day or take more pride in making the best hay possible in the available weather. If he built you a fence, why you could count on it to be the best fence you'd ever had built.

But Gussy never successfully got into the cow business on his own. The management end of things just wasn't his cup of tea.

For one thing he thought too much of horses and too little of cows. When he should have been buying heifers, he was dickering for cayuses or grub-staking himself to a winter chasing unbranded wild horses off the Big Bar Mountains along the Fraser River.

Still, he'd found a way to make a living in ranch work, notwithstanding that he never built an outfit of his own. He built instead an unassailable reputation for hard work, dependability, and good faith: a man whose word was worth more than many a written contract any day. If he said he'd cut and stack your meadow at seven dollars a ton, why, count on it man, he'd stack your meadow and give you the best hay he could, no drying it out and fluffing it up to stretch the tape at measuring time.

No, the Old Man made a good decision, putting Gussy on contract and hiring other crew himself to try to be done more quickly if he could. And he'd have done all right, too, except for the weather.

The rains came without mercy. They began with the first mowing; they were still coming with cruel regularity in the fall.

Not once all summer did we put up a stack from hay which had not been rained on once, or several times, and dried out in between. This fussing about, raking it up only to get it wet, scattering it out again afterwards to dry, ruins the hay while it doubles the costs. There was no chance of the beef shipment that fall paying for the kind of harvest we were having.

The intervals of sunshine were always long enough to let us start something, never to finish it. We'd rake some hay, planning to top the bunches into watertight cocks by hand. With the hay half in the windrow and half in the bunch, the cocking only started, the clouds would blow up from nowhere and rain would be there.

Or the Old Man would have a stack half finished. He'd wait until the weather looked settled, then send us out to load our sloops while he'd open up the stack, spreading the emergency top he'd built at the onset of the last storm. Maybe he'd pile a few loads in and maybe he wouldn't, but sure as he had the top of the stack flat to spread out a few more tons, a savage wind would tear through the valley and before he could close up again, it would be raining.

At the Milk Ranch for a month doing two weeks' work, we then moved to the Morton meadow. It rained so much we forgot what a jack pine tree looked like without water dripping off its needles.

Just camping a crew that size in a wet summer at the Morton was bad enough, let alone try to hay as well. Olie and his family took the only cabin, an old one, where his wife could care properly for the two small children. But it was a small cabin and to have no other refuge in a spell of wet weather was no easy matter. It didn't leak but it grew dismal and depressing under the eternally sunless sky.

The Old Man and Bill slept in a fair-sized tent with a fly, an extra piece of canvas the size of the tent roof, stretched over it to be sure it didn't leak. But everything in a tent dampens in wet weather and soon the Old Man was walking half sideways, twisted painfully with rheumatism. He rustled up an old heater from somewhere, setting it up in the tent, and gained some relief from that.

Roger and I shared a badly built pole shack with room in it for two narrow pole bunks, nothing more. It would have been suicide to put a stove in it. Nonetheless it seemed to shed the rain, though damp clothes and bedroll were a constant discomfort. The shortage, too, of hay dry enough for bedding became so acute at one point that we worked down to the knots on the pine poles in the bunks and had nothing with which to replenish the padding.

One night the sky exploded. Torn from sleep by the sheer pain in my ears, I was instantly blinded by a flash of lightning that poured through the cracks between the poles as though the shack weren't there.

I twisted on my bed, burying my face in the blankets, grasping my ears, frantic to shut out the next searing crash of thunder. Before the light was gone it was there, drowning out everything in one's consciousness save the trembling of the bed and the terrifying conviction that the shack would get it next.

After an eternity of ripping crescendos, the echoes died away, leaving a silence so complete one could well wonder if this wasn't eternity itself.

"Roger. Are you there?" It was an exploratory question.

"I ain't nowhere else on a night like this. Sufferin' cats! Here it comes again!" In the brilliant light I caught a glimpse of him then, propped on an elbow, staring into the violence of the night. But only a glimpse, for I threw my face down and covered my ears once more.

Practically no interval before the first clap, we knew the bolt had come to earth within feet of the camp, perhaps in the yard itself. Again we endured those seconds of unholy fury as though we heard the sky itself ripped to shreds, cast into a wild, cosmic confusion. Still, the very fact we heard it assured our safety until the next bolt.

A horse whinnied a scream-like cry of panic and then the bunch raced by, running the yard from fence to fence, pounding hooves close together, in terror, bewildered, running aimlessly but running, for it was all they knew to do.

"You think they'll try to go over the fence?" I wondered aloud.

"Nah. They're scared so bad, you couldn't fence 'em out of camp right now."

Another bolt came but we didn't flinch this time. The brightness was noticeably less and I counted four before the blast of sound.

"Gone over," I observed.

"Yep. Listen, there's the rain."

Down it came, in great solid sheets, splashing on the ground, splashing against the shack, the sound of it running everywhere. I thought of the Old Man and knew how he'd be lying awake thinking of it, thinking of his hay, of how the meadow was wet enough now without all this, of how if something didn't happen to change the weather there wouldn't be hay to winter half the cows, suppose he sold everything but breeding stock at sacrifice prices.

"Dammit, the shack's leaking!" Roger brought me back to our own problems.

"Where? Hell, it never leaked before."

"It's leaking now! Right over my bunk."

"My gosh. Well, there isn't much we can do about that till morning. Roll your bedding to a dry place and climb in here."

"You got room?"

"No, but you gotta squeeze in anyway."

He did have to squeeze in. His bedding was drenched by the time he got out of it. We huddled together on a bunk I reckoned was too small for me alone and there we toughed it out till morning, listening to the rain fall without letup into daybreak.

Fortunately for all hands, the rest of the camp came through dry. One spot leaked in the tent but was out of the way of bed or gear. The cabin took it. The big bonfire we kept burning in the yard had drowned out and as soon as there was the least break in the rain we fetched dry wood from the shed behind the cabin to nurse it to a blaze again.

Roger brought his bedding and we held it against the fire to dry in the lulls, dashing with it to shelter whenever the rain started up afresh. The shack quit leaking and by the time his bedroll was as dry as we could make it he was able to take it back. His meagre supply of hay shot of course, I split what remained of mine. That put us both on the pine knots but good.

Life in camp went on. We all crowded into the cabin three times daily for meals but beyond that there simply wasn't room. Mainly we kept the big fire burning and stood around it, drying the rain off one side, soaking it up on the other.

Sometimes we built fence or slashed brush to extend the yard. At first we went out only in the lulls, but after a while we went out regularly, preferring to be wet and occupied as against just wet. Olie started making logs for a new cabin and then we all helped with that until the logs were gathered and the slow, more skilled task of raising the walls began. At that point the Old Man left Olie one helper, usually Roger, while the rest of us turned back to brush and fencing.

I worried about the Old Man, watching his face grow more weary daily. It seemed one man alone couldn't stand it and yet he plodded on, looking westward at the sky more frequently as time went by, waiting for the break that would show there, had to show there eventually.

"Pretty tough ain't it ... I mean, isn't it, Dad?"

The Old Man looked at me thoughtfully a moment, in an oddly affectionate way. "Do you think you'll stand it?" he asked.

Puzzled, I replied: "Sure, I'll stand it. I was thinking about the hay and all this rain."

"Oh yes, that," he said, and suddenly I knew just what a great big man my old father was. The rain seriously threatening to force a sacrifice of half the herd he'd been years putting together and by the Lord Harry what ate him was the lot of us having to put up with some weather, nothing more important on our minds than three squares a day and keeping dry at night.

The water began to rise in the meadow. This was worst of all for now even if the rains stopped, we could hardly mow hay that stood in several inches of water.

"I think," the Old Man decided, "I'm going to dig a ditch, a damned great long ditch, and get rid of some water."

I pictured a mammoth canal, cut across the vast Cariboo plateau, draining the sky itself. Maybe the weather was really driving him around the bend, more than we knew. "How," I asked, "do you figure to do that?"

"With shovels. How else?"

"Oh."

He called Bill. The three of us trudged down to the far end of the meadow, carrying shovels, a fork, a scythe, and a hay knife, a contraption like a straight-ended shovel only jagged and sharp which one uses by thrusting it downward into the stack to cut the hay when one wishes to use one end of a stack and leave the remainder untouched.

"Now," he explained, "there's a piece of low ground here at the end of the meadow. We dig a ditch, not a big one, starting here in the bush. Then we dig back into the meadow. If water runs in our ditch, we keep on digging. We dig as long as there's water. Got it?"

I could see us going through a powerful lot of shovels before we ran out of water. But we began. Soon our ditch was into the meadow and a current was running, carrying water into the bush and away on a gentle drop of land beyond; such a pitiful trickle though when you compared it to the acres of water sitting on the meadow, it was hard to believe in what we were doing.

We scythed the grass out of the way and with the hay knife we cut the sod into square chunks in a strip two feet wide. Coming behind the knife with a pitchfork, we lifted each square of sod out, tearing it loose at the bottom. We worked in water over our ankles, our feet sodden. As each piece of sedge root sod came out of the ditch, water replaced it.

We'd go home at night after a day of this and peel dead, white skin from our feet. Our boots were ruined. Nonetheless we stayed at it if for no other reason than that we could no longer stand to watch rain pour out of the sky. Our ditch grew longer and longer, farther into the meadow than the Old Man had planned, and we were encouraged by the increasing flow of water.

We hoped with all our might the rain would quit. It kept on coming down. Now at least what fell on the meadow had somewhere to go, though there were parts of the hay land so boggy that we could never cut them that year. Would we ever now have sufficient hay to feed our cattle in the coming winter? It was impossible to be hopeful.

Then the weather showed signs of change. Even before the rain actually stopped, the Old Man took action. "Bill," he instructed, "you put on a pair of chaps to keep your legs dry and go out there to mow hay. You keep on mowing no matter what."

Mowing hay in the rain was contrary to everything I had learned about haying. Again I wondered if the Old Man wasn't suffering a mite too much under the strain. "Still rainin', Dad," I said casually, to make him realize what he was doing without letting him know I suspected the worst.

"I know it's raining, you silly ass! But if I cut the hay now, there'll be hay down to dry when the sun does come out. It won't come out for long, you can count on that, and we won't waste it mowing. We can rake as soon as we dare." He tamped his pipe thoughtfully with a calloused thumb, impervious to the burning of the tobacco he had already lit. "And," he added, "if it doesn't work, it won't make any difference. We won't get the hay up anyway."

The change held. Soon we were haying and none of us had ever known anything so good in our lives. We still had rainy days but little by little we made progress.

Other grief beset us. The stacking poles we used were several years old but, carefully laid up on blocks each winter, they gave every sign of soundness. Dry and light, they handled well and to cut new poles would have seemed most unwise.

We were halfway through the first stack and all pressing ourselves, knowing the urgency the weather had put upon our every move. I came in with a heavy load, some of it dangerously wet but not that much that the Old Man couldn't work it in by spreading it along the very edges of the stack. Hurriedly I set the blocks, unhooked from the sloop, picked up the derrick cable, and tightened the slings. I always looked back at this point for a signal from the Old Man, just to be sure he was ready.

He waved me on. "Git!" I urged the team and quickly the load lifted from the sloop, rising fast up the front of the stack. On it went, higher, over the lip, now a foot of clearance, now two, now five, and that's good enough.

"Whoa! Whoa, you horses."

In a clean, unbroken movement the load came to the end of the rise and swung in over the stack. The fore line tightened, grabbing the poles, arresting the swing. The load went on and I wondered if the Old Man would trip it now or catch it on the first swing back. He'd had trouble grasping the trip rope as it went by and he might not judge his moment to pull. I readied myself to unhook the second the slings would burst, spilling the hay.

My stomach wrenched into a knot as I saw the load go on, the left pole splinter apart halfway from the stack top to the peak of the derrick, the crash of shattering wood hard on the sight of the right pole swinging crazily, then plunging down, driving the broken end like a skewer into the hay.

The Old Man had thrown himself into the stack, head down, crouching for what protection it might give him. I'd seen him go from sight and the broken pole end follow him into the hay but whether hurt or not I couldn't know from where I was.

I backed the team to slack the derrick cable. Somehow in spite of the trembling that seized me I got the cable ring off the doubletree hook. I dropped the lines and turned to run for the back of the stack where the Old Man had a ladder when, brushing hay from the back of his neck, he rose slowly up from the stack to survey the damage.

"You all right?" I shouted.

"Oh hell, I'm all right." Then thoughtfully: "We ruined us a pole, didn't we?"

I gulped. "We sure did. I guess I made my load too heavy."

"Oh, no. In a summer like this all the loads are too heavy. I just misjudged the poles, that's all."

We untangled the mess then and shut down to fetch new poles, losing precious hours of stacking weather, followed by the inevitable shower just when the new poles were ready to go.

As if bad luck haying wasn't enough, we had to have it other ways. Bill and the collie had become inseparable companions. Wherever he worked she followed. If he was out with the mower, she'd make the first round or two with him, then find a sheltered place in a nearby bush to lie where she could see him, to join him again when it came time to return to camp.

We were cocking hay one afternoon when a threatening shower had stopped us stacking and compelled us to top up the remaining bunches. Bill worked from bunch to bunch near one of the islands of timber in the middle of the meadow. The old collie left him briefly to explore the bush along the edge and suddenly came running back to him, crying in an agony of pain.

Bill knelt with her, talking to her, trying to quiet her whimpers, at a loss to know what afflicted her. Her pain increased, she went into convulsions and in moments, her head resting in his hands, she died.

Then we knew. She had picked up a strychnine pill set out for wolves which, despite the Old Man's scrupulous efforts to recover all the poison he'd set out, had lain there since last winter.

Bill picked the old girl up in his arms and walked away across the meadow to the timber to find a place to put her away, hobbling along pitifully on his bad feet. The first spattering drops coming as he started, it was raining so hard when he reached the trees you could barely make him out.

We all put our forks at the stackyard, to trod wearily back to camp. That night Bill didn't come for supper.

Occasionally we saw something of Gussy. He'd ride over once in a while to see the Old Man, or perhaps one or two of us would visit the Blaze to pass the time in the eternal wet. He was making no more progress than we were. He had also a share of bad breaks. One night a porcupine chewed the front guy line while the poles rested on the back line. When the first load went over the front line tightened and snapped, the poles crashing to the ground behind the stack, shattering themselves and the stackyard fence at the same time.

Haying done that fall, we were terribly short of winter feed. So was every other cowman in the country and therefore there was none to buy, suppose there had been any money to buy it with after paying the costs of the haying. All we needed was a long tough winter and it would be a hard row to hoe indeed.

The Old Man knew he would have to ship every animal that could sell to advantage, maybe some that couldn't. The season dealt him one backhanded stroke of luck, if you could call it that: the bears had killed so many calves on the summer range that he had nearly a carload of dry cows and heifers in butcher-fat condition. They brought a better price, with more poundage, than they would have had their calves been with them.

Roger and I, of course, had to leave the camp before the end of haying to return to school. In the last few days I was almost sure I looked forward to it. I had grown sick of hay and sick of fighting it in bad weather. Our every hour revolved around it. We fed it to our horses, we pitched it on our sloops, we cocked it up in the face of oncoming rain, we even slept on it.

The Old Man drove us out of camp to our mother's house in Williams Lake in the first week of September and for the first time in many weeks we slept in a proper bed. No sooner there and surrounded by comforts, I fell in an agony to be back on the ranch. I would have traded the soft mattress of my mother's house for the jack pine poles and swamp grass of camp on the instant, were it my choice to do so. Unhappily it wasn't, though wisely so, no doubt.

CHRISTMAS IS LIKE ANY OTHER DAY

 The cards were called between the Old Man and Mother that fall. While it is not part of this yam to hang old washing on the line, some matters need explaining.

Back before my time, the Old Man had the Eagle Lake ranch, ten miles farther out on the road beyond Spout. Business took him away from the place to Victoria, the capital of the Province, on Vancouver Island. In that city he entered the Jubilee Hospital to be rid of an offending appendix and, lo, he met my mother nursing there. In time they married.

A painting hangs on my study wall. Centrally, one sees a typical small log cabin, chinked with mud, a Yukon chimney poked through the roof, a whiff of wood smoke trailing from it.

Around the cabin runs an old log fence and inside the fence a tent is pitched, no doubt to accommodate crew or other extra persons for whom there is no room in the cabin. Behind the cabin there is a clothesline, hanging from the visible part of which one sees the bright blue of denim, the ranch man's favourite cloth.

In the background rise the trees, the jack pine and spruce of the Cariboo country which, wild and untracked, reaches hundreds of miles in many directions before it comes to more than a trapper's shack or another such isolated piece of hay land around which some hardy devil is trying to make a ranch.

In front of the cabin, outside the log fence, there is a pile of firewood drying in the sun. Beside it a black border collie rests, looking enquiringly away to the right of the picture where there is another log structure, perhaps a tool shed or barn or smoke house for curing ham and bacon. Contentedly, oblivious to his certain fate, a hog roots about in the soft earth searching for tidbits, company, in the absence of any other, for the dog.

To this my mother came as a bride. It is little wonder, I suppose, after the environs of the city that it was more than she could adjust to. Although the Old Man moved the headquarters of his operation close to the highway, selling the Eagle Lake ranch and building a log house second to none in the territory, in 1941 Mother left the ranch for good and went to live in Williams Lake. The Old Man sold the big house then and the Milk Ranch, hitherto the nearest of the hay lands, became the home place of the ranch.

Mind you, it was not only that she never really was happy with ranch life. Without saying more, their natures were vastly different. Had Mother been more inclined to the ranch, they might have bridged the other gaps. Had they not had other differences, she might have adjusted to the ranch. But in the aggregate a situation existed which was clearly irreparable, which it would have been folly to try to repair and which the Old Man finally realized must be struck from the books for good.

Divorce in the air that fall of 1944, Mother decided to move to Vancouver, putting the Cariboo itself behind her. When school closed in mid-December she left for the coast, and Roger and I for the ranch for a few last days before we, too, would go to the city. She asked us to join her before the twenty-fifth of the month so that she might not be alone for Christmas. Roger agreed but I refused. I could see the need to leave the ranch for school, but for no other cause would I set foot off my father's ground. She did not press me.

We joined the Old Man at the Milk Ranch. Bill was at the Morton with the cattle and we spent a few days poking around the home place at the odds and ends there were to do: splitting a little wood, some fixing in the barn, and a bit of riding, more for the joy of it than anything else.

I got to thinking of Bill, alone at the meadow cabin. I'd grown genuinely fond of him and knew I'd not see him again for several months. We were running out of odd tasks around the Milk Ranch and, with Christmas only a couple of days away, the Old Man had to see Roger off to Vancouver.

"I think," I proposed at supper, "I'll ride out to the Morton tomorrow to see Bill. Maybe I could go see Millie too."

"Fine," the Old Man agreed. "I'll follow you out in a day or two. Take some eggs to Bill. It'll be all the change he'll have for Christmas. When I last saw Millie she said to come that way for Christmas Day if we had no other plans. And I guess we haven't."

I guessed not, too. The possibility of the Old Man and me rigging up a tree in the old frame house at the Milk Ranch and batching our way through a festive dinner was more or less preposterous.

I struck out on the Eagle Lake road early the next morning, eggs wrapped in gunny sacks behind the saddle, no bedroll, for the Old Man had left plenty of blankets at the Morton cabin for both of us. I arrived in good time in the late afternoon.

"Bill, you old convict! How are you?"

"Fine! Fine! How's yourself? Put your horse in the barn and come on in. I've done feeding. Is this Christmas Day? I've kind of lost track of the calendar."

"No, tomorrow's Christmas. Look here, I broughtcha some eggs."

"Bully for you, boy. That'll be a good change from porridge and bannock."

He took the eggs while I tended my horse and soon I was back to the cabin. "What's for supper?"

"Eggs, of course. What do you think?"

"Well, gosh, Bill. Those eggs are for a change for you. You should keep 'em till I'm gone."

"No. It's Christmas and we'll have eggs." He broke one to drop it in the pan. It wouldn't come out of the shell. "Hey, boy, you froze these eggs."

71

"No! Did I? Aw, Bill, I'm awfully sorry. I wrapped 'em in two gunny sacks and I didn't think it was that cold. What'll we have now?"

"Eggs. What the hell you think? Pass me that spoon."

I passed him the spoon which he used to scoop the eggs into the pan where they sat like translucent golf balls, the bacon fat spattering around them furiously until gradually they melted and adopted a posture reasonably appropriate to an egg.

"You think they're gonna be all right, huh?"

"Haven't the foggiest, my boy. Haven't the foggiest. But I do know this much: they'll be no good at all if they thaw out before we cook 'em." With that he put on another pan and scooped in the rest of the dozen.

So it happened that on Christmas Eve of 1944, Bill Wilson and Alan Fry consumed a dozen eggs for supper, among other cabin-crafted rarities like greasy bacon and tough bannock, then sat around in the lamplight to the wicked hour of nine-thirty trading yarns, at which time I rustled around in a big dunnage bag full of bedding till I came up with some suitable blankets and we socked off for the day, bringing in Christmas dead to the world.

We let ourselves sleep in till daybreak for I had told Bill I'd help him with the feeding before I rode on to Spout. I lay on the spare bunk looking up at the decrepit ceiling of the cabin. The new cabin Olie had begun wasn't ready for use yet, wouldn't be until another wet summer provided an opportunity to finish it. Daylight was seeping in the only window and I wondered if old Bill was awake yet.

"Bill? You awake?"

"Sure thing."

"Merry Christmas, Bill."

"Same to you, boy. Merry Christmas. Though I guess it's not a very merry one for you this year."

"Oh, I wouldn't say that. It's really no different from any other day anyway." Then: "Christmas hasn't been much for you for quite a few years has it, Bill." I said it more than I asked it.

"No," he agreed. "It hasn't. But that's the way it is when you're a hired man, from one place to another. Christmas Day the cows have to be fed, like any other day, and chances are you're away out in the sticks somewhere like this. But I don't mind. Like you say, it's no different from any other day."

We quit philosophizing and crawled out into the cold air of the cabin. Before long Bill had the place hot as sin with the tinder-dry pine he laid on the heater fire. Then he started the cookstove and put on some porridge.

"That's breakfast, huh, Bill?"

"That's breakfast. That and canned cow and coffee."

I thought about that for a while, my natural yen for protein in the morning rebelling at the idea of plain untarnished porridge with condensed milk. "Bill, you better fire the cook."

"I thought of that, but I don't know where I'd hire another one so cheap."

"Well," I acknowledged thoughtfully, "that's a point."

"Anyway," he went on, "if I fire the cook, the maid'll quit. Then I'll *really* be up a creek. No grub, no bed made."

I looked at Bill's bed, which hadn't been made in weeks and had the appearance of being stirred up daily with a stick. "I think," I observed slyly, "you better have a word with the maid *about* making beds. She's obviously too darn tied up with the cook."

I leaped for the door, barely escaping as Bill, joyously, came to the attack with a broom. He failed to follow me out into the snow, however, so I immediately fetched the axe from the woodshed and approached a hind quarter of meat I'd seen hanging in front of the cabin on my arrival.

It hung from a crossbar between two trees, the bar fitted with a pulley for easy raising and lowering. I dropped the meat to a convenient height and in a couple of mean whacks with the axe had two thick chops taken from the round, across the frozen grain: tough frying meat but frying meat just the same.

Bill accepted my peace offerings graciously, frying them up while we ate the porridge, and allowing in ominous tones that the Old Man would have something to say about the mess I'd made of a good roast of moose.

Soon we were out with the team hooked to the big sleigh with the hayrack, trotting briskly along the broken sleigh trail across the meadow to the open stack where the cattle already were gathered outside the stackyard fence, bawling hungrily for the late feeding. They didn't appreciate that it was Christmas, though we couldn't have been more than an hour late.

I dropped the bars and Bill drove in alongside the stack to load. The bars up again, I took the spare fork I'd brought along and climbed the ladder at the back of the stack. Still in the exuberant mood we'd created earlier, I leaped into the hay, lifted a hefty forkful, threw it on the rack.

My throat seized. I dropped my fork, coughing furiously, the white cloud of must I'd raised drifting slowly away from the stack.

"Whooee, that's awful hay!" Tears in my eyes from the fit of coughing, I picked up my fork, approaching the task more cautiously.

"You saw it go in last summer. I'm afraid it's all like that."

It was bad hay, no two ways about it. Everywhere it was musty, some places it was black and had heated. It occurred to me too that not only was this the sort of hay the Old Man had, it was the sort of hay every cowman in the Cariboo faced the winter with. That was a dismal prospect.

We scattered the load out in a long oval, and as the cattle strung out on it to feed, Bill stopped the sleigh to take the daily count that warned him if any animals were lost. While he counted I studied a few beasts feeding near us. There was no use denying that what I saw was ominous.

"Bill," I said, when he was done counting, "they're not in very good shape for the end of December, are they?"

"They're in bloody bad shape for the end of December."

"How long we been feeding?"

"Early November. The first snow came then and it jolly well stayed."

"Hay's going fast."

"Going fast, there isn't much of it and what there is, is poor quality."

There was no use going on talking about something so depressing and obvious. We began joshing around again the way we had at breakfast and in that mood we put on a small load for the stock around the yard, the weaning calves and a few weaker animals receiving such limited special care as a man could give.

I stayed with Bill for the noon meal, then promising I'd be his way again on my return, I took the road to Spout, riding in to Buster's camp with a couple of hours to spare before dark.

I went directly to the house where I found Millie making Christmas dinner.

"Merry Christmas, Millie!"

"Merry Christmas, Alan. Where's Julian?"

"He was at the Milk Ranch with Roger. He was going to come out soon as he got Roger away. I'd have thought he'd make it today but he might not get out till tomorrow."

"Well, put your horse in the barn and hurry back. Rex is here."

I put my horse away and soon was sitting with Buster and Rex by the heater, asking after Tom and generally catching up on news. I learned Tom and Rex had made a deal whereby Rex would go out for one holiday, Tom the other. Millie had a big spruce tree decorated — it reached to the ceiling — and with Roy running around excitedly why, heavens, it was Christmas.

We ate a dinner fit to bust our belts. Buster had come by a turkey somehow and Millie made the best Christmas cake and steam pudding a boy might ever dream about. I couldn't help thinking of Bill, who'd be sitting down alone in the old cabin to that crusty bannock he lived on, probably little else.

We gathered around the heater again after dinner. Rex idly suggested if only there was another player, he and Buster could engage in a wee game of poker.

"I can play poker," I said.

"Maybe you think you can play poker."

"No, honest," I protested. "A couple of the guys in Williams Lake showed me how. I played a coupla times."

"You got any money?"

"Sure. Four, five dollars." Now four or five dollars was an immense sum of money and I'd played poker for pennies so there was little doubt in my mind I was more than flush enough for a little cards. Oh, how the sheep rush off to slaughter!

Millie protested, but uselessly. Buster and Rex decided if I was bent on a lesson in cards, it would be better I had it from them than some others who might care less for me and more for my money. Buster rustled up a deck and we began to play.

Now I did have a fair grasp of the game, in fact a good grasp of the game for having played so little. I knew the relative value of the hands without hesitation and understood more than vaguely the chances of bettering a given beginning. We stuck to draw poker which helped me to put those chances in a reasonable perspective in my mind.

My weakness was that I invariably stayed in the pot to have a look at what was against me. Whether this was more curiosity than a failure to realize that when to stay and when to get out is the key to success, I cannot say. Anyway I stayed, if I had so much as a pair to stay with.

A good run of cards kept me above the surface in the first stages of the game. I bettered several pairs to three of a kind and filled more than one straight, once a flush. A number of high pairs did me more good than they ought and I began to have a mite too much faith in a high pair.

My tendency to stick by a weak hand soon was obvious to Rex and Buster who need only wait for a good turn of cards to clean me out. In the meantime they worked against each other's resources and Buster, having almost no cash in the house, soon was pledging squirrel skins as Rex gained a steady upper hand.

Then the cards turned, only slightly really but I began to lose rapidly. My opponents need use no caution in building the pot for I hadn't the discretion to scare out. Millie saw my dwindling reserves and protested, again to no avail.

"Alan, what will your father say?"

"Nothing. We won't tell 'im."

My situation became critical, I could see that. I did begin to throw in the poor hands then so I might stay in the game which I was enjoying immensely, not for the gambling of course but for the feeling of being accepted among men. But it was rather too late. Even throwing in the poor hands before trying to improve them in the draw was not a sufficient economy.

Just at the end of my funds, three or four fair hands came my way and I won on them. My previous failing did me a good turn for now Rex and Buster both rode the pot, thinking I was probably only going to the end out of curiosity but with poor cards. Then I lost again but, with some caution now, not all I'd gained.

I assessed my situation. The few pots I'd won had really done me well and the subsequent losses still left me in a position to recover the evening if I could corner one substantial pot. How to do this? I couldn't seem to draw the cards to do it. How else? I decided on one magnificent bluff and in pulling it would capitalize heavily on my inexperience.

I waited until the deal came around so that both Buster and Rex would be betting ahead of me. I picked up my hand and looked at as dismal a collection of garbage as ever a card player caught. No mind. The cards weren't going to win this one.

I kept quiet just long enough for Buster to bet and Rex to raise. Then I made my big play.

"Zowee!" I cried, as if for the first time I discovered I had a good hand. "You know I nearly never saw that. Say, I got you guys good this time."

"Well, my goodness," Rex declared patiently. "You should keep quiet about it. If you'd jumped out of your chair like that when you first picked up your cards, there'd be no money in that pot at all."

I resisted the temptation to say I know, for of course that was precisely the point of my timing. I merely went on being excited and of course raised to the limit on top of Rex's raise. Since they each already had an investment in the pot, they met the raise to see cards though it took Buster awhile to decide since he had two raises to contend with. But with plenty of squirrel fur to back him, he felt he could afford to draw.

Then I sat pat. Neither Rex nor Buster drew cards that could beat a pat hand and they tossed in. I slid my cards into the deck so there was no chance of anyone disregarding the rules to see what I'd done it with and scooped the pot, which, had I genuinely held pat cards could have been played differently and built considerably more, was still sufficient to put me within a few cents of breaking even.

The hour had grown late. We played a few more cautious hands and then called the game for the night.

The Old Man arrived Boxing Day and we stayed over another night. Then we rode back together, stopping by the meadow to see Bill. The Old Man had a good look at the cattle, and discussed matters generally with Bill, promising to be out immediately after the New Year to give him a break from the routine.

"How is the water holding out?"

"It's going down pretty fast. It'll be gone before the hay." We had a water problem at the Morton. The pond we used to water the stock usually went dry in January and the cattle would have to be moved to the Blaze, the remaining hay hauled over in daily round trips, a tiresome task on a cold, blustery day.

"Can't be helped. We'll move them as soon as they're not getting plenty of clean water. Means more work but you have a better cabin at the Blaze."

I said a fond farewell to Bill, then we rode on to Wright's and after a visit there, the Milk Ranch. A few eventless days later I had to go. We spent several hours on a cold afternoon starting the pickup truck, heating water on the stove and lighting fires under the oil pan. The road open to car traffic from the Milk Ranch out, at midnight the Old Man took me to catch one of the two trains a week providing passenger service from Quesnel to Squamish, connecting with a ferry service to Vancouver.

The station was around the end of Lac la Hache, on the south side of the lake. The truck wouldn't climb the last steep hill so the Old Man parked it, threw a canvas over the hood, and lit a lantern under the engine block to prevent the water in the cooling system from freezing before he returned.

Then we walked to the station where we stomped about on the platform to keep warm, the station being one of many unattended whistle stops on the Pacific Great Eastern line that boasted a heater and a freight room but no one to light the heater and rarely any wood for it.

The train arrived. We said an oddly casual goodbye, neither of us much of a hand at such a moment.

"Sorry it was such a dull Christmas for you, boy."

"Oh, shucks, that's okay. Christmas is really no different from any other day."

I swung aboard. The train started up again, jerkily, and a trainman showed me to a bunk on the left side of the aisle. I slipped through the curtain and rubbed the mist from the window. Far down the station road through the trees I could see the light of the lantern glowing from under the truck engine. I thought of how the Old Man even now would be striding along in the snow back to the truck and I watched the yellow glow of the lantern until at last I could see it no longer.

TOUGH WINTER, LATE SPRING

I f Williams Lake was remote from the life of the ranch, Vancouver, Canada's largest city on the western seaboard, was a great deal more so. I felt out of time with the clanging, rushing tempo of the city itself; I felt strange and awkward at school; I grew most unnecessarily difficult in my mother's house.

I inflicted on that poor woman my distaste for where I was. The only diversion that intrigued me was the heart of the city at night. I began going downtown on the pretext of a movie on Friday after school or Saturday, not returning until the small hours of the following morning. In appearance I was safely beyond the curfew age, though not of course in fact.

Mother worried herself sick, literally, but was powerless to put an end to my explorations. In truth of course, my activities were innocent. I knew no gangs of youths, nor joined in any riotous revelling. I only observed, intrigued by the life I saw in the side streets and backways of the city. I watched broken men in filthy rags, shuffling through their wasted lives, begging dimes for endless cups of coffee they never drank and matches to light the cigarette butts of the gutter.

I saw a kind of woman I had never seen before, saw her walk along the ill-lit sidewalks or watch in windows, waiting for the inevitable man to join her. One night I realized the woman had never seen the man before and what had been a word in a grown-up's book became a reality before me.

The more I saw of the city, the greater was my longing for the ranch. The days dragged slowly by. The weeks reluctantly crawled into the past, while the months it seemed never would. But in the end Easter came, letting Roger and me take a bus going north. Overnight we left the soft weather of the coast and found ourselves in the interior where winter clutched the land in a last stubborn grasp.

What we learned at Lac la Hache, where the Old Man met the bus with the pickup truck, was far from happy news. The cattle had failed terribly on the inadequate amount of musty hay available to them at the meadows. Every pound had been fed out the week before we arrived, and the Old Man had driven the herd out in an agonizing trek of weak and hungry beasts to the Milk Ranch.

Some hadn't travelled. One cow, already calved, remained at the Blaze with a last pitiable forkful of hay; she would have to be moved on a sleigh rack. Two more fell aside on the road in, too weak to come farther. Already a sick cow with a calf born the day after arriving was bedded in the corral where the Old Man could try to doctor both to survival.

It would have been a tough winter, even with adequate hay. The snow had begun to accumulate in early November. By January a man could play out a grain-fed horse in a couple of hours on an unbroken trail.

With the snow came the cold, a persistent enduring cold that ate at a cow's stamina, demanding more heat from her hulk than the low-grade hay could let her make. Even the sun swinging high again in February made no difference. For weeks the mercury never came on the top side of zero, plunging at nights anywhere to fifty below.

March came and went, but winter hung on like an unwanted cousin at a funeral. April should have seen a break, but it didn't. The temperatures rose, slowly and reluctantly, but not enough to move the snow. Desperate for green grass in May, not a cowman in the Cariboo could believe he'd ever see it.

The Old Man had only the Milk Ranch hay left and it would barely stretch. Still, the cows must calve on what there was of it and what little they could rustle of last year's dry grass as the snow melted. There were sure to be calving losses and adding that to the bear losses from last year, the past twelve months had cut a devastating slice out of the Old Man's hopes to build his herd up over two hundred head.

But now there was work to be done. Roger set to helping Bill put out hay while I saddled a horse to go with the Old Man, who was taking a sleigh to the Blaze to pick up the cow and calf there. We took some hay to feed the cows still on the road and threw this off as we came to them. The first lay by the side a mile and a half beyond Wright's, the second nearly three. With two and a half miles between Wright's and the Milk Ranch it made a hell of a walk for a cow too weak to stand up, a cow carrying a calf due within the month.

The second of the invalids lay in the middle of the road. The Old Man stopped the sleigh and tied the lines.

"Come on, Al," he said, jumping down. "Let's try to move her."

"Right with you." I dismounted and joined him. Together we tried to move her. She wouldn't get up. She wouldn't even struggle. We put hay beside the road, thinking her desperate hunger would inspire her to try harder. She would only stretch her neck in the direction of it.

"It's no use," the Old Man concluded. "Put the hay here in front of her where she can eat it." He kicked fresh snow toward her that she might lick a cleaner drink from it, then went back to take the lines again. He backed the team a few feet, then swung the left horse off the broken trail. Seeing what he was about to do, I jumped into the snow and marked a track for the outside horse, crowding as close to the trees as possible. The horse followed and soon a fresh set of sleigh tracks showed what would be the road for all who might come that way till the cow would get up and move, or die and be dragged away.

The cow at the Blaze loaded easily. One realized too well the weight she had lost when, after taking her feet from under her and tying them, we inched her easily up a couple of planks onto the rack by hand.

Then we tied her only so much as we must to prevent her lunging from the rack in fright, doing the same with her calf, placing the wee beast where the old cow could nuzzle him for comfort to them both. It was already after noon and the Old Man pulled some sandwiches in a brown bag from the big pocket of his sheepskin coat. "You hungry?"

"Yep. Let's light a fire in the cabin."

The Old Man looked thoughtfully at his watch after much labour to get at it in his heavy clothes. "It would be nice," he agreed. "But look at it this way: if we stop now, we'll be late to the Milk Ranch. Do you want the time in the middle of the day or the end of it?"

"The end of it, if you put it like that. Let's eat and go."

"Right. Here you are." I took the big sandwich he offered and we ate beside our patient, stomping around in the snow to warm our feet for the journey.

Soon we left. I rode behind, preferring the saddle to the hayrack. It was only a while before the old girl reckoned she'd had enough and burst into a wild struggle against her ropes, head thrashing, horns striking the deck of the rack, her exposed bones literally rattling on the deck poles.

The Old Man pulled up. I swung out, came alongside the rack, and reached for her horns, vacating the saddle and wrestling with her all in one movement.

The Old Man had tied the lines up at once and was free to tighten the ropes. Weak anyway, the cow's exertion had exhausted her completely and it was no task to resecure the bonds. We shifted the calf so, should she struggle again, he would not inadvertently be struck by a horn. We were reluctant to tie down her head, knowing the discomfort that would inflict on her over the long haul home.

"Well done, old chap," the Old Man declared, surveying the subdued patient. "You'll be a good bulldogger with a little practice."

"Perhaps," I acknowledged. "Provided they'd starve the critturs first. This old gal hasn't got much left in her, has she?"

"Not very much at all, I fear. You want to ride the sleigh or your horse?"

"I better ride the sleigh. Wait'll I tie my horse." I slipped the bridle off the mare and tied her to the back of the rack by a lead rope short enough she couldn't put a leg over it and we started out again, the Old Man driving the team at a fast trot, me squatted down where I could stop the old cow before she hurt herself when she tried to struggle. Several times during the trip I twisted her head back by her horns, holding her thus until she fell quiet again.

Our hope in bringing the saddle horse was that we might herd on in closer to the Milk Ranch the two cows still on the road. This was out of the question with the weaker of the two, and the other had finished her hay, then of her own accord moved on a surprising distance. We decided against pushing her and threw her a bit of hay instead, the last we had on the rack, so she might eat again and come farther if she felt like it. We went on to unload our cargo.

The following morning the Old Man helped me tie a bundle of the best hay we could muster onto a pack horse and sent me back up the road to feed the stragglers again. I met the first of them soon, resting, but having come past Wright's and, if she could keep up her pace, in good prospect of reaching the Milk Ranch by evening. I dropped off her share of the hay, then went on.

The other beast lay where we had left her. Again I put her hay by the side of the road to induce her to reach her feet to get to it, but no attempt to herd her so much as a few yards would bring her up.

Off my horse, I pushed at her from behind, uselessly trying to lift her in the back quarters. She was agitated plainly enough but it failed as surely as anything to get her up.

I went in front of her. Taking her by the horns, I pulled her to the right by her neck, since to rise she must begin by shifting her body weight directly over her feet.

Suddenly, in a final violent surge of strength she came to her feet. I jumped back and to one side. In the same motion that brought her up she came for me, ears straight out, eyes wide in wild, distraught panic. I jumped again, somewhat in panic myself, off the road into the untramped snow. She followed in staggering lunges but within a few paces her knees buckled, her valiant charge ending in a crumpling collapse into the snow.

I put the hay before her and left, hoping that her next attempt to rise might see her stronger and even able to walk a few feet toward home. Little by little, if I came each day with hay she might make it. Alternately, we might bring the sleigh and load her on. But all this was so much speculation. The next day she was dead.

By contrast, the other straggler reached the Milk Ranch and was never any trouble again. But more cows weakened on the feed ground, particularly those calving too early. The barn and the yard around it became a veritable infirmary. The sickest cows rated a bedding place inside and the less sick a dry spot outside. The Old Man concocted mixtures in a beer bottle reputed to help an ailing beast. He'd tilt a cow's jaws up, pouring the stuff down. Half would go into the cow, the rest down the Old Man's jeans, kill or cure. Mostly the cows died but more in spite than because of the home-brewed medicine.

If not hauling in a sick cow to calve, we were hauling away a dead one that hadn't made it. When the calf survived, we'd take it up to Burt Wright who always had enough milk cows around to care for one more young one. We weren't milking and hadn't time to fuss with an orphan calf unless we were. Under these circumstances, you give the calf away for the trouble of raising it.

I hated more than ever having to leave for Vancouver to finish the school year. It seemed the Old Man shouldn't have to bear his grief alone, no family around to make the bleak days warmer. I think it was then I began to see what a hell of a lonely life he must be leading, what an empty refuge it must be to go to a cold and empty house at the end of a day of trial and worry, no comfort there but what little he might stir up for himself. It wasn't the struggle of the ranch itself that made his burden great, it was carrying it without the warmth of home to give him strength.

A boy could see this only vaguely. The hardships all part of it, the ranch was the central substance of my own life. I reckoned on as little schooling as I could get away with, to return to the ranch and its annual cycle of activities. As bad as the Old Man's lot seemed now, it would be better then for sharing it. And had the Old Man's grief been only the ranch, he'd have asked no more than his boys to help him run it. But a man's needs are greater than that alone.

I had no thought of my own needs in more mature years. How to make enough of a living to support a family, indeed how even to find a woman in this modern day to put up with hay camps and lonely weeks feeding cattle in the long winters, these were no problem at a newly turned fourteen years. To me it was simple. I would grow up and ranch.

Many tried to discourage me, including Mother. She had promised herself her boys were going to be somebody, someday. Being somebody had nothing to do with ranching. Of all those who attended the log schoolhouse of our first days, she reckoned we were the ones to go on and be a success in life. She was wrong of course, though one could barely blame her for her error. In truth no man is more successful than that one who, whatever his calling or education, fulfills his duty to himself, his family, and his community, living in peace and dignity with all three. If I could be as successful as my neighbours on the Eagle Lake road, I should have little complaint with my station in life.

It was popular to look with contempt upon those who worked the land or tended stock. The word "farmer" was a term of derision at school, spat out in scorn. Argue the worth of the land? You were shouted down by jeering hordes.

Even those who wouldn't trade the hard work and good health, the ups and downs of ranch life for anything in the world spoke against it. Bill Wilson, dear old cuss, and I argued the matter fiercely.

"Ranching's the best way to live," I contended. "Look at those men who work in stores and offices in Williams Lake. You think I want to look like that, with soft hands fit for only a woman? This is the life. Work hard, eat lots, no worries about a depression." I recalled the latter part of the thirties when men drifted, weary and despondent, up to the ranch, humbly begging work, asking no more than tobacco and board.

"And what the blazes do you think your dad's giving you an education for," he retorted angrily. "So you can chase around after a bunch of cattle, putting up hay, feeding it out again, same old thing year in, year out? If you got any brains, you'll stay in school. Wish I'd had the chance."

"Dad's educated, and he's a rancher."

"Sure, and look at the struggle he's having. You got a chance to do better and you want to throw it away. You're a stubborn, crazy kid. You better smarten up."

Well, we went at it and come time to chore up we were so mad we wouldn't talk. But old Bill meant well and I loved him for it. It was only that he couldn't understand. Nobody much seemed to understand and the Old Man carefully didn't try to influence me either way.

He had his reasons. In June of that year he sold the ranch.

Sale

T hat came as a jolt, but when the Old Man explained it, one could see readily enough why it had to be. Mother had decided to move back, not only to the Cariboo country, but to Lac la Hache itself. This, the Old Man acknowledged, she was free to do. But if they were either of them to succeed in building a new life, it would help no end if they didn't try to do it two and a half miles from each other on the same stretch of country road.

There was a position open as Secretary of the British Columbia Beef Cattle Growers' Association and the B.C. Livestock Producers' Co-operative Society, two jobs rolled into one, each organization paying part of the salary, in Kamloops, a hundred and fifty miles southeast of Lac la Hache in the heart of the beef country of the province. The Old Man applied for the position, went for an interview with the directors of both organizations, and it was no surprise shortly after his return that he was accepted for the job.

He was through ranching and all that was left to do was wind things up. There would have to be an auction sale to unload the grand collection of ranching equipage, and likely the cattle would best be sold by private treaty. The herd was ranging north of Spout Lake on territory now given up by Tom Barton and Rex Williams. They had been there since shortly after turnout time and it was now June. The Old Man decided to bring them to the big lease next to the Milk Ranch field until they could be sold.

I undertook to go to Spout to bring the cattle around the lake, to start them toward the ranch on the Eagle Lake road. Roger and the Old Man would come out early the following morning to help through the hard part of the drive, the territory between five and ten miles from the Milk Ranch where our cattle had been used to ranging and where, at this time, cattle from two other outfits were scattered throughout the bush and partly open hills. One rider alone could not come through without losing many head, to be rounded up later in piecemeal lots, something we naturally wished to avoid.

Taking the best horse in the corral I made my way to Spout, arriving in midafternoon. Too hot to start the cattle, the flies having driven them into the spruce thickets, I did some visiting.

Millie was making bread. It seemed she was always making bread, huge tasty brown loaves, baked in the oven of a great wood stove. I settled on a kitchen chair to watch her work, calculating the time before the first loaves would come from the oven.

"Your father's selling out, I hear."

"That's right," I said.

"How do you feel about that?"

How did I feel about that? Not so good, really. The ranch going out from under a boy left him feeling a little lost. His parents going separate ways, knowing it was all inevitable didn't make it any easier to grow used to.

"I'm kind of unhappy about it, but there isn't much else the Old Man can do. No use crying over the pieces." At fourteen a boy wanted pretty hard to be a man. Taking things in your stride was part of it.

"You'll make your own life sooner than you think, and then it won't matter so much."

"I try to think about that but it's hard to picture things. I can't see how it will be when we don't own the Milk Ranch and the meadows and the cattle any longer."

"Oh, you'll find your way. There are a lot of things to do in the world and you may wonder someday why you thought cows

89

and horses were the only thing. I don't mean there's anything wrong with ranching, there isn't. It's just that it seems like everything to you because you haven't seen much else. And maybe you will go on to be a rancher on your own — there'll be nothing wrong with that."

Millie went on talking in her comforting way, making the problems seem far less pressing than they were, bringing me to realize that in some ways I was taking myself all too seriously. I thought how kind and sensible she was, and before long the only really important question was how soon the bread would be out of the oven.

"Are you hungry?" she asked, smiling at my impatience.

"I'm always hungry."

"Then there's nothing much the matter with you." Soon she turned the great golden loaves from the pans and if she hadn't been there to remind me of it, I'd never have gone after the cattle. I was too busy melting butter into slice after slice of the hot, fresh bread.

"I'll stop on my way back for more bread," I promised as I went out to mount up, a last thick chunk still in my hand.

"See you do," she replied.

The cattle gathered easily out of the open aspen growth north of the lake and in two hours I was pushing the herd through Buster's camp. The last reluctant calf across the creek and headed for the Eagle Lake road, I doubled quickly back for the last treat of bread that Millie held out to me so I needn't dismount.

"Thanks. 'By."

"Goodbye. Don't ride too hard." She waved to me until I was gone across the creek, up the rise of the bank, and into the jack pines after the cattle.

The cows travelled well the first few miles. Heading back to more familiar range, they moved readily along, heads up, the leaders moving almost too fast for the small calves at the drag.

This couldn't last, of course. I had taken them just as they came out of the thickets for their late afternoon feed. Hungry, having laid up out of the flies since morning, they would soon begin to feed at all costs. The mosquitoes began to be intolerable with the coolness of evening and the cattle drifted into the brush to wipe them off. Knowing they would only move slowly southward now, no danger of them returning to the north of the lake, I called it quits for the day.

The nearest cabin was at the Blaze meadow. I rode through the scattering cattle and in a few minutes reached the turnoff. A steady trot took me down the Blaze meadow wagon road and with darkness settling in on the forest, I reached the cabin.

There wasn't a shred of last year's hay around so I couldn't corral my horse all night. At the same time I daren't turn him loose in the big yard without watching him. The possibility of a low spot somewhere in the fence, which I could hardly check for in the dark, was unlikely, but the consequences of losing the horse were too great. I compromised, making hobbles of the halter rope that kept his front legs out of use except for an ineffective creep. Then I went to the cabin to see what sort of camp there was for myself.

I lit a match and peered into the darkness of the small room, finding a stub of a candle on a shelf. This I lit in turn and stuck it to the table with drippings of its own wax.

Hanging from the ceiling timbers by a rope was a rolled up mattress. Stored thus it was safe from mice. I untied it, heaving it out on the inevitable pole bed in the corner. Then I searched for bedding but found none, much as I expected. Sort of vaguely thinking I would be at Spout for the night when I left the Milk Ranch, I had failed to tie the usual roll behind my saddle. Oh, well. Worse camps were made.

I brought in my saddle, throwing it to the head to use the seat for a pillow. Then I blew out the candle and lay down, taking my chaps off to throw over me as a sort of futile blanket. It was comfort enough. I slept.

In the misty grey of the dawn I was up again, fetching my horse from where he fed in the big yard. I stripped the make-shift hobbles, saddled him and mounted up. Odd, I thought as I rode from the yard. The last time I came here it was to load a sick cow that later died. Why, there lay the planks we used to skid her up on the rack. Now it well might be that I would never camp here again.

The sun stole over the treetops, spilling its early morning gold across the meadow. A mule-deer doe with her fawn browsed in the buckbrush by the pond in the middle of the big open. I slipped into the timber, and she watched me warily as I left the peace and the early morning sun to herself and her spotted young.

Back at the Eagle Lake road I picked up the cattle tracks, following them wherever the night's wandering had led the herd. Here they left the road, there they bedded down. Here once more they began to feed before the dawn, soon travelling from little meadow to little meadow through the jack pines, striking the road again several miles farther on.

Here I caught them travelling fast, much too fast. The sun told me the hour was still early. Only now would Roger and the Old Man be stirring at the Milk Ranch. The cattle had come too far in the night and were going to be into crowded range long before I would have help to keep them sorted from two other brands. There was going to be the grandest damned mix up you ever saw.

Only a mile away from trouble, I rode to the lead to try to hold them back. It was useless like trying to tie back the wind with a lariat loop. I could only watch them go by, using the opportunity to take a count. I found I had them all. I knew I wouldn't have for long.

We came out of the timber into the semi-open country where the other cattle ranged, only half a mile away. Then it was a quarter mile, and soon the whole herd was racing down the last hill, bawling and bucking, the strange cattle of the other ranches pawing the dirt, heads down, squaring off for battle.

Into this melee I rode full tilt, furiously herding along everything carrying the J over E brand, trying to maintain the momentum of the drive to push them through.

92

That scheme was useless. While I bowled one cow over and pushed her down the road, sixty others went in all directions. Calves were lost from their mothers, everywhere there was a constant din of bawling beasts, and three bull fights began at once. I decided I could only hold all the cattle in the clearing, something between two and three hundred head of them, until help should arrive. It was a fantastic undertaking for one lone rider, but I went at it, driving a still reasonably fresh horse to the limits of his endurance.

Everywhere cattle were drifting into the bush. No longer could I stop to discern a brand. I rode around and around the herd, everywhere at once, fighting for time that would bring assistance, doubting with every moment that I could hold so much as half our own cattle.

Riding the high ground, I saw a bunch of twenty or more a hundred and fifty yards away slipping out of sight below me. The incline was gradual. I turned my horse, touching the spurs lightly to his hide. He struck out in the new direction in big strides, lines loose, head out for the run. I relaxed for the moment, feeling the thrust of the great muscles beneath the saddle.

With shocking impact the ground rose up. I rolled loosely and lay still, stunned by the suddenness of whatever had happened, waiting to see if the feeling of unreality wouldn't go away and perhaps I would find I was on my horse again, nothing really having happened after all.

My horse. Oh God, a gopher hole! But no, there he stood, a few feet away, snorting and blowing but sound on all fours by the look of him.

I got up, gingerly trying myself out. Arms, legs, everything worked all right. I talked some gentle nonsense to the old gelding till he let me have his head again. Leading him a few paces, I saw he wasn't limping. I couldn't see what he'd stumbled on and wasted no time searching. Already the bunch I'd gone for were out of sight, and others were making tracks for the timber, the situation hopeless.

Mounted again, I brought back the bunch I was after and then went on as best I could, holding everything in sight, but everything in sight became a lesser quantity of cattle as the minutes slid by.

At long last my kinsmen arrived, but not until I'd blackly concluded they'd overslept the alarm, deliberately dawdled over breakfast, and wasted an hour on the road in idle talk. Nonetheless they were there and before long the cattle were travelling again, remarkably enough only twenty to thirty head short. A day's gathering would pick them up, once things settled down on that piece of range again.

By midafternoon the cattle were in the big lease and I was stretched out on a bunk at the Milk Ranch, where I stayed until the sun was up the following morning.

My brother wasn't around much after that. Mother was building a house at the highway and he went to help her. It was the last time, save an interval at boarding school, that we shared a roof. We never worked side by side again, and just as well at that. Roger was growing serious; I was developing a streak of hellery. He felt offended by my frequent disregard for my mother's feelings; I swore it was none of his business. So it often is with brothers. I knew he was a rare person, genuinely good. But I fought him like a bear cat at the drop of a well-intended word. It was good that he went his way and I mine.

I helped the Old Man until he cleaned up the sale of the outfit. I brought in the last of the cattle and one day a buyer came to dicker miserably with the Old Man. A disreputable cuss, he made his living buying cattle from one man, selling them to another. The price was not good but there are times, and we were in one of them, when you sell to whoever will put up ready money.

The buyer asked me to take the cattle up the Cariboo road toward Williams Lake. He would send a rider to meet me and with fenced hayfields bordering the road most of the way, one man could handle the lot quite readily.

I asked the Old Man what I should do.

"You go ahead. It won't take you a couple of days and you'll still have time to bring in the horses before the sale. Charge him plenty."

"How much is plenty?"

"Oh, six dollars a day for yourself and your horse."

Six dollars a day was more than my wildest dreams had made me worth. The cattle buyer agreed to it as though such a huge sum of money was parted with daily to cowboys, and the next morning I started up the road with the herd.

It was a simple drive. I had only to push them along between two fences and help the occasional car through the bunch. At a little before noon I passed the 122 Mile House on the road where Gilbert Forbes, himself a rancher and also a deputy brand inspector, made out an inspection slip which would follow the cattle for the rest of their journey, proof that the herd was the property of the man under whose direction it was travelling.

Late in the afternoon I met a rider. He sat on his horse on the bank above the road, letting cattle go by him till I approached. Then he came down to the road to join me.

"You Fry's boy?"

"That's right."

"Davidson sent me. I can take 'em now if you want to turn back."

If I want to turn back. Well, yes, in a moment I would turn back, all right. But a little longer I would ride behind them, looking at one and then another. There was the brindle we'd milked the past two summers. That roan there, the big one, she'd been in the herd since before I could recall, bearing a whopper of a calf unfailingly every spring. Here on the drag with the calves was one of the cows from the Hance herd the Old Man bought in the thirties, with the knife wattle high on the back of the right hind leg.

A hundred and some head of cattle, the bulk of the herd save a few head sold to a neighbour. Not a big bunch — they made my father a small man in the cow business but still they were what he'd put the labour of his back and the worry of his mind in since before I was born or thought of.

Until a big decision a month ago, they'd been the hub of my plans and hopes for the future. Around these cows, these run of the mill Hereford beef makers, had been run a ranch and that ranch had seemed to me to be my only proper way of life. Now I was going to draw up my horse, say goodbye to a stranger, and see these cattle for the last time ever.

Well, it had better be done. I reined in. "I'll leave you now," I said.

"Fine. See you around some time."

I crossed my hands on the horn and rested forwards in the saddle. The cattle and the stranger soon drew away. It was only moments before they were gone around a bend, a cloud of fine dust rising up behind them, dust that I knew from long experience smelled and tasted heavily of cows and cow manure. I turned back the way I had come.

Once more at the ranch, I rounded up horses. The Old Man set a date for an auction sale. He had Gussy with him and they hauled machinery down the road to the big barn he had borrowed for the sale, along with almost every piece of gear accumulated in twenty years of ranching. He held out some odds and ends which might be useful in his new life, but these were few.

It was without doubt the most exhaustive riddance of a man's possessions I had ever witnessed. There were mowing machines and wagons, rakes and harness, saddles and milk cans. He had built up a good blacksmith shop, so a fine old anvil along with a complete line of tools went into the heap. There was household equipment, including a kitchen cabinet of an ancient design which had been around since long before I could remember. There were kegs of nails and nuts and bolts, and odds and ends of iron.

Under a hot sun before a crowd of people who had been the Old Man's friends and neighbours for twenty years, the auctioneer began his chant. In his own words, the Old Man was paid for his junk, while his equipment was stolen from him. So it is with dispersal sales.

It was exciting to see the crowd gathered about the familiar objects, bidding now slowly, now quickly. It was strange for a boy of fourteen years to sit on a corral fence, or stand in the big barn and see the symbols of his life go over the auction block.

The last of the sale was devoted to what were left of the horses. It was disappointing, to say the least. The best blood brought into the territory in years, animals costing a hundred or more to raise, drew high bids of fifteen dollars.

The Old Man let some good mares go, then he would stand it no longer. I remember him striding into the corral in a fury, stopping the auctioneer. "Dammit! Nobody buys my horses for stud fees. Roger! Open the gate."

Roger, standing near, swung the gate open, pushing people back. I was mounted, as I had been bringing the groups of horses in and out, so I went quickly in and hazed them through, away from the auctioneer. He grinned, raised his hands in a gesture of well, what's the use, and the sale was over.

The Old Man made an arrangement with Gussy to bring the horses over the Mount Olie Trail to Kamloops in the fall, after haying, where other means of marketing might be tried. For the time being, we turned them back on the range.

REAL COWBOYS

Bordy Felker, a hardy German-Scots son of a pioneer, who ran more than a thousand head with the Lazy R brand on the ribs, bought the Milk Ranch. Gussy made a deal for the Blaze, while Wright bought out the Morton and the Alfie. Thus the Old Man's holdings were absorbed by the other outfits around them and one less rancher occupied the valley.

Gussy took the Blaze for horse hay, his home at Whitehorse Lake not really capable of keeping the cayuses he had to have around him to be happy. He would go out later to put up the hay there, but for the time being he contracted with Bordy to put up the Milk Ranch. Already there to help the Old Man gather up for the sale, he need only bring some horses and gear from Whitehorse and he'd be ready to hay.

The morning after the sale the Old Man loaded the pickup with what little was left and was ready to go. He was delaying going a bit, taking a last look at the Milk Ranch field, the barn, the corrals. I joined him, leaning against the hood of the truck.

"Well, Al, it's goodbye for a while at least."

"Oh, yes," I agreed, cheerfully. "But not long, I don't suppose."

"You better go down to the road right away. You have to stay with your mother once I'm gone, you know that."

"Yep, I know that." I must have said it a little flippantly.

"Now, no shenanigans, boy. You have to mind your mother, do what she says."

"Okay," I said, impatiently. "I will. Don't worry about me."

And with that he was gone, though I'm pretty sure he worried about me and went on worrying for a good long time to come.

The truck out of sight down the road to the highway, I went back in the house. Gussy was preparing to go for a few horses, then begin haying the next day. Maize, Marvin, and young Verne would be his crew. I thought of Maggie's cooking and how if I stayed with them it would still be home for a while longer.

"Gussy, I'm lookin' for work. Can you use me?"

"I don't know," he said thoughtfully. "I'm short on money. My bills are gettin' ahead of me. I couldn't pay you much." Staying square with the world was Gussy's main concern and he didn't want to be unfair with me either. I could understand his position, but what I wanted was to be with him at the Milk Ranch.

"I don't mind what you pay me. I just want to stay with you folks."

"What about your mother?"

"It'll be all right with her. I'll ask her, if you say you'll take me."

"You go down and ask her. I'll give you what I can spare."

I left at once, my own saddle horse still in the barn. When I told my mother I wanted to work for Gussy for the rest of the summer, she agreed. She may well have realized I would be little use to her while she worked on her house. I'd have been scrapping with Roger, and my heart would have been away in the hayfields anyway, making me impossible to get along with.

Marvin and I were overjoyed to be together again and we gave Gussy a few grey hairs, you can count on that. Once we nearly ruined little Verne.

I was stacking, under regular supervision from Gussy each time he brought a load in. This time he was out in the field and Marvin had a load to go up. Verne was with him, watching what was going on.

The poles hadn't been swinging properly. I had tried various weights on the guy lines but nothing worked. The poles would start over before the load was raised above the stack and the constant drag was messing up the front of it.

Marvin started his team and, seeing the poles lean over too soon, shouted at Verne to grab the guy line, to hold it down. It never entered his head the boy wouldn't let go in time.

The load reached the top and over it went. Verne rose as the guy line tightened, flying in an arc around it, twenty feet in the air. I saw his face in a grimace of terror and pain, the rope singeing his palms. Throwing myself toward the trip rope, I grabbed it, releasing the load.

The guy line let the boy gently to the ground. He clutched his hands, tears forcing through, streaming down his cheeks. Marvin rushed over to him, shouting a hero's praise, and Verne managed a grin. Then of course we all laughed like jackasses, boys being what they are.

We were back to our old tricks in the evening after work. There were some bulls ranging up the road and, it being breeding time, they would occasionally get to fighting. But a Hereford bull is slow to start in a scrap. A pair will bellow and paw the dust for two or three days before a blow is struck.

This wasn't good enough for us so we'd promote a bull fight. We'd find two raging around a bit, bellowing and screaming, maybe a day or so away from the first blow. Down on the ground, behind logs or under a fence out of sight, we'd crawl as close as we dared.

From long practice we could bellow like a bull in his ultimate rage. From our hiding place we'd start to add our own screaming to the commotion. The effect on the bulls was remarkable, to say the least. They dashed around in confusion, their anger mounting at every thrust. With any kind of luck it wasn't long before they were rushing and smashing at each other, crashing through the light brush, thundering over windfalls and generally putting up the best show on earth. We relished every crash, every bang, terrified though we were at the battle we had started.

Failing bulls to victimize, we'd saddle our horses in search of other devilment. There was some old fence in the big lease, most of it fallen over but a few stakes still standing.

A boy would ride by fast, drop a lariat loop over the stake, take a quick wrap on the saddle horn and wait for the rope to tighten up. Sometimes the stake would fall over easily. Others, there would be one hell of a jolt, the horse caught mid-stride, struggling to keep his footing, the boy to keep his seat.

We had a little mare the Old Man had left in Gussy's care. She was a fine little cow horse, hard working and intelligent. She couldn't stand, try as she might, someone riding double behind the saddle. So we doubled on her, taking turns riding behind, betting on how long a fellow could stay there, the little mare bucking for all she was worth.

This was hard on the tail bone and hard on the horse. "If you young hoodlums don't respect good horseflesh," Gussy finally ordered, "you better have sense enough to leave it in the corral." We went back to promoting bull fights.

We found another source of amusement that summer. A couple of greenhorns, real cheechakos, came to work for Percy Ogden at the road. In conjunction with his store, he ran a small herd of beef cattle and put up a big field of good tame hay. Hay men hard to come by, he hired these two doubtful looking fellows when they came up the road decked out in cowboy gear, looking for work.

I don't know where they came from, nor where they went. But memory is enriched with a chuckle or two for their having been there that summer long ago.

We heard of them, long before we saw them. "You see Percy's cowboys yet?" a neighbour would ask, going by on the road.

"No," you'd say, shaking your head, wondering what Percy would hire cowboys for at this time of year, or any other for that matter. A man was a man and he did everything on a small ranch: hay, ride, fix fence, dig ditch, irrigate, carpenter, cut wood, feed cattle, shoe horses, repair harness. There wasn't an outfit in the valley big enough to hire a man to cowboy and nothing else. "What you mean, cowboys?"

"Oh, *real* cowboys. Two of 'em. You never saw such cowboys." The way it was said you couldn't help catch on. You knew there were a pair of dandies to be seen, you could hardly wait to see them for yourself.

The first I saw them, Percy had them cleaning out a deep section of irrigation ditch in a spell of wet weather that shut the haying down a few days. Marvin and I happened to ride by the ditch and there they were, big fancy hats, embroidered vests, coloured scarves, brand new jeans, and inlaid cowboy boots. What a sight that was, in a ditch to their shoulders, those beautiful boots squelching around in the mud.

Archie Ogden, Percy's oldest son, who looked after the ranch work, was with them and introduced us all around.

"Howdy, boys! Howdy," they greeted us while we looked at each other, then grunted a short hello, not really quite sure how one should meet these rare specimens.

They wanted to ride of course, more than anything. Percy had no riding to do and had he, he wouldn't have entrusted it to them, but he let them use a couple of gentle horses he had so they might have a taste of saddle leather in the evenings and on Sundays. They became a common sight at the road in off hours, riding along together in their finery, very pleased with themselves indeed.

There was a low hill across the highway from the store. Being so close, not a hundred yards away, it hid the landscape behind it, the sky itself rising up from its crest. On this hill, carefully striking a moving-picture pose on the skyline, these two cheechakos often sat so they might be seen by all who came in an evening after work to the store. They made quite an impression but not, I fear, quite the impression they sought.

Roger had a mare, a devil of a fine little animal, that he passed word around he wanted to sell. We kept her at the Milk Ranch and I had undertaken to display her to what advantage I could to any prospective buyer who might enquire. One of Percy's cowboys had a month's wages coming, and one evening when Marvin and I had ridden to the store, this one approached me.

"That the hoss yore brother reckons tuh sell?"

"Yes. This is the mare." I made a point of my pronunciation. The fellow was riding the animal Percy allowed him and he stepped down, handing the lines to his partner nearby. "Heah, Slim. Hold mah mustang while ah try out this crittah."

"Why shore, Bud," the other said, grasping the lines.

Caught off base, I let him take her. Marvin sidled over to me. "Wish to gosh she'd buck him off," he said, his voice low for privacy.

"So do I" There was a remote chance of it. The mare was touchy, but the greenhorn did nothing out of the way and apart from being confused the little mare found him tolerable.

Roger happened along, the store, or the area in front of it, being something of a gathering place at Lac la Hache in the evening. "What the hell is that guy doing on my mare?" He gave me an accusing look for which I could hardly blame him.

"I'm sorry," I apologized, and I explained how it had happened.

"Well, I don't want to sell him my horse, no matter if he has the money or not." It was clearly a question of having respect for good horseflesh.

"I'll see to that. You mind if I spook her a little and scare him off a deal when I get back on?"

"Go ahead."

Marvin was listening. "When he comes back we'll get on our horses and ask them if they want to ride home aways with us."

Soon the one called Bud was back from taking the mare a few turns across the road. Marvin and I mounted up, just as planned, and the prospective horse buyer told my brother how he thought the little mare was suitable to him and he'd maybe make a deal after he collected his wages at the end of the month. Then we invited them for a short ride with us and we all four started up the Eagle Lake road.

Passing a low hanging limb, I snapped off a sharp twig an inch or two long, hiding it in the palm of my hand. Another hundred yards or so up the road I jockeyed into a position between our new-made friends and reached behind my own saddle, unobtrusively, jabbing the sharp stick down firmly on the mare's backbone.

She exploded on the spot. My knee caught the one called Slim on the way by, twisting him around in the saddle. Then I was out in front, carefully holding the mare up from really going at it but nonetheless creating a lot of noise and dust. If she'd got down to business I couldn't have ridden her with resin on my chaps.

Then I calmed her down and dropped back into the group. "Trouble with this mare," I said, heaving a sigh. "Busts loose like that when you least expect it."

There was a silence in which I looked at the fellow, Bud, out of the corner of my eye. He was pale and shaken at the very thought of what might well have happened to him, or so he believed, right there in front of the store.

At last he spoke. "She do that often?" He'd lost the Texas drawl completely.

"Oh, no. Maybe once a day. No more'n that." Roger lost a buyer, then and there.

We met them another evening, a little earlier. Marvin invited them along, though, less imaginative, I couldn't see why until he turned off the road onto a trail that led several miles through the bush and out again farther up toward the Milk Ranch. Crossed up badly with windfalls, taken at a run it made the kind of steeplechase a ranch boy loves and, ho ho, a greenhorn fears.

I needed no instructions from Marvin to know what to do. I let our friends go by and fell in last, tearing off a long willow switch from the side of the trail as I did so. Soon Marvin was up to a jog, then a fast trot, finally a pacemaking gallop.

Bud and Slim were soon in agony. Clinging with the off hand to the saddle horn, they had no arm free to ward off the stinging slap of the light brush. We came to the windfalls and they banged around unmercifully in the saddles as the horses broke over one after another of these obstacles.

The thin one, directly in front of me, began in desperation to rein in his horse. Prepared, I crowded up, catching the beast a sharp swat on the back leg, dropping the switch promptly at the same time, not wanting to be seen with evidence in my hand. The poor devil on board caught the horn with both hands, slacked the reins, and hung on in terror.

I thought Marvin might ease it up but he didn't. A first-class bushwhacker, he set a pace even I found breathtaking at times. Once my heart stopped, I feared disaster so certainly. Bud, the one directly back of Marvin, hit a heavy limb, all but tearing himself from the saddle. Fortunately he hung on and before long we reached the Eagle Lake road, bringing the chase to an end.

They didn't ride with us again, but they remained in the community for the rest of the summer, amusing us all with their affected drawls and their ignorant ways. Percy hadn't work for them both and finally laid off the less useful.

This one approached Gussy. "Mistuh Hallah, you all lookin' fo a top hand?"

Gussy surveyed him from head to foot. "You seen one around?"

"What ah mean, do yuh have a job fer me?"

"Can't say I have."

Finally they both left the valley and so far as I know, none of us ever heard of either of them again.

The summer drew on. Late August saw the Milk Ranch in stack and Gussy preparing to go to the Blaze. There was little point in my making the move with him since I had to leave for boarding school in Vancouver at the end of the month. A mare the Old Man had sold to a woman in Williams Lake was reported missing by her new owner and I had said as soon as I was done for Gussy, I would take a look on the mare's old range and if I found her, bring her back. It was a task that would pleasantly fill out the last days of the summer.

With Gussy gathering his gear to move, I rode into the back valley, a stretch of horse range beyond the big lease, not our big lease now, where our horses had run in the summer months.

I found the mare with a band of twenty or more, some four or five miles from the corrals in the big lease, my most logical catch point. I unrolled my lariat to have a try at saving my horse some running but, inexperienced with the rope as I was, I missed by an ear's breadth. The mare squealed and ran, kicking her heels in the air, starting the bunch. I rolled up the rope and gave chase.

We ran through the timber where I headed the bunch onto the trail I wanted. Just as I tried to turn them westward into the big lease and thence to the corrals, they doubled back into the thickets.

Another two miles of hard running and I brought them around again. All asweat now, they took the turn. Before long I was at the corrals with the bars up. It had been a tremendous run and it left me happily exhilarated.

Gussy came riding up to the corrals. "Just thought I'd see if you got yourself lost."

"Nah," I said. "Not me."

I slipped into the corral and when the mare wouldn't let me approach her, I popped the lariat loop on her neck as though I'd never known what it was to miss.

"Good boy! You'll make a cowboy yet."

"Think so, huh? I'll be a long time tryin' if I don't."

We rode together to the Milk Ranch where we would all be staying one last night. I was strangely very happy to be riding side by side with this odd cuss of a man who had been friend and teacher to me so many times in so many ways. I thought not of how we would soon say goodbye, for in that would be sadness.

But the following morning it was goodbye and we said it briefly. Then I was gone up the road, riding one, leading the other, to Williams Lake, an uneventful trip at the end of which I delivered the mare to her grateful owner. I lodged my horse at a livery barn and found a room for myself in town. The next morning I was up early and on the road again.

Halfway back to Lac la Hache I turned into the timber on an old wagon road shortcut to Spout Lake. I'd never been that way before and when I came to a forks, I could only guess at which was the road, which a byway to an old homestead. I guessed wrong. The wagon road dwindled to two poor paths, eventually one. The one petered out, growing less and less distinct until, as the Old Man used to say about that sort of track, it turned into a squirrel trail and ran up a tree.

Doggone it, I was lost. I debated about turning back, but I'd come a long way since the wrong fork and was reluctant to give up that much distance.

Climbing a tree, I could make out Spout Lake Mountain. There was a forest fire burning at the westward end of it, not more than a spot fire that would go out with the next rain, but it produced a visible column of smoke. I decided to head through the bush, hope for the best, and keep an eye on the smoke.

Burned in places many years before, the country had patches of thick, second-growth pine on it, impassable to a horse and rider. Skirting these, I came to impenetrable bogs, great reaches of treacherous mud, full of half-sunken snags.

By the time I realized I should have turned back, I was too far in to believe turning back would be any better than pushing through a barely passable stand of the small pines.

I crossed small meadows where the untouched grass reached to my stirrups. Here and there we watered at a slow-moving stream. A hot and lazy afternoon, the buzzing of the occasional fly would have lulled me to sleep in the saddle had I not a growing concern to get out of the bush before dark.

Cheechako, I thought, not a little amused. We laughed at Percy Ogden's greenhorns but by golly I was a bit of a cheechako myself. But not so much a cheechako as to lose sight of that column of smoke, by golly.

The shadows raiding more ground, I began, unwillingly, to look for a place to make a crude camp. I came to a wider meadow than I'd come to all afternoon. Finding it solid, I crossed it. The closer I came to the opposite side, the more familiar it looked.

Ha, I thought. The Eagle Lake road isn't spitting distance through this last bit of bush. And it wasn't. In a moment I came to it, not ten minutes ride out of Buster's camp. I'd crossed a meadow he used for hay for his hunting horses, but he'd not cut it yet that season.

That was fun, I thought happily, a sense of accomplishment making my misadventure a pleasing experience. "Fun!" Buster snorted when I told him where I'd been. "You dam nearly got hung up in the big swamp and if you had, you'd have been bones before we found you."

I stayed two happy days with the Hamiltons, then rode on out to Lac la Hache. I turned my horse loose on the range, knowing he'd care well for himself till I needed him again, and resigned myself, out of necessity, to a year in boarding school at Vancouver.

GOOD TIMES

We attended Vancouver College that fall, a private school in the city of the same name, a place to which boys came from all over the world. It was fun to know a hulking great logger's son from the west coast, a "pineapple" from Hawaii, and a boy once an inmate of a Japanese prison, all in the same dormitory.

But still it was a blue business. The activities out of class weren't my ticket somehow. Everybody became enthused as Old Nick over the football team, going to all the games and shouting rah, rah, rah. I tried it. It was fun while the game lasted, but it looked pretty ridiculous afterwards.

Sports were for the athletic. The rest of us took part in a half-hearted gym program, and once I took a little boxing. I didn't learn much, I guess. Annoyed at the pushy ways of one of the older boys, I took him on. That Queensberry business went all to flea powder as we fought scrap and scramble over the whole of the rec-room floor. It was still a draw when, twenty minutes later, the dormitory master caught us at it and cancelled the next two weekends.

For once in my school career I got down to business over studies. I think it was a form of escape. I got up at four in the morning to swat, staying as late in study hall at night as rules allowed. My marks good at Christmas, they rose to a phenomenal ninety-four per cent average at Easter.

109

But it was all meaningless to my heart. Inside I longed for the free air of the Cariboo country. I wanted to feel saddle leather and make a fire of dry jack pine wood. I wanted to trade the whole caboodle for a pitchfork in my hands, for ten long hours under a haymaking sun.

School would be out in June. In May I asked to go home on the strength of my good marks, saying my mother needed me. This was allowed, and I explained it to my mother by saying the chaps with top marks were let out early. Then I went looking for work.

I walked to Whitehorse Lake to see Gussy, finding him in the barn brushing down a horse. So glad to see him, I could have hugged him right on the spot, but you didn't exactly go around hugging old Gussy right on the spot. He seemed pleased to see me. I asked him if he would be doing anything I might help him with.

"No," he replied. "I'm not contracting this year and I don't have much to do for myself. Lester and Clarence are home and they're talking about making mine props. You better see them." These were his older boys, home from the war.

"I'll do that. By golly I will. Where's Marvin?"

"He's working for Percy. I think if they start on these props he's goin' to come home."

That did it. If I could spend the summer with Marvin I would be home again. I went to see Lester at once.

"You use an axe, boy?"

"You damn betcha I use an axe!"

"Okay, Jack. You got a job."

"M'name ain't Jack."

"That right? Okay, Jack." When Lester felt that way, everyone was Jack. Marvin came to work and it was old times once more.

The Hallers were a happy crowd and though their ways didn't lead to much material prosperity, there was everything about them to appeal to an imaginative and impressionable youth.

Gussy was born in the Big Bar country, along the Fraser River, in the late eighties, when the interior was yet in the hands of a generation of pioneers. Maggie was part Native, part Spanish, part a lot else. They married young. They never knew easy times, nor jealousy or weakness in their marriage. She bore ten children of whom eight survived. A son was killed in a rodeo at Lac la Hache and a daughter by a cause never clear to me.

Gussy worked from job to job to feed these many mouths, often some homeless lad as well. An excellent workman, he always found a hay contract or fencing job with one of the ranches in the territory.

Other times he chased wild horses out of the mountains along the Fraser River to break and sell as saddle stock. A vicious business, this, it gave him every abuse. Broncs wore away at him, he was thrown down mountainsides and smashed against trees in the wild chases after the timber-bred mustangs, the cold of winter riding took toll of his great stamina. Still, he was happy, his only wish that he might do it all again.

Maggie followed wherever he went. When I first saw her she was a healthy, upright and hard-working woman, and she remained so well into her later years. At ninety she was named Mother of the Year by the Canadian Legion in Merritt and charmed a gathering of sixty people in a kick-off ceremony for the annual poppy drive. She was reported then to have forty-four grandchildren and sixty-two great-grandchildren.

She was the best hay-camp cook I have ever known. I have spoken elsewhere of her proficiency in providing for a crew under difficult circumstances. She would pitch hay for a change from the stove and the dishpan. She treated me well when I was a boy, overlooking my faults, filling my stomach three times a day whenever I was part of her family.

The boys they raised are a hard-working, hard-playing strain of men and, true enough, they haven't gathered much moss. But I take men the way they treat me and among my finest friends, I count the Hallers.

Yesterday is memories, tomorrow only hopes. If today can be filled with hard work, hard play, gaiety and song, why, so it should. Each played some musical instrument and when they gathered they drummed up the rhythm of an old-time dance. Sure too, they drank, not in poisonous nibbles but in great man-sized draughts during mighty celebrations liberally scattered throughout the times of hard, labouring work by which they made their living. A lad found life with these an inexhaustible round of adventure and excitement, though the work was hard, the days long.

We made mine props till we thought we looked like them: eight-foot pieces of peeled pine, averaging six inches in diameter, destined for the United Kingdom. We felled tree after tree, barked them, skidded them in with horses, bucked them in lengths, piled them, swore at them, made jokes about eating them, and concluded nobody would ever earn a fortune cutting them.

Felling was a tricky business. The tall slender pines grew in tight groups and pockets. As carefully as a fellow chipped out the undercut, calculating the lean and the breeze and the weight of the heavy side of the branch cluster, there were times when he couldn't lay the brute out through the slender corridor available to get it on the ground. She'd hang up on her neighbours.

Then you'd begin calculating on the tree holding up the tree you just cut. Cut her so, she'll go thus. Hmm. Maybe a little tiny bit heavy this side. All right, hold the cut t'other way. Have to watch those three big ones. Get her in there, you'll have a sweet time getting her out.

Well, maybe the wind changed or she wasn't as heavy as you thought on the offside. Anyway, she hung up on the three big ones. So then you started figuring those out and before you knew it you had a network of half-fallen timber above you that was going to come all acrash when you took the last whack on this crucial one right here in the middle, and no man was fast enough on his feet to be sure he'd get out in time. But you cut her anyway because you couldn't leave a mess like that and all of a sudden you had enough stuff on the ground to keep you peeling till quitting time.

It was good work, but it grew tiresome. Marvin and I found it harder and harder to be conscientious about getting a good, full count by five o'clock. We told ourselves the timber was getting tougher as we cut farther into the stand but the truth was that we were weary of the axe and the peeling spud. We worked an eight-hour day, but I longed to trade it for the ten or twelve hours of the hayfield.

Then Lester made a great announcement: we were going to hay the Milk Ranch. Bordy had given Lester and Clarence a contract.

"When we leavin'?" I asked, as though it were a big move, when of course it involved only three miles.

"Maybe tomorrow. You in a hurry?"

"I'd rather make hay than props any old day."

"Think you can hay?"

"Can I hay?" I cried, incredulously. "Sure I can hay!"

Then I could see the twinkle in Lester's eye. "We'll see if you can hay," he said with a chuckle.

Gussy provided the horses for this venture and while he had few good ones to spare he had plenty of the half-broken, ill-bred kind running on Peavine Ridge, a hill country beyond Burt Wright's ranch, east of the Eagle Lake road.

We went for them the next day, late in the afternoon, Marvin, Lester, and myself. Just at dusk we found them, a band of thirty or more, Gussy's and others, ranging high on the ridge and as spooky as mule deer.

There was a corral at the foot of the ridge by the trail we'd come in on, but when the band started there was clearly little chance of taking them to it. We came on them from the east and they lit out to westward on the dead run, heading for another trail that would take us out on the Eagle Lake road several miles north of Wright's buildings.

We weren't heading them, you couldn't call it that at the start. We simply flung ourselves down the long slopes of the ridge after them, sometimes seeing one or two tails swinging in the diminishing light ahead of us, other times only hearing the thunder of hooves above the clattering racket we made ourselves, tearing through the light brush, scrambling over rocky patches.

The band split and we split with them. I found myself alone with a handful of horses on a side trail above the main route out. Lester and Marvin must still have been with the rest on the trail we had somehow to keep to there in the dark, horses scattered to hell and gone through all that timber at the foot of the ridge.

Suddenly I was on top of the few I was chasing, in utter confusion, all blocked up on the trail, crowding to turn back. A big sorrel mare, white eyed and wild, saw me there, snorted, bolted off the trail to the low side, the others crashing after her into the thick of the timber.

"What the devil!" I cried audibly, to nobody in particular.

Then my own horse was up on his hind feet, fighting the bit, fixing to get to blazes out of there the first chance I'd let him. At last in the dark I was close enough to see the big bear blocking the trail, head down, motionless, confused as I was. I spurred my horse to put him all fours on the ground again, standing him fast while I watched the bear. In his own moment of sudden decision then, that fellow bolted, back down the trail he'd come on, just as fast as four furry legs would carry him. I turned off after the horses.

I could hear them still and I made my way as best I could, knowing they would join the main bunch, now they were going in the right direction. Finally we came to the other trail and turned westward. Before another three quarters of a mile Lester and Marvin moved off the trail to let my little bunch by into the rest of the band and we were together once more, everything settled to a walk now, the big initial run behind us.

"Where you been, boy?" Lester asked. "Get lost?"

"Just sight-seeing over 'yonder aways."

"Watcha see?"

"Bear."

"Big one?"

"Fair to middlin'."

"Why you didn't rope it?"

I looked at the coils of the lariat strapped to my saddle. Suppose I had been that good with a loop, a bear was the last thing in all creation I'd care to be tied to by the saddle horn there in the dark. It was just the kind of thing Lester would like to do though, never mind how it would all straighten itself out afterwards.

"I figured you fellas'd be lonely without me so I didn't spare the time."

The horses went well after that. It was only a matter of time and a fast pace before we corralled the lot at Burt Wright's barnyard, picked out the best, and turned the rest loose again.

Maize came to cook for her brothers. Besides Lester, Clarence, Marvin, and myself we gained one more member, a lanky, dark-skinned, onetime cowpoke of the grandest sort whom Clarence rustled up. His name was Garnet Johnson, but he liked to toot and any time after the first drink you asked him how he was doing he'd fix you with an eye like a Christmas tree light, wiggle the handle bars of his moustache and holler: "Jolly fine!"

So we called him Jolly Fine.

Some task it was to get going, with that rangy lot of horses. We matched them as best we could, hooked them up, and started out. Horses, men, mowers, and hayrake went every direction. Jolly Fine ran over a hornets' nest, flying across the flat like a Roman at war in his chariot. He outran the hornets, but he did his team in for the morning.

Marvin's horses balked. He tried to make them go, but they jackknifed in the harness, tangling it all to hell. He went to their heads to straighten them and one pulled back. Furious, he hit the beast with his fist. Unhurt, the horse stared in wide-eyed wonder as Marvin danced around the hayfield, clutching his hand in pain.

Clarence inspected his fist, telling him to quit jumping around. "If you'll keep still for a minute I can put your fingers back in their sockets." Clarence took one finger, pulled and pushed in a quick movement, restoring the joint.

"Yeeow!" cried Marvin, leaping about again.

"Gi'me your hand, there's still one more needs fixin'!"

"Yeeow!" again, and Clarence was done with him.

115

We tore up some rigging and had to fix it again, but in time we got going and made a lot of hay in a day at that. We worked long days and hard, harder than I had ever worked, trying to keep up to Clarence and Lester, each of whom could outwork two average men any day they chose, and most days they chose.

And we didn't only hay. Sitting around together after the evening meal, Lester eyed me craftily. "Al, you ever see the stars in daylight?"

"Nope. Don't figure to either." I wasn't going to be a victim of any half-baked, practical joke. Lester saw my scepticism.

"Haven't you heard how you can see the stars in the daytime from the bottom of a deep well?"

I had heard this, but never verified it. I acknowledged as much.

"Well, you can do the same thing with a piece of stovepipe. Even a coat sleeve'll do if someone holds it up for you to look through."

"That right?" I found it hard not to be interested.

"'Sfact. Maize, bring Al his coat. C'mon Al, we'll go outside and I'll show you."

So we went outside and I peered up my coat sleeve, Lester holding up the other end. It was darker than the inside of a black cow.

"See any stars yet?"

"Not yet."

"Takes a minute sometimes for your eyes to adjust."

"Oh."

Suspicion was creeping in pretty strongly when the water, the whole cold bucket full of it, tumbled down the coat sleeve onto my expectant, upturned face.

"Keeripes!" I leaped back, throwing away the coat, pulling the wet shirt away from my skin. Everybody was slapping their knees and guffawing at a great rate. I knew enough to laugh when the joke was on me, so pretty soon Lester was pounding me on the back, saying what a good sport I was, slyly setting me up for the next one. It had to do with holding a bowl of water against the

ceiling with a broom handle. Try that sometime and see if you
don't get wet.

We had a little mare that could buck fairly proficiently and I
said sure, I'd try her out. Lester held her while I piled into the
saddle, fixing the halter shank in my hand, tucking the loose end
under my arm the way he instructed.

"You ready?"

"Ready as I'm goin' to be."

"She's all yours."

He let go the halter. I threw my heels up, hitting the little mare
in the shoulder. She got the idea in a hurry. Down went her head
and high in the air went her withers. Up there in the sky she
twisted, then came down hard. Up she went again and I lost track
of her.

"You don't quite got the idea," Lester suggested as I rose from
the ground, scooping the mud out of my left ear.

"So bring 'er back, I'll try it again."

He brought her back and this time I pawed around up there for
a couple of jumps before the curtain. Then Lester put an end to it.
Not good for the boy or the horse, he reckoned.

After that he climbed on, to show me how it was done. He sat
up there on the saddle with the most magnificent impunity, his
off arm waving in time, both feet reaching from the mane to he
flank at every jump. The mare couldn't budge him, try as she
might. I shook my head, doubting that I'd ever be a bronc stomper.

When Lester and Clarence cut the stays loose on a Saturday
night, why, so did Marvin and I. Big boys for our age, we did a
man's work. Nobody doubted that we had a right to a man's good
time as well. More than once we passed ourselves off in the dark
as a lot older than we were when the jug was going the rounds
behind a jack pine bush at the Saturday night dance at the
community hall. Whooee!

I remember a morning after a night of this. The sun was up,
warm and pleasant. In front of the house at the Milk Ranch,
Marvin promenaded about, big as life, playing the violin. Everyone

else was sleeping off the effects of the night and, listening to Marvin's music, beautiful restful music, not the least impaired by his condition, I wanted to sleep too. I found some clean grass and lay down.

Marvin discovered he was alone with his music. Putting his violin away, he dragged me up by an arm, took me into the house and directed me to a chair. "You set right there, boy. About now I am agoin' to make some hotcakes."

Not long ago I had concluded an experiment with a quantity of rye whiskey and I wanted no part of the kind of hotcakes Marvin was likely to whomp up at that moment. I waited till his back was turned, then headed out the door, back to my patch of grass.

The creek water spilled over my head and shoulders, drenching the thin shirt. I had resistance to the stuff by then. I peered up at my persecutor.

"Are you comin' for your hotcakes or do I gotta take you?"

"Eatcher own blasted hotcakes."

"I'm goin' for another bucket of creek water."

I contemplated that last threat, weighing it against the hotcakes. It was mighty cold water. "Okay, I'll come." I ate those hotcakes too, but it was enough to drive a boy to the pledge, suppose there'd been anyone handy sober enough to administer it.

But life wasn't all play and hellery. We still went out there into that hot hayfield for ten to twelve hours every day the sun shone, and in the best time I ever saw it happen, the Milk Ranch went into the stack.

We moved back to Whitehorse and, riding several miles through the timber every morning and evening, we put up a little meadow for Clifford Eagle, Buster Hamilton's half brother, who had a small ranch to the northeast of Whitehorse Lake.

That done, we went back to mine props, piling them up into great mountains of peeled wood, white in the August sun. Another brother, Henry, came with a three-ton truck to begin hauling and soon the props were disappearing from Whitehorse, to pile up at the railway siding around the end of Lac la Hache.

Still, the summer could not go on and on, however much I wished it to. The day came that I must say goodbye to the Hallers once more and return to my mother's house, to make ready to go back to school. I took my horse to the far barway and let him out on the range. I gathered my bit of gear and said I'd leave my saddle in the barn, where it might be some use to someone over the winter. That done, I left. "You turned out to be a pretty good sort of a boy," Lester acknowledged when I took his hand in parting. Those few words meant more than ninety-four per cent in the Easter exams ever could.

Rodeo

 School was harder to bear than ever. I found the regimen of boarding-in hopelessly dull after the freewheeling approach to life I had experienced in the summer. The temptation grew to throw it all in, to go find a job feeding cows some place for the winter. But at fifteen I still respected my parents' wishes, if only enough not to bolt.

A classmate, Colin Hudson, one who also found the school a burden to bear with no compensating joys, wanted to join a local Reserve Army unit, the Irish Fusiliers, an ack-ack regiment with a drill hall just off West Pender Street, perhaps half an hour's ride from the school by bus. There was one evening parade each week, occasional weekend exercises.

"Why don't you join, too? If we can get permission from the warden, that is. Come on. You can join as a boy soldier after you're sixteen, and nobody'd think you weren't sixteen."

It sounded a fair lark to me. "Okay," I said, and we sought out the principal who agreed readily enough that a bit of parade-square snap would do both of us good. We were granted thereby an evening out of the school every week.

Off we went to the recruiting office. Colin stepped up first and soon was a boy soldier in a sort of provisional class of service for standard training with regular enlistees.

Came my turn, I gave my age as eighteen. Nobody looked twice. Down it went on the form and I swore to it. Colin, standing by, kept prudently silent. Then we moved off smartly to another part of the drill hall to receive our kit.

"Whatcha want to lie about your age for so much?" Colin demanded indignantly. "Sixteen was all you had to say. What difference does it make?"

"I think," I said, "it means I can drink beer in the men's canteen and you can't."

But even with a night of soldiering every week, which I thoroughly enjoyed, I found school life growing more and more tedious. No longer throwing myself into studies as I had the year before, I worked only so much as to bring off passing grades, no better. I wondered more and more seriously if there wasn't some way at least to get out of boarding school and Vancouver, perhaps go back to Williams Lake.

Fortune showed the way. Late one night in my sleep, disturbed by a strange commotion in the big dormitory where seventy of us in the main building slept in long rows of cots and double bunks, I grew increasingly annoyed. Would they not shut up? Something like a message tried to get through to me. Either I rejected it or it couldn't break through the barrier of sleep. I made an effort, tried, hazily confusing the noise and the message. I began to register a word. What was it? Did someone say …

Fire! Keeripes! I came out of the cot in a leap. Bedlam surrounded me. I thought of my brother in the next upper. I saw him dropping down, reaching for his clothes.

I grabbed a pair of trousers, pulling them on while I searched for flame and smoke. There was none in sight.

"Hey, I can't get inta my pants!" It was Roger, fighting a pair of trousers half his size. I looked at the offending garment. It was no wonder: the pants were mine.

"Here!" I cried, whipping out of the ones I'd hauled on. "Here! These're yours. Gi'mme them!" We traded pants, solving that problem, and with a little more caution assembled a few more garments.

I could see order growing from the bedlam. Boys, once clothed to their own satisfaction, were leaving the dormitory by the main door. With some this meant topcoats, others pyjamas. I settled for shoes, pants, and jacket and made my way the devil out.

No fire could be seen in the hall. I turned quickly down the stairs to the lower hall, turned again to leave the building. A burning cinder fell by me as I passed out the door.

The whole top storey gymnasium — recreation room, cafeteria — was ablaze. Already the trucks were arriving. In another minute the building was vacant, in another two the water was going on. We milled about to watch her go.

By the most remarkable efforts the firemen held the blaze to the upper side of the top floor. Subject to water damage, everything in the dormitory came through. Fire touched none of the classrooms. After a night in emergency accommodation in private homes in the city, we were able to enter the building and gather our wet belongings, to pack them as best we could for the trip home.

Trip home it was, of course. Now early December, the school could not possibly function before January. Christmas therefore was a long holiday which Roger and I spent at our mother's new house at Lac la Hache.

I successfully persuaded her to let me go to school in Williams Lake in the new year. She was going there herself to work and live in at the hospital, to use her home at Lac la Hache on weekends and days off. She had a car to drive the forty-five miles on what was now a much improved highway.

Roger returned to Vancouver, while Mother arranged my board with a family in Williams Lake. I secured a discharge from the Reserve Army by mail on the grounds that there was no available unit training in my new locale. My ties with the city were cut. I had achieved my purpose, but one might well ask for what.

I was growing truly aimless. Nothing held my interest save the prospect of saddling a horse again, or taking up a pitchfork when summer would come, bringing complete freedom. I cared for no subject at school. No sport, no chum could absorb me. Discipline was low and sometimes I slid away, missing classes for other pursuits such as snooker, pool, and poker.

The community at Lac la Hache held a rodeo on the twenty-fourth of May. I found a ride with a friend to my old home and soon was walking out the Eagle Lake road to Gussy's turnoff to fetch my saddle and see my friends.

Lester was there, greeting me royally. I told him what I was about. He looked at me solemnly, shaking his head.

"No brains, huh?"

"Nope. None at all."

"That's the stuff, boy!" He was on my side, I could see that, and Mrs. Haller shook her head in dismay as we went to the barn to fetch my rigging. Gussy, a great believer in everybody making his own mistakes, had no comment.

I wanted to stay at Whitehorse that night and of course I knew it was my privilege to do so, but I had to be at the rodeo grounds early enough to enter and Gussy couldn't be sure he'd be there as soon as that. Therefore I walked out carrying my saddle and before long had a lift from a stranger going by in a pickup truck.

The saddle bronc ride under the rules at that time lasted eight seconds. Your time began when the chute gate opened, spilling you and your squealing bronc into the open arena.

When he took the air in a great bucking leap, you reached for his mane with your dull-rowelled bronc spurs. As he hit the ground you raked him back to the flank, then reached for his mane again, and look out if you were late doing it. If your feet were back of the cinch on the up, you'd probably find the ground on the down. Keeping in time was important.

One hand gripping the halter shank, the other stayed clear of the rigging on pain of disqualification. For eight hard seconds you rode him thus, then the pickup men moved in on trained horses from both sides, one to take the halter shank, the other to take you clean out of the saddle, slip you onto the back of his own rig, and drop you safely to ground on the other side. Great sport that. Ruins horses and kills men. I was all for it.

I put the night in at my mother's house and after a light lunch the next day at noon, made my way to the rodeo grounds. Already a crowd of spectators had gathered, cars lining the arena, two deep in places. I could have done without the crowd. The gut-twisting scariness of what I was doing suddenly moved in on me. I thought I might be sick.

I ducked under the fence, carrying my saddle across to the chutes. Leaving it there, I went to a table set up at one side of the arena where entries were being taken.

I strode up to the table, my mouth as dry as the dust underfoot, twenty dollars clutched in a sweaty fist for the entry fee, three weeks' poker winnings in a game of ten-cent limit with my schoolmates.

Rex Williams sat at the table, a shoe box of money before him, taking the entries. He looked up, squinting into the sun. "Where you going, dressed up like a cowboy?"

I gulped, searching around for my voice. "Put me down," I said, "for the saddle broncs."

"How old are you, Alan?"

"I been sixteen for a month."

He shook his head, took my money, gave me a flag with a number on it to pin to my shirt, and wrote my name down.

The saddle bronc contest makes the main event, taking up the first couple of hours of an afternoon show. Then the bareback riding, steer riding, calf roping, and what have you are run off. The pattern is much the same for two- or three-day shows.

I hunkered down near the chute, by the arena fence, out of the way, to watch the broncs boil out, their riders fighting to stay in the saddle. I hoped to be up before long and I might as well see a few others take their licks in the meantime. A fist-sized knot churned around in my insides.

A couple of riders came out, performing passing well. Then there was a delay at the chutes over something, accompanied by a great lot of cursing and hollering to look out.

The crash of splintering wood sent the crowd in front of the chute scattering for safety. I jumped up in time to see a big horse all but clear the releasing gate, hooves flailing against the timbers, his great neck arched in a fury of effort.

He came down in the chute and two alert saddlers grabbed his head, haltering him in a deft split second. They both jumped clear as he reared again, but the man on the far side had the halter shank. He soon wrapped twice on a timber, forcing the brute's head against the chute, holding him still at last.

"My Gawd!" the other exclaimed. "You think we'll ever saddle him?"

"You betcha. Where's the rigging? Where's the cowboy?"

I'd seen his number and picked up my saddle. "Over here. Both of us." I spat in the dust and passed up my rigging, mustering a weak grin. They mustered the biggest belly laugh I think I've ever heard.

I wasted no time. The saddle once cinched, I climbed up on the chute. The big horse was under me then, every muscle tense, legs braced, fourteen hundred pounds of untamed dynamite waiting for a chance to explode. I shivered, in spite of the heat and the sweat, and spat again, but the taste of fear stuck to my mouth like lye.

The gateman readied himself. The chap on the other side, holding the shank, gave me a nod. I lowered myself into the saddle, fixing my feet in the stirrups.

Quickly, when I reached for it, the shank man passed the rope. I measured it, tucked the loose end under my arm, clamped my arm down on it, leaned back a little.

"You ready, young fella?" It was the gateman, a little anxiously.

"Give 'im air," I said, remembering I'd wanted to say that.

The gate swung open. The arena waited like a yawning pit of destruction. The bronc wasted a moment in indecision. Then in a bellow of fury, he threw himself in the air, plunged down his head, tearing at the shank.

My legs weren't mine. They held in their own clutch of fear to the battering saddle, yanking me everywhere in inescapable jolts. Come out reaching …

I tried to catch track of the jumps, vaguely knowing the pain of coming to ground had happened twice already and this was three and I hadn't hit his shoulders yet, never would now.

Four, and the saddle was getting farther away from centre. Five. The saddle? No, me. There were two hands on the shank. Disqualified. How? I didn't ... But I must have, of course.

I came to ground rolling and stood up unsteadily, immersed in a vast weariness. There was a big noise and I wondered what was wrong around me. Then I realized it was the crowd, and I was ashamed for pulling leather. But maybe they didn't know about that.

I walked back to the chute slowly, nothing much to hurry about. In a way I didn't want to go there where so many men stood about, men who'd seen what I'd done, who must know now how scared I'd been, so scared I'd tasted it, foul in my mouth.

A big man, stranger to me, came forward, grabbing my arm. He was grinning through a layer of dust and perspiration.

"How ya feel, kid?"

"Okay." Then: "I made kind of a mess of that."

"So what? You think there's many would do better? You drew a tough horse."

"Did he look bad?"

"Damn bad. You better go take it easy."

I saw Gussy in front of the arena fence, off the end of the chute, and made my way over to him to sit down. He said nothing as I joined him.

After a bit I volunteered: "I need some practice."

Gussy thought awhile. "Yes," he said at last, "you do. But this is a poor place to get it. And you'd be a whole lot better off if you was to forget the whole idea."

In the realm of advice, that was a long speech from Gussy. We sat thereafter in silence.

There was another rodeo at Williams Lake a few weeks hence, so I wasted no time gathering funds one way or another to be sure I had an entry fee. A two-day event, it gave a man two rides, but he paid proportionately more for them.

Alfie Eagle, after whom one of our meadows had been called and who now lived a quieter life than when he was the champion bronc stomper of British Columbia, was chute judge and general sergeant-at-arms in the busy area of the arena immediately in front of the gates.

My horse in, I passed up my saddle. Alfie, who had watched me grow up my few short years, spared a moment to stand by me while I watched the saddlers.

"How do you feel?"

"Scared."

"So's anybody here if they're normal. You'll be all right once you're on. Try to get in time with him. And come out with your feet in the mane."

The saddlers done, I climbed the gate, dropped into the saddle, fitted my feet into the stirrups. Alfie reached through and straightened my chaps to be sure there were no wrinkles under my leg, instructing the saddler to do the same on the other side.

I measured the shank, tucked the end.

"You ready?"

I nodded.

The gate opened. The horse stood there, suspicious of the arena, trembling and white eyed. I struck him on the off shoulder with the spur.

He bolted, out the gate on the dead run into the arena. Oh, hell, what luck! I threw my feet up to strike his shoulders, raking back to the flanks.

My feet back, he exploded straight in the air. In a futile second I fought to get in time, spurs ahead on the up, back on the down. I couldn't. Another jolt tore me sideways. I felt the hard impact of the ground against my back.

Perfectly conscious, I couldn't move. But the thought that ran through my mind had nothing to do with the paralysis. I need more practice than I can get this way, I swear. I've gotta get hold of a couple of broncs and a piece of soft meadow somewhere, get used to that damn …

Then voices gathered and a man asked me a few questions, did some gentle probing, rolled me onto a stretcher.

It was cool in the tent and a pleasant, middle-aged woman sat with me, asking if there was anything I wanted. She raised my head just enough that I could drink some cold juice, then I rested some more.

"You're young," she said, looking worried as though she'd just realized it. It was a statement of fact I was growing used to hearing.

"A lot younger'n you think, at that." I grinned at her to show her everything was all right. "C'mon. Give me a hand. I'm okay now. I'm gonna get up and walk outa here."

I had been cautiously aware of the feeling coming back into my legs and back. There was one devil of a sore spot in the small of my back, right on the spine itself. I knew enough anatomy to conclude that the impact had temporarily suspended the transmission of command in the main line.

"Do you think you should?"

"Positive." I rose up slowly, and hesitantly she helped. Once sitting, I sat awhile, then dropped my legs over the edge of the cot to which I'd been transferred from the stretcher. I paused again at that stage.

"Another drink of juice?"

"I'd love it." I drank another glassful. Then I thanked her for her kindness, stood up and walked out to go fetch my saddle, which by now would have been brought back to the vicinity of the chutes, then find a shady spot out of the way where I could watch the remainder of the day's events.

I didn't ride the second day, Alfie saw to that. He turned my horse out when it came in the chutes and I knew better than to protest, to dispute his judgement. My short venture into rodeo riding had fizzled out in ignominy. I was indeed a sad boy.

Runaway Boy

S chool was a hopeless task thereafter, and time due my books fell to debating the use of the coming summer, though in truth my mind had been made up for many weeks, only the details left to be planned.

I would leave the Cariboo, going in search of work on the ranches out of Kamloops, seeing something again of the Old Man. My parents now divorced, each married again, I had been assigned to my mother's care. She'd blow a gasket, no two ways about that, if she knew the mischief I was brewing.

But I was beyond her wishes. Stronger by far was the urge to see new country, new men, get a new job on some distant, unknown cow outfit. Even seeing the Old Man again was not the greater part of it: the wanderlust was in my bones and trail dust alone would quench it.

The last agonizing days of school dragged themselves away, let me free once more. Exhilarated, light and carefree, I'd lost what little conscience I might have had over what I was about to do. I told my mother I was going to Lac la Hache to look for work and caught the first bus down the highway.

I went to her house to roll together some blankets and work clothes, then walked out to Whitehorse Lake where once again I had left my saddle and gear, where, after all, home was, if indeed home was anywhere. Maggie set another place at the table the way she always did when I showed up.

I needed Gussy's help, but at the same time I didn't want to burden him with bad secrets. I asked if I might borrow a horse for a day or two.

"My horse must be running in the back valley," I conjectured. "I'd like to bring him in."

"You take old Shorty then, but you be sure you don't run him any more'n you have to."

I promised I wouldn't, and the next day found me searching for horses in a big chunk of country east of the Cariboo highway at the 111 Mile. I found no horses, but I narrowed the search and around two o'clock the next afternoon I came on thirty or more, my own among them.

We tore out of the hills at a breathless pace, crashing through light brush, scrambling down the slopes toward the road to the corrals at the 111 Mile. With luck I reached the road, the bunch still together, still running hard. More luck and I was down the road, a cloud of dust rising high behind in the hot, June air.

Within the hour I'd reached the corrals, spun out a lariat loop, and brought my horse abruptly up in front of me. I turned the rest out, then rode up the highway to Ogden's store at Lac la Hache, four and a half miles away, leading my much subdued saddle stock behind.

I stopped at the store to buy a pair of gloves, an item I had realized I was short while handling the rope.

"Your mother 'phoned from Williams Lake and wants you to call her. She said to tell you if you came in the store." It was Mrs. Ogden who gave me this message.

I experienced a sudden sinking feeling. How is it one knows the worst has happened, no need to confirm it? How did she find out? Who had I told? Only an Indian boy, a friend who might himself be going to Kamloops, and innocently I'd said I might see him there. That figured. She'd have seen me with him and asked him afterwards what I'd said. The Indian lad wouldn't have known not to tell. Oh, how foolish!

I made the call. It is useless to relate those words. I had lied, saying I was going to look for work at Lac la Hache when in fact

I had no such intention and now, confronted with it, I was ashamed.

I would not lie again. She said I must not leave, that she forbade it. I said I would, that nothing would turn me back.

Her words still in my ears, I hung up the receiver, much as one would make a quick cut with a sharp knife. I stood looking at the telephone, realizing what I had done, suddenly knowing what it was to turn my back on my own kin.

"Is anything wrong?" It was Mrs. Ogden.

I quickly recovered. "No," I said. "No. Nothing's wrong. Thanks for telling me about the call."

I left the store, mounted up, rode quickly out to Gussy's. It was late afternoon and if necessary I would ride out that night. But first I must tell Gussy the score for his own sake. He might have second thoughts about aiding a runaway boy.

He absorbed my explanations thoughtfully. "What you're up to is your business. You want to stay here, that's fine. You want to go, that's up to you. What's between your mom and you got nothing to do with us."

"I'd like to stay tonight, but I'll sleep in the barn. That way I'll hear if a car comes in, and I can be gone and nobody any wiser. You won't need to tell any fibs for me."

I put up in the barn just as I'd said, my saddle handy to the horse, nothing to keep me from riding out but to throw it on him and tie my bedroll back of the cantle. But it was all a needless caution. Daybreak found me crawling out of the loft, brushing hay off my shirt and hoping Maggie was up early making hotcakes.

She was, and I stoked up on a big heap of them washed down with steaming mugs of black coffee. Gussy ate in his usual near silence. Only once he ventured into conversation.

"You goin' to take the Mount Olie trail?"

"I figure on it. I'll lay up a day at Bill Wilson's place at Bridge Lake. 'Sabout eighteen or twenty miles to the trail from there I understand."

"You'll need shoes on that horse."

131

"I know. I didn't want to ask you for any. You been too good to me already."

"Well, that don't matter. But I got no shoes'll fit 'im. Bill won't have none, either. You gonna have to shoe up at the Hundred Mile."

"Yes, I guess I will." I said it with a sigh, knowing what it might mean. All the way to Bill's homestead at Bridge Lake I could stay in the timber, safe as a mouse. But at the 100 Mile for shoes I was vulnerable. Still, there was no avoiding it. "I'll have to take that chance."

Gussy said no more. I finished the last meal I was to eat at Maggie's table for many years to come, then rose to go. There were no elaborate goodbyes. We weren't that kind of folks, I guess. I just gathered my hat, accepted a bag of sandwiches from Maggie and a wish of good luck from Gussy, then was gone, onto the timber trail.

It was by no means a full day's ride to the 100 Mile, but not wanting to arrive there any earlier than I must, I dawdled along in the bush, coming out above the ranch buildings at about five in the afternoon.

The 100 Mile House on the Cariboo road in the early summer of 1947 wasn't settlement enough that you would call it more than a village. The big ranch house lay west of the highway and the barn lay east of it, then down toward the old store on the opposite side again was the bunkhouse where the ranch help lived. On one side of the store was a café, catering to the traffic on the road that once was a wagon track to the gold fields. Beside the café a garage building was going up, with a basement in and the first floor down, the framing started.

I sought out the ranch foreman. I knew nobody here; nobody knew me. The foreman therefore was the logical man to see. "I need shoes for my horse," I said, finding him. "I'd have to borrow shoeing tools too, to put 'em on. I can pay you."

"That's okay. Come over to the barn." I followed him there, where he gave me what I must have. I set about fitting the shoes, nailing them on.

He started to go, then turned back. "There's a spare cot in the bunkhouse where you can lay your blankets tonight if you want. You can leave your horse in the barn. There's grain in a box in the saddle room." It was a clean offer, no who are you, where you come from, where you going, attached to it.

"Thanks," I said. "I'd been figurin' on the timber east o' here, but maybe I'll take you up on it." I'd begun to feel safe enough, thinking Mother would probably have accepted the inevitable.

Finished shoeing, I put my horse in a stall and fed him, both hay and oats. Then I took my bedroll off the saddle and made my way to the bunkhouse, a hundred yards or so down the road. There the crew, fresh in from the day's work, showed me an empty cot. I left my blankets and went across the road to the café.

I took a stool at the counter. A pretty woman with a freckled nose — and at sixteen I knew enough to appreciate a pretty woman though she was probably seven or eight years my senior — asked me what I'd have.

"Coffee, please." I felt no hunger at the moment, deciding therefore that I might eat later. Anyway I had no abundance of funds, and if I didn't eat at all it would be no hardship.

Nearly done the coffee, I glanced out the big front window of the café. The Greyhound bus had just come in from the north. Already the passengers were alighting.

A sudden feeling of disaster swept over me. I'd caught sight, I thought, of a certain face going down the aisle of the bus to the exit door. The bus windows were at eye level with the café window. I jumped to the window to be sure, in the instant confirming what I'd seen.

It was the face of a man of sixty, the man to whom my mother was married, a man with whom I had no quarrel but with whom I had no intention either of discussing my differences with my mother. He was also a lawyer. I, of course, was grossly in doubt about the legal propriety of my exodus from the Cariboo, and I wanted no opportunity to have it explained to me.

There was no going out the front door. I turned back, looking for the woman who had served me, knowing there was only a moment to spare before everyone from the bus would be in the café for the evening meal stop.

She saw my agitation. "What is it?"

"Quick. Which way do I get out the back?"

"Go into the kitchen. There's a door out that way. What are you …"

But she had no time to finish. I bolted for the kitchen, stopping to look directly at her before slipping through the door. "If someone asks you, you haven't seen anyone who looks like me. Promise?"

"But why do you … All right, I promise."

I fled through the kitchen past an astounded cook and out the back door. I waited until I thought he must have reached the café, then ran to the partly constructed garage, leaping a pile of earth, ducking through a door in the foundation into the basement.

There was a window at eye level that would be above ground when the backfilling was complete. As it was, I could see part of the bus protruding past the café and people still coming out, walking from my sight to the café entrance.

I caught my breath. The one from whom I had fled, curses that I should flee from *him* anyway, was looking thoughtfully toward the garage. Had he caught a glimpse of me running? Perhaps I had misjudged the moment, running between the buildings too soon.

He began walking toward me, butting a cigarette as he did so. I'm in better shape than you, old boy, I thought. I can take you if I have to. But what would that do for me? I wanted no trouble, only to have my own way.

He still advanced. I looked quickly about. A disorderly pile of construction material lay in a far corner. I ran there, leaped the pile and dropped behind it, quickly seeking a place to peer around without being discovered.

He entered the doorway and stood there, perhaps waiting for his eyes to accustom to the dark. It seemed my breathing would surely give me away, so heavy it was with my heart pounding behind it.

He looked directly at the pile of material behind which I lay. Then he fumbled for cigarettes, found them, lit one. He moved again. Two steps. Then he stopped, as though debating something. I wondered how long I could lie there, tense as a tight-wound spring, without involuntarily doing something rash and sudden.

He shrugged and quickly walked away. I sighed and closed my eyes. Sweat had drenched my shirt. I knew the meaning of sweet relief.

I changed my plans for the night at once. It would be too easy to be caught. I watched the bus load again and the old chap got on with the rest. When it pulled out I walked back in the café.

My abettor approached me cautiously.

"Could I have another cup of coffee?"

"What are you up to?"

"Does it matter?"

She brought the coffee. "I don't know. You look like you're just a kid to me. I shouldn't have helped you, but you caught me so sudden."

"Well, you helped me, and thanks. An' you got a pretty nose."

"You brat!"

"Aw, I'm sorry. I just got tired of everything being so serious."

She blushed and I thought it might be wonderful to be more her age. "Anyway," I went on, "I haven't done anything wrong. I'm running away from home, sort of."

"That's not very smart."

I passed that up. She said no more while I finished the coffee. I thanked her again when I paid for both cups — I'd bolted before paying for the earlier one — then went to the bunkhouse to fetch my bedroll.

"You ain't stayin' long," commented one of the men, while I bundled up my blankets.

"Nope," I said. "I'm not, at that. Kinda changed my mind."

"Where you gonna sleep tonight?"

"In the timber."

"You on the run?"

"Sort of." With that I left, feeling terribly mysterious and excited, knowing there'd be some wild speculating in the bunkhouse that night.

Mount Olie Trail

I poked along till dark that night, then slid well into the timber out of sight of the track I followed, a side road of fair proportions which led from the Cariboo highway to Bridge Lake, the jumping-off-place for the Mount Olie trail that came out on the North Thompson River and country kin to Kamloops, not the Cariboo.

I staked my horse by a forefoot, with enough rope that if he had the sense not to wind up he'd have room to crop a feed. Then I picked as friendly a looking spruce tree as I could find and lay out my blankets.

It was in Bridge Lake country that Bill Wilson, good old stick of two summers ago, had his pothole homestead and there, I planned happily as I tossed around on the spruce roots trying to make comfy, old Bill and I'll trade a passel of yarns before I cross over the Mount Olie trail.

That was a rough camp and the mosquitoes were bad and before daybreak I was hungry and there was nothing to eat. I rolled out of the blankets in which I'd slept but little and fetched my horse. He'd eaten the grass to the roots in the circle of the stake rope. Chances were he was hungry again, but I threw the rigging on him to move out at once. It couldn't have been more than four-thirty in the morning.

I made good time, pushing along steadily at a mile-eating trot. I reckoned it to be near forty miles from where I'd camped to the

Bridge Lake store and though I knew this country only vaguely, I could count on finding Bill once I reached the general store where it seemed he must deal for his supplies.

I passed farmhouses where the smoke had yet to rise from the chimneys, then one or two where the first flush from lighting up belched out of the Yukon pipe. I thought about stopping to dicker for food, but thinking was as far as it went. I pushed on.

The sun rose high and the day grew hot. Once I passed a herd of cows, grazing untended in the timber by the road. One of the cows had an infected jaw, probably from an encounter with a porcupine who'd left a quill or two behind as a reminder of his virtual invincibility. A distended pouch of skin, full of poison, hung below her mouth. She was quite unable to graze. I pitied her but stopped only long enough to see where she was branded, not long enough to sort out the brand itself, a poorly applied splotch of a scar.

A while later I came to a wagon track leading away from the road. In sight was a log house and some outbuildings. I paused, then turned in.

A big woman met me at the door.

"There's a cow down the road with a poisoned jaw. I thought I'd best tell someone."

She looked at me, pondering what I'd said, no doubt also wondering who I was. "Oh," she said at last. "Well now, I wouldn't know anything about that. You tie your horse in the shade and come in while I call my boy."

She went back through the house and I could hear her calling out the far door. "Harry! Hareee! There's a man here to see you about a cow."

I tied my horse and went in, taking a chair close to the door. The room was cluttered but comfortable and scrupulously clean, typical of the dwellings of poor but dignified farm folk, one hell of a stride ahead of our old meadow cabins. Soon the woman came back, accompanied by Harry, a man of perhaps thirty. It was only then I realized the woman must be fairly elderly.

"How do y'do? You say somethin' about a cow?"

"There's a cow about two miles back has a bad jaw. Maybe a porcupine quill. She doesn't look like she can eat any more. Thought I should tell somebody." I described the cow as well as I could, explaining about the poorly made brand.

"That's my neighbour's cow. He don't tend his stock no better'n he brands 'em. I'll go down'n see what I can do. Where you from?"

"Up around Lac la Hache."

"Well really it ain't my business, is it? You come a long way. You had anything to eat?"

Already his mother had gone to the kitchen to make a meal for me. I could hear her stoking the wood stove and clanging the pots and pans. "I don't want you to go to any trouble. That isn't really why I stopped. I thought I should tell someone about that cow." Inside of course I was ravenous and the thought of food was terribly welcome.

"Oh, that's no trouble. You have to have some food once in a while or you get weak. Least I sure do and you don't look no tougher'n me."

I assured him I didn't think I was. Then he insisted on taking my horse to the barn for hay and grain while I sat down to eat a meal that made up completely for the fact that the last thirty-six hours or a little better had been passed only on Maggie's sandwiches. When I finally took my leave, it was in the conviction that henceforth I must regard a cow with lump jaw as a good omen of the first order.

The sun was over the hump and there were many miles yet to go. I trotted along persistently, promising my horse at every mile that he was earning a layover of at least two days, starting tomorrow. It was more a promise to myself, really. I'd been out of the saddle a long time and to ride so constantly before hardening into it was tough on the seat of my pants.

Come early evening, I reached the Bridge Lake store. A few directions from the old merchant there set me off again, but now not far from corral and cabin. I found the wagon tracks and following them, came to the meadow. Across it, smoke drifted out of the chimney pipe of a sod-roofed shack, everything about the place telling me here was old Bill.

He was the most astounded man in all creation to see a strange rider coming around the edge of his little meadow, approaching his cabin, finally identifying him to be no other than the ornery boy he had known so well in the Old Man's hay camp.

"What the blazes are you doing here?" he cried in astonishment.

"Lookin' for grub and a place to throw my bedroll. I'll be damned sore if I don't find it, too."

"Well, I might know that much, but what else?" So while we put my horse in the corral and gave him feed, then gathered spruce boughs to lay on a corner of the split-pine floor for a bed, I told Bill what I was up to. To hide a runaway boy, especially me, tickled Bill no end. Had he the chance, he'd have joined me on the trail.

There I spent two good days. Bill showed me about his place. He hadn't enough hay or pasture to make a living, supposing he had the money to stock the place, which he hadn't. He scraped along, going out at times to work, living frugally off the land when he was home. More than anything, Bill treasured his own horses and his homestead. Though it gave him no living, it gave him something to live for.

He was prone to accidents. His team would run away or his saddle horse fall with him. Often hurt or beset by other bad luck, he bore his difficulties with good will and nature, returning happily and optimistically to his cabin, after each time away to work for money to pay his bills, or to stay in hospital to mend a bone.

His cabin was a most primitive affair, poorly put together out of unbarked pine logs. The roof was of split pine and earth, the door of rough boards, hung on leather hinges. Even the floor was split from pine, the halves turned up and hewed as smooth as Bill could manage.

But it was a homey little den just the same. Bill's few belongings cluttered it up magnificently and if he wanted something, he hadn't far to look. The furnishings consisted of a camp-size cookstove, a rough table, and a pine-pole bed with spruce boughs in it for a mattress, which, clearly, Bill didn't change nearly so often as he should. An item of gear had to be on stove, table, bed or floor, and only by hiding under something else, could any of his stuff get out of his sight.

Bill was poor, all right, from a belongings point of view. His funds were exhausted at that time and he was living largely on potatoes and cheap pilchards, a bottled fish he bought at the store on credit he'd go out to work in the summer to pay back. He was a poor hunter or he'd likely have had game instead.

But all this was of no consequence. He was absorbed in his simple existence and the frugal meals he sat down to daily were part of it. He shared what little he had with a joke about its meagreness, knowing full well it was all one damn fine time to me.

Fine as it was, I must go. On a rainy morning I said goodbye, riding across his meadow, the way I had come. Even yet I see him, standing by the sod-roofed cabin, waving his big hat until I was gone from sight. It was the last I saw of Bill. Then I turned my eyes to the road ahead. I must reach Little Fort on the North Thompson River by nightfall, over twenty miles of road and twenty-five of trail.

I pushed along quickly, mostly at that mile-eating trot again, for the trail would be a slow business and I must be on it as soon as I could. At nine o'clock I passed the Bridge Lake store, at ten o'clock the Boultbee Ranch, and by ten-thirty I reached the start of the trail.

Here and there, carved on trees, were the names of men who had ridden across this stretch of wilderness and the times it had taken them. Some had been ten hours, some fourteen or fifteen from Little Fort. I did a bit of calculating, hoped to be through by late evening.

Little used, the trail was badly obstructed by windfalls. I had no axe, though I knew I should have, and had no little trouble with trees across the. trail., too high to jump, too low to crawl under, and surrounded by other windfalls in a thick, jack pine jungle. Many times I dismounted to force my horse to scramble through as best he might.

At times the trail dropped down to the valley bottoms. We waded fast running streams, pushed through treacherous mudholes. The rain let up and the sun turned hot. The flies pestered my horse and the mosquitoes went after me. Then the trail would go high again, where we'd scramble along a shale slope, struggling to keep from sliding hundreds of feet into the tangle of rocks and trees at the foot of the talus.

The long day wore on. My horse tired of the trail. I tired of the saddle. Often I walked, resting my horse, giving myself a change. Though there was little time for it, twice I stopped by one of the many streams we were obliged to cross. My horse drank and grazed while I took off my shirt to wash in the fresh, cold mountain water. At one stop I ate the sandwiches I had brought from Bill's meagre larder. But mainly I had to keep on without thought of my horse, nor, for that matter, myself.

I had started before six in the morning. It was now well on for evening. I must be close to the end of the trail. It had been rumoured the Department of Public Works were starting to push a road through the mountains to provide another car route from the Cariboo to Kamloops country. If this was the case I must soon come to construction machinery and a road camp. I might even find a meal at the road-camp cookhouse, the few sandwiches long since gone and me very hungry.

I rode on, encouraged that I could not be far from the camp. I was not. In the half hour, I was dismounting as a crew of men gathered around to ask how my trip had been, was I hungry, my gosh, boy, your horse is wore out, and will you have some grub and coffee. In this welcome there was an element of great surprise.

"You missed your dad by no more'n ten minutes."

The Old Man! How could that be? How did they know who I was? I searched for the one who had spoken. "I don't understand," I said.

"Well, seems your dad knew you'd be comin' through here about today, though he said you wouldn't know he knew. He had a horse trailer hitched back of his pickup."

I began figuring hard and guessed rightly that in her anxiety my mother had telephoned him, maybe blaming him for what I had done, though it was all my own contriving. "When did he come in here?"

"Around two this afternoon, wouldn't you say, Jack?" He turned to another, who nodded assent to this estimation, then went on: "He waited till just a few minutes ago now, then said he had to get back, he couldn't stay any later. He told us, watch out for my boy, he said, and tell him to let me know when he comes out."

It was a fair tribute to the Old Man's reckoning that he had come so close to meeting me. I looked up the road, along which even yet he would not be far, but without a telephone to send word ahead of him, he was out of reach.

"Give me your horse, lad. I'm going to take him along the creek here to feed while you have some grub. Jack, you go with the boy and see Cookie gives him something to eat." With this the one who had spoken took the bridle reins from my hand, leading my horse away.

The chap called Jack took me to the cookhouse, on the way forewarning about Cookie.

"He ain't much of a cook and he's a crabby old beggar. He'll cuss you out for botherin' him, but you just shut up an' eat an' I'll take care of him." I would have weathered more than a cussing out to get a meal. "Whatever you say," I agreed.

"Cookie, we want some grub for the boy here. Fix up a plate."

Cookie was washing dishes and he went right back to them after a savage glance over his shoulder.

"Some grub for the boy here, Cookie." My champion wasn't losing his temper, but the tone of his voice made it plain he wasn't settling for anything less than he asked.

"What the hell do you think this is, a restaurant?"

"Never mind. Just fix the boy a plate of that damned swill you feed us."

The cook leaped around in a fury. "You get the hell outa my cookhouse!"

142

"Just fix some grub."

I sat through all this in wonderment. I'd been around some for a boy my age, but this was the finest rough and tumble of words I'd ever laid an ear to. Jack didn't raise his voice or make any threats, but he had his way. The cook glowered at him, in some inexplicable way coming to the conclusion he'd feed me. It wasn't a bad meal at that, though one had to use one's knife on the pie crust.

Thanking these rough-cut benefactors, I took the road once more. Close to dark I came to Little Fort and the broad, swift waters of the North Thompson River.

Little Fort was no more than a small village, once a trading post, boasting a store or two and a ferry crossing, with a few small farms around, up and down the road.

I confronted the only man abroad in the village. "Where do you suppose I might find a stable for my horse for the night?" I enquired.

The fellow thought a moment. "You see that farm back up the road past where you come? You come down that way, didn't you? Well, you see the folks at that place, they'll fix you up."

I thanked him and turned back up the road a quarter mile to some farm buildings. I came first to a barn, beyond which was a small house set in among some apple trees. I remember that because of course in the Cariboo one does not see apple trees: they won't survive the winters.

I found a young man at the barn.

"I'm on my way to Kamloops. Could I put my horse up in the barn here for one night?"

"Sure," the other nodded. "I'll show you." He led me in and indicated a stall I could use for my tired mount.

"Would it matter if I went into the loft with my bedroll? I won't smoke in the hay." He thought this odd, but said it was fine, then left me. Soon I had fed my horse and was sound asleep, purging my young body of a great weariness.

The first sound in the morning was of milk streaming into a pail. I lay for a moment, gathering where I was. Then I slipped into my denims and boots, rolled up my blankets, and went down the ladder into the barn. My host was busy milking a cow in a stall near my horse.

I asked if I might borrow a hammer and have a few horseshoe nails. He told me where to find these in a sort of gear box in a corner of the barn, and I set about tightening up a shoe which had come loose on a rocky piece of the trail. I was bent over thus, the hoof secured between my knees, when I discovered I was confronted by a trim and husky little woman of perhaps forty-five years. She had slipped into the barn unnoticed, and I must say I was taken off my nerve to find her standing there, glaring at me so.

"You slept in the hayloft last night! What do you mean by sleeping in the loft like that? Look at the seeds stuck in your hair!"

I couldn't think where else I might have slept. Why did the man tell me I could if it was forbidden? I looked over to seek his aid, but he kept his head down, intently drawing milk into the pail. Clearly, he was no match for this woman, probably his mother. I had the distinct feeling he had already heard about it for letting me sleep in the loft.

"Well, ma'am, I didn't think it would ..."

"I don't think either of you thought very much!" She cut me off crossly. I tried to explain that I knew better than to smoke in a hayloft, but fared no better with this. Could one escape? I had my horse and all my rigging in the barn and anyway there would be no going by that determined woman, standing as she was in the doorway. I felt the colour rush to my face as I stood there, helpless, having let the hoof to the ground again.

"Do you think I keep beds in my house to look at? Sleep in a barn indeed! That's just the sort of thing you kids would do. You're a brainless lot. What would your mother think if she knew you'd slept in our barn with empty beds in the house? Eh? What would she think?"

I reflected that where I slept nights wasn't what really bothered my poor mother, but of course there was no use trying to explain all that. "I'm sorry, ma'am. I'm used to camping and sleeping out and I never really give it a thought."

"Well, finish fixing that shoe and then get up to the house at once. I suppose you'd have gone on the road with no breakfast, too, if I didn't stop you. Where did you eat last night?"

The way she said it, I could see she was going to be sore about this too if I didn't look out. "I ate at the road camp on this end of the trail."

"You sure about that?"

"Honest I did. I came through there close to six."

"We keep food at our house, in case you didn't think so. You hurry up now." She left me with that, and I finished up. The young man passed out of the barn with nary a word, but I thought I saw a thoughtful smile on his face as he walked by. Once done, I tied my horse back in the stall, fed him, and then went to the little farmhouse in the trees.

Maybe I felt more alone in a strange country than I knew. Sitting down to that woman's table as she piled a breakfast in front of me fit to bust the best of men, porridge and bacon with eggs, strawberries with rich cream, toast and coffee, I had to blink hard to see properly. What if she should discover this? Heaven knows what that blessed and generous little woman would have tried to do for me then. Fortunately I was alone at the table, the others having eaten, and soon was all right again, occupied completely with that mountain of food.

She never asked me about myself. She let me eat, and when I rose to go she handed me a bag. "Here's a few sandwiches for you. You'll be hungry before you know it." Then she touched my arm in a tender way, that great facade of harshness completely gone. "You're young to be on your own," she said. I thanked her as best I could and left.

Sixty miles down the river lay Kamloops, the bustling centre of British Columbia's beef-cattle industry. Fifteen miles this side of it lay Heffley Creek and there I aimed to be by nightfall. I had known two boys, Jim and Bill Palmer, fellows about my own age, while I was in boarding school. They had come from Heffley Creek and I thought perhaps their father, Doug Palmer, would give me work on the ranch I had heard them tell so much about.

Again I pushed my horse, eating up the forty-five miles of road with an hour to spare before dark. Coming to the store at Heffley Creek, I asked directions. I was shown the foot of a trail which would take me up a short way above the valley floor into the hayfields of the Seven O Ranch.

I knew Doug the moment he answered my knock at the door, there was so much in Bill that was like him. A big man, hearty and talkative, you wondered sometimes whether he was gruff or kind or maybe both. I told him who I was, and Bill came out of the house at the same moment to confirm it, asking me if I was lost or something, so far out of my own bull pasture.

"I need a job," I declared.

"Your dad said to take you on if you passed the once-over," Doug informed me. So the Old Man guessed right again.

"You think I pass?"

"I think so. Put your horse in the barn. Bill, show him the bunkhouse."

The next morning I took a place at the table in the cookhouse to become part of the outfit, borrowing use of the telephone in the ranch house after breakfast to tell the Old Man where I was.

146

BIG HORSE, BAD TROUBLE

The Palmer ranch headquartered at the place near Heffley Creek and, unlike the outfits in the Cariboo, grew all its hay at the home place. The climate in the southern part of the North Thompson Valley was much milder than the Cariboo, and great fields of alfalfa produced more hay to the acre than I had imagined was possible.

Next to the hayfields was a hard-grass pasture for spring and fall use; fifteen miles away at Pinantan lay the cow camp where a rider spent the summer keeping an eye on the seven or eight hundred head of cattle carrying the ranch brand. This summer range was in high country more like the Cariboo, a rolling country where the cattle grazed under an overstorey of open timber.

I found myself in a new atmosphere, one I had not experienced before. This was no small, friendly, family crew such as we had known on the Old Man's place or working with Gussy. In that gathering of neighbours there had been some concern for one's feelings and a little regard for a boy's attempts to learn his trade — attempts that do not always turn out happily.

There was none of this on the Palmer ranch. With eight men in the bunkhouse and Doug with his two boys, we were a crew of eleven or thereabouts, depending on some coming and going. Some of the men were surly and disgruntled, showing it in everything they said. One was the same as another to the ranch.

If he did the work, he stayed; if not, he went down the road. What he was like apart from that made no difference to Doug.

When I made a mistake, and a sixteen-year-old boy on a new outfit is going to make mistakes, I found hard words from the boss, contempt from the crew.

The first afternoon three of us had been sent to reset posts in a fence. We went along testing the posts and when we came to a rotten one we'd free the barbwire and break the post off at the ground. Then we'd dig out the rotten butt and rebury the post, putting the top end down, tamping with the shovel handle to make it firm.

I had just reset a post and more to make friendly conversation than anything, I spoke to the chap working one post up as I tested the firmness, shoving at it with my hand, "You think that'll do?"

He turned on me with a scowl. "Can't y'tell? You got a head on your shoulders. Why'n hell don't you use it?" He couldn't have cut me more with the heel of his boot. Green, a stranger in new country, I'd have given anything for a word of friendship from someone. I turned to my work, silent and miserable, completely abashed.

I'd have quit, but I had no promise of other work, and would it not be the same anywhere else I might go? I wanted no reputation as a quitter, so I determined grimly to take what came, work as best I could, hold on at all costs. I learned again what every young hand must learn that experience comes the hard way and you don't earn a place in the scheme of things to call your own with pride till you've endured all the abuse the old hands feel like heaping on you.

Still, I was the only one on the outfit in the least worried about me, which, in a reverse way, made the harshness easier to bear. Instead of taking hurt, I learned to cuss under my breath, to turn to my task more earnestly than ever. I could handle the horse-drawn machinery well enough, and this I was given to do.

Then for me the summer came abruptly to an end. The Old Man had been boarding a horse on the ranch that he was disinclined to sell. A big, long-legged gelding, sired by a near-loco racehorse out of a chunky brood mare we once owned, the Old Man thought a lot of the critter. I didn't, mostly because he was so much farther off the ground than any horse I'd ever used. A frisky brute, at least once he'd laid the Old Man up a few days, tossing him down a hillside back of the Milk Ranch.

Nobody had been riding him, so I decided to take the edge off him. I brought him in on a Sunday and put my rigging on him. I led him into the big corral behind the barn to pile aboard. I don't know quite what he didn't like about it, but before long he was rearing back on his hind legs, making a devil of a fuss.

I slapped the back of his neck with the end of the lines. He plunged down on all fours, started to buck. I loosened in the first jump but tightened up in the second. Soon I had the hand of him and was doing fine, one arm out for balance, taking the jolts as they came.

I could have ridden him out if I'd left it at that. But I was bent I was a bronc stomper and nothing would do but I shoved my feet up and socked the spur rowels into his shoulders, trying for his neck. Go to it, cayuse. I got your measure.

He exploded sideways and in the instant I knew I'd opened up more horse than I could handle. I fought for the saddle, driving my spurs for the cinch, bringing down my spare hand to try to lift his head.

It was all useless. In another twisting leap he threw me against the corral fence. I crashed on the rails and fell to the ground.

I moved and a searing pain shot through my left shoulder, into my neck. I lay back again, debating what I should do.

I reached with my good hand for the fence rails and drew myself up, taking the pain. Once up, I clutched my left arm against my side with my right hand, keeping the shoulder rigid. The pain still there, the sharp stabs of sheer agony lessened a little.

The big horse stood at the watering trough, eyeing me doubtfully. I threw him a curse and walked slowly out of the corral. There was more wrong with me than laying around the bunkhouse a couple of days would fix and I needed help.

A few of the men were lazing away the day off on their bunks. They jumped up when I entered, seeing immediately I was hurt.

"It's my shoulder and I think it's bad."

"Lie down on your bunk, Al," one instructed me. "I'll fetch Mrs. Palmer. Doug's away somewhere with his boys, but she'll know what to do."

"The horse is still in the corral with the saddle on. Maybe someone could strip him and turn him out."

While the first man went for Mrs. Palmer, another set off to unsaddle the horse. The remaining men stayed to talk to me, to take my mind off the pain in my shoulder. For a rough crew, they'd turned a leaf of kindness.

Mrs. Palmer arrived, bringing the pickup truck. She asked me a few questions, soon concluding I'd broken a bone. She strapped my arm to keep my shoulder rigid, then had me climb into the truck. On the way past the house she stopped to telephone to town so a doctor could go to the clinic to meet us, at the same time sending a message to the Old Man. Realizing the trouble I was creating all around, I wasn't in too much pain to feel a bloody fool.

The Old Man was at the clinic. "Hullo, boy," he said. "You been overdoing it?"

"I guess I have. I'm sorry about all this grief." I knew what, in a way, was the worst feature of the whole business. "You'll have to tell Mother, won't you?"

"I'm afraid I will, old chap."

"I never thought anything like this'd happen. I only wanted to work around for a while. I thought maybe once I was here she'd kinda get over it and I could stay with you for school this fall. That is, if I gotta go to school."

"You 'gotta' go to school all right, count on that. Never mind the rest of it just now. I'll see about all that."

The doctor looked briefly at my shoulder, then sent me with the Old Man to be admitted to the hospital, a large building on the south side of Kamloops, overlooking the city. There he left me, promising to see me again as soon as he could.

I had suffered no more than a broken collar bone. The worst feature of all was being confined to a hospital bed. But events moved quickly. The following morning an orderly came at an unearthly hour to subject me to unthinkable indignities in preparation for the operating table. Then at ten o'clock I met the doctor again in the operating room.

"How are you, young man?"

"Fair enough, considering. What now?"

"We cut you open, wire your bone together, sew you up again. Okay?"

"Sounds fine. Do I get to hold hands with the nurse?"

"You're too young for that."

"I could try."

The nurse wasn't missing any of it. "You'd better not try," she declared. But she was smiling and the banter made me happier than I'd been for hours.

I came to in the late afternoon, a nagging ache replacing the earlier sharp pain, a dressing and a lot of bandages binding my upper arm and shoulder.

There were curtains around my bed, shutting me off from the rest of the ward. Soon a nurse appeared through the curtains, to see how I fared. It was the same young woman who had been in the operating room.

"You're awake at last."

"What time is it?"

"Nearly four. You're a terrible youngster."

"What do you mean?" I was dopey, but this assertion concerned me. Maybe I *had* tried to hold her hand.

"You talked under the anaesthetic. Your language was frightful."

I cringed with shame. I'd the repertoire of a mule skinner, developed behind a wide variety of knothead horses. But it was unthinkable that a woman should ever hear me. What could I possibly say to make amends? I pictured the worst and it was a wonder she would even speak to me.

"I'm very sorry," I said, inadequately.

"Really?"

"Really. Terribly sorry. Honest." Then cautiously: "How bad was it?"

She laughed. "You're properly worried, aren't you?"

"Well, yes. I know some pretty awful words." I was confused now. "It was bad, but nothing I haven't heard before."

I felt greatly relieved. "Then you never heard the half of it, miss. You never heard the half of it."

All this while she'd been efficiently fixing my covers and, of course, taking my mind off my injury. Now she popped a thermometer in my mouth and gently took my wrist in her hand to count my pulse. Her fingers felt soft and cool. I smiled as best I could past the thermometer and decided there were some distinct pleasures in being an invalid.

The Old Man came in the evening. He'd telephoned my mother and in an unexpected turn of acquiescence she'd said I could stay with him. Maybe it was more, you can have him if you can stand him. I guess I was an awful burden to any parent.

My shoulder made good progress. I began to be interested in my fellow patients in the ward. Next to me on the right lay an old Scandinavian whose only pastime was chewing snuff. "Yesus," he'd say, "but dot stoff iss too strong for me, but I got de habit and I cain't quit." The nurses grimaced when they came to take away the bag he'd been spitting in.

Over the aisle was an old fellow with bladder trouble of some nature. He was talkative and cheery and somehow he'd brought with him a bottle of medicine of a brand he'd been using to keep himself regular for nigh on twenty years. When the nurses brought around the prescribed laxative we all took to overcome the effects of our inactivity, there was trouble.

"But Mr. Gatby, everybody takes this medicine, every morning and evening." It was a mixture of something white and something chocolate brown. True, we all took it, but we none of us liked it.

"I don't need it," stoutly maintained Mr. Gatby. "I'm regular as clockwork. Don't need it at all."

152

"Please now, Mr. Gatby. Don't be difficult."

"I'm not being difficult. I just won't take that stuff. 'Tain't necessary."

"Mr. Gatby! You must take this medicine!" She looked severe, commanding him.

"No," he said quietly, a twinkle in his eye.

"Oh but Mr. Gatby, please take it. Just for me." That approach would have had me, personally, taking straight iodine, her voice soft and mellow, her eyes appealing. But I guess he was too old to be moved by it.

"Look," he said, pulling his bottle of patent medicine out of its hiding place. "I take this. I don't need that."

"Mr. Gatby! You can't have that in here. You can't bring your own medicine into the hospital." She reached for the bottle, but he clutched it tightly.

"G'wan. If'n I didn't take this, that stuff'd be useless. I been takin' this for years. Wouldn't be without it."

"I'll tell the matron," she said, that being her invincible trump card. "I'll tell the matron." She couldn't conceive of anyone defying the matron.

"Go 'head. Tell 'er."

"Okay, I will." But we knew she wouldn't, for how could she admit she was incapable of giving Mr. Gatby his medicine? He stayed regular after his own fashion.

The days went by and the pain in my shoulder diminished. The bandages reduced in number and while I had to use some caution, I could move the arm about a little. One feature of the entire situation continued, however, to plague me. Several times daily I must submit to a needle in my backside.

I didn't mind the jab. That was nothing, even after the skin grew tender from many jabbings. What bothered me was the embarrassment of having to bare my anatomy to the young lady with the needle. There was something excruciatingly undignified about the entire procedure. I did my best to expose only the very necessary patch of hide, adroitly covering around it with nightgown and bedding. Still, it was a devil of an experience.

But there was to be an end, even to that. The day came that I could leave the hospital. In the morning the nurse brought my clothes and drew the curtains around my bed.

"Here," she said. "You can get dressed and go down on the lawn. But don't go away. You won't be discharged until eleven. I'll call you out the window when it's time." She left me and I dressed, then did as she suggested. It was a sunny day but not yet hot, and I was glad to be outside. The Old Man would be around to fetch me after eleven and there seemed no better way to spend the morning.

I found I was not alone on the lawn. Already there, stretched out to his full six feet and propped on an elbow, was a man of perhaps thirty-five or forty, wearing jeans and riding boots, a plain shirt and a wide-brimmed hat. His face on one side was completely covered by a dressing. I'd not seen him before, so he must have been in another ward.

"Pull up some grass and sit down," he invited, seeing me approach.

I dropped on the lawn beside him. "Are you going out today, too?"

"No, 'fraid not. Wish I was. I come down here every day for a bit. I can walk around all I want, but I got to stay in awhile yet. What's your grief?"

"Broken collar bone. Landed against a fence."

"That's bad. You got to avoid that. I did that once, in a show at Sedro-Woolley, Washington. Broke my left arm. Where'd it happen?"

"On a ranch, back of the barn." I felt that must sound awfully tame and unglorious. "I ain't done much rodeo work. I only got started this year."

He looked at me for a long moment, sizing me up. "So you caught it back of the barn from a cranky cow horse, huh? Well, let me tell you, you got nothin' to be ashamed of." Then he started talking as if he'd been waiting a long time to find someone to sound off to. It wasn't hard, as I listened to him, to put together a picture of the life he'd led.

He'd come from a small town in southern Alberta, but his family weren't ranch people. Still, he'd soon caught an interest in horses and before long he was out with boys his own age on nearby ranches, becoming fairly proficient in the saddle. Once he owned a horse of his own which he kept in rented pasture just out of town.

As he grew older he began going to round robin broncriding practices on Sunday afternoons. At first he picked the easier horses, but soon, finding he had a bent for it, he tackled tougher ones. He'd been athletic and the hurricane deck came to him like football does to the city youth with better than average strength coupled with good co-ordination.

By the time he was eighteen, he was a rider to reckon with at any local show. In another few years he was on the rodeo circuit, going from one show to the next, making a living from it except perhaps for a few months in the winter when he'd take any job that came to him on a ranch or any place else.

It had been a grand life for the first few years. Even the occasional injury hadn't dampened his love of it. He was young and strong and bounced back quickly. There were good times, easy money, and plenty of women but never, for some reason, quite the one he'd want to marry and settle down with.

As time went on the injuries came more frequently and he stiffened up in different parts of his body. It was an effort now, each time he made a colourful ride on a good bucking horse. In fact, he suspected, his riding was no longer as colourful as it needed to be. Younger men made more points on less adequate horses.

He thought of quitting, that it was time to get out, maybe take a job on a ranch. Still, he really knew nothing of ranch work and the hundred and one skills that are all part of it. And, too, he'd never learned to put up with the drudgery of any steady work. If there was ever a job with long days of sheer toil attached to it, it was ranch work, he could see that.

He talked on, and I said nothing, taking in the feelings of a man who'd been a success at something I wanted to do and now was strangely bitter about it all. His present injury perhaps had capped matters off for him. He'd caught a hoof full in the cheek and the injury threatened to ruin his appearance completely.

"And you were raised on a ranch, huh? You know about makin' hay and tendin' cows and all that, I guess. Well, you stick to that, boy. It'll do you a hell of a lot more good in the long run. Take it from me, I know. I been findin' out."

I thought about what he was saying and couldn't deny there was sense in it. Too, I didn't really stand the chance of success he had. He'd been athletic, you could still see it in him. I wasn't and never had been. I could easily end up like a mediocre hockey player, better maybe than average, but never good enough for the big league. I'd hate to try my best and never be a top rider. It was sobering to hear him talk. Only a rodeo rider, of course, could have spoken these truths and made me listen. If it had been the Old Man telling me the same things, it would have been in one ear and out the other.

Then I heard the nurse calling me and had to go. "Glad to meet you, mister," I said, getting to my feet.

"So long, boy. Go back to your pitchfork. And any time those cow horses are going easy on you, don't think you're smart and try to liven 'em up."

"I'll remember that."

I went in the building and up the stairs to the ward. The nurse was waiting for me. She had a needle.

"I thought we were done with those."

"Not yet. One more. Just slip into the ward office here and we'll get it over with."

We went into a small room in which there was a desk and all sorts of hygienically white apparatus that smelled of disinfectant. She closed the door.

"I guess my arm'll do, huh?" I began rolling up my sleeve, hopefully.

"No. Regular place."

"You mean ..."

"Yes. That's what I mean. Hurry up, give me a bare spot."

"But nurse, I'd have to ... That is I ..."

"Oh, come on now. Hurry up. Turn around and down with the trousers. You can lean over the desk."

Mortified, I obeyed. It was quickly over, but I promised myself faithfully that never, never would I let anything happen to bring me to such an undignified posture before a woman again.

That rodeo cowboy had omitted the very worst part of it all.

I'VE GOT TO RIDE HIM

 I lived that winter with the Old Man and Dulce, the blessed and exuberant woman who'd made life worthwhile for him again and borne him my sister, Joan. My financial embarrassment was acute. Since my twelfth summer I had not failed to earn enough to see me through the winters. But now not a penny rattled in the pocket of my denims.

The Old Man made me a small allowance which, while it met my needs for tobacco and papers, left me uncomfortably indebted, if not in fact, certainly in my sensitive imagination.

School was no happier a venture than it had ever been. My longing eyes looked out often to the sagebrush hills across the river and I wished with all my soul that I might be out in the rushing wind and fragrant air. I was a difficult student.

The following June it was over at last. I wrote government exams in two subjects, my marks sufficient in the others to be recommended for graduation. I met Doug Palmer on the street one day and asked if I might work for him again. He agreed, and the Old Man drove me out the very day that, in a sense of unbelievable relief, I threw my books into an obscure corner of the basement of his house.

At seventeen it isn't imperative that one decide on a life's vocation or take it up in earnest. Still, when one has high school at long last behind him the suspicion begins to dawn, in one's

158

own mind and that of others, that a worth-while boy should show his mettle in some persevering interest which will lead to a suitable work in life, one that will draw on his abilities, providing him, and the family he will have one day, with a reasonable minimum of material well-being.

In this day in the ranching industry of western Canada, ranch labouring does not meet these requirements. It is also impossible, starting on a ranch labourer's wages, to one day own one's own outfit. Ranch labour pays little, and the capital required to go into the business is great. These truths did not escape me.

Still I had no other thoughts. I knew one trade: to do with horses, cows, and hay. No simple work, it demands a resourcefulness and a diversity of ability not often found in the city-bred specialists who look upon it with contempt. A good ranch worker is cowboy, hay hand, mechanic, amateur veterinary, axeman, carpenter, blacksmith and, if he is to be left much on his own — if he is any good he will be — he must know how much time he may put into a specific task before it has reached the point in time and material consumption that it is no longer good business.

To be genuinely a master of his trade, and he must be this if he hopes ever to operate on his own, he must understand basic soil science, irrigation, drainage, crops of hay and grain with their growing requirements, and be a competent student of range management. This subject alone is researched annually by government departments at a cost of thousands of dollars.

His eye must respond to good cattle when he sees them and tell him the point at which beef is ready to market. If he would be up-to-date, he will think about rate-of-gain testing in the search for beef that will convert all the produce of the soil — hay, grain, and grass — into the most marketable beef on the least number of hooves in the shortest possible time at the least possible cost. I don't say every ranch hand will study these things, but he who would paddle his own canoe one day must come to understand them to some degree at least or he shall not succeed, supposing he works the virtual miracle of finding capital to get started.

Working this virtual miracle was my stumbling block. Still, since I was young enough not to be conscious of future responsibilities and since I had no other thought about what I might do, it made sense to turn to that which I knew, understood, and liked. There was much to learn and it seemed sensible to go out to learn it, the while making my living in the way I had begun. This I did.

When I arrived on the Palmer ranch in that June of 1948 Doug was about to take a crew of riders into the Kamloops Indian Reserve to gather the several hundred head of cattle he had there on a range-fee basis, then move them out to the summer range at Pinantan. This reserve, fifty thousand acres in extent, is a mixture of open range land, sagebrush hill country, and in the higher parts, mature Douglas-fir forest.

Centrally lies Schiedam Valley; at its floor, Schiedam Flat. Down through this formation flows Paul Creek to the North Thompson River. The road to Pinantan leads through Schiedam Valley and on it the cattle must travel to the summer range, after a big gathering on the flat.

There was the matter first of giving men their horses to ride. "Fry, you take your dad's big gelding. He hasn't been earning his keep."

I kept the tight knot in my insides to myself, accepting this instruction as though it were no more out of the way than being told to go rake hay or fix fence. Maybe it was Doug's way of forcing me to face something I would have to face for my own sake sooner or later anyway.

I put him in the barn, all seventeen hands of him, giving him a feed of oats, just to make it fair. I wondered at the worth of that bit of bravado, lying awake through the night, waiting for the dark hours of the morning when we'd saddle up.

Then the waiting was over. We were all in the barn, saddling horses, making a last check of our rigging, tying the lunch we each had from the cook on with the saddle strings. Everything done, nothing left to put it off any longer, I took the gelding outside and tried to make the seat.

160

He was impossible. I'd reach for the stirrup; he'd strike away. I'd try to turn him in a tight circle toward me that would help me up at the crucial moment of going for the stirrup; he'd leave me. More experience with this kind of a horse was what I needed, and I lacked it.

"Take him back in the barn, Al." It was Mike Ferguson, Doug's head rider, the best cowboy I've ever known and a man with, I think, a little more sympathy than most around that outfit.

"I got to ride him, Mike," I said.

"I mean you to ride him. But I want you to get on him in the barn. He won't buck in there and when you bring him out you can keep him moving so he'll settle down."

"He wouldn't start to buck right in the barn?"

"Haven't seen the horse that would."

I reflected that it would be a short matter if he did, but I respected Mike's greater experience, so did as I was told. Back in the barn with the big horse up against a stall partition where he couldn't get away from me, I spat to rid myself of the collywobbles, swore for courage, reached for the stirrup, and took the saddle.

I waited until everyone was out of the barn and riding off. This way the gelding's concern would be for catching up, not so much for starting his own private rodeo there in the dark. It was the only hope I had, short of tying myself on with the saddle strings.

Then we went out of the barn. He pranced a little, bounced a little, whinnied for the other horses, and then started off to overtake them at a fast, level trot. I drew a sigh of immense relief and relaxed at last. The saddle felt good again.

Dawn broke on us in a thick fog coating the high hills above Schiedam Flat. One might have been anywhere. Clarence Jules, a cheerful young Indian riding in the outfit, was detailed to keep half an eye on me. We paired off from the rest, gathering cattle as we went along. Cows and calves showed up in every little draw and in the shelter of cotton-wood thickets near water holes. Before long we had twenty or more cows ahead of us, their calves tagging along behind them.

161

As soon as you start moving cows and calves, the cows set up a bawling to keep track of their young and they stay with it all day long until you let the herd stop to sort itself out. Our little gathering began this old familiar noise and every so often one heard the sound of other cattle bawling in the fog.

We came to a level area. "Stay here and hold these cattle. I'm going over into a couple more draws and I'll be back, then we'll move down the hill. Can you handle 'em?" Clarence barely waited for the answer, just giving me time to say, sure, I could handle them, and he was gone. The fog was still as dense as dirty creek water and I felt very much alone in a strange chunk of country. I rode around my little herd, pushing back the cows that tried to stray.

Clarence failed to return. I began to grow anxious. The fog was thinning, but I had no idea what I should do. I had been told to wait and felt I must, considering that I didn't even know where to take the cattle. The cows were more and more restless and soon it was difficult to hold them together. I was riding hard to be first on one side, then on the other.

Then the fog lifted, letting the morning sun break through. At a great distance down in the valley bottom a huge herd was gathering. Riders came in from every direction, pushing along their cows and calves. I looked all over for Clarence but I could not see him, nor could I identify anyone down on the flat. I had been told to stay put, but now perhaps it was time to use my own discretion and move off. Much could happen to prevent him returning as he had planned.

The more stubborn cows were impossible to hold. Everywhere cattle were moving and to keep a beast still on such a morning, with the main herd bawling and milling over half a mile away in the valley below, was impossible.

Nonetheless, I hated to move off until absolutely certain Clarence could no longer intend to keep the rendezvous. Unknown to me, of course, he had come on a much larger group of cattle than he had expected and was obliged to go downhill with them, leaving me to my own devices.

162

Naturally, he thought I would use my head, move off as soon as it became impractical not to do so. In thinking this he did not allow for the fact that it was my first experience in working on a roundup with so many cattle and riders. I was more than a little uncertain and reluctant to act on my own decision. The inclination was much more to do what had last been laid on.

Finally a cow got away from me and I acted, moving off immediately, pushing my little herd down the hill. I didn't catch up to the cow that had escaped and I knew this was not good but not, I thought, unforgivable under the circumstances. Soon I reached the main holding ground where a dozen riders ringed a herd of several hundred cows and calves and odds and ends of other stock.

Doug saw me arrive. He rode to meet me. "Dammit, Fry, I don't know what kind of pets you kept for cows in the Cariboo, but you're on a real ranch now."

Moments later he drove out a big black cow, obviously dry, without a calf. I wondered why, for when she went by I could see the Seven O brand on her hide as clear as print on paper. Then I caught on, for as soon as the old cow was some distance away he shouted for her to be brought back. I thought someone else might go, but Doug pointed at me and shouted again. I turned to go after her.

Never a tougher cow was calved. She had her mind made up: come hell or high water she wasn't going back in the herd. I got around her but she'd dodge this way and that, making ground all the time. The big horse was no cow pony but he was intelligent. Soon he was onto the principle of changing direction the instant the cow did to block her way again.

Still, it seemed hopeless. I could never bring her back without help. I checked, turning to go for help. Then I stopped. I looked at the cow, heading off, taking advantage of being left alone. I looked at the now distant spot where the rest of the cowboys were pushing away the strays and holding the milling cattle.

I might as well go down the road as ask for help. If I wanted to be part of the outfit again I had to come back on my own and bring with me that she-devil of a black cow. I was nearly certain I couldn't, a lot more certain I had no alternative.

So I went for her once more. I stayed on her tail through brush and draw, over knoll and ridge. I headed every chance I got. She still gained ground, but at more and more expense and effort. I lashed my horse, lunging him into her, setting her off balance. Time after time, whenever the chance came, I made the big horse strike her with his chest.

She began to give in. Froth hung from her mouth. She puffed and heaved for air. My horse grew a white lather. I was sore and bruised with holding a seat on the horse, jolting and jarring as he switched on her every time she dodged to put us off her tail.

I knew I had her whipped. In my direction now, not hers, the distant holding ground was growing bigger, not smaller. Then she gave up the fight and I drove her briskly, in a straight line, right into the herd.

I looked at Doug. I thought he might have something to say. He looked at me briefly, saw the black cow was back, and went back to his work. So much for that. I took up a position in the holding ring and went to work too.

In two more hours the strays were pushed out and a few steers moved off by three or four men to a nearby corral. From there they would be picked up later, taken toward the ranch. Meanwhile, the rest of us moved the big herd maybe a couple of miles in a northeasterly direction, through a fence into a holding pasture. We ate our lunches while the cows sorted out the calves.

The cattle quiet, we left them to return to the ranch. On the way we picked up the steers, taking them to the hard grass pasture where we turned them loose. Then we rode on down to the ranch, put our horses away, and kept a rendezvous with the cook. It was late afternoon. We had been up since two in the morning. We were to be out again the next morning equally as early. I sought my bunk.

We gathered for another three days, during which time I traded the weary gelding for a ranch horse. Then we moved the herd to the summer range. The night before we moved, instead of returning to the ranch, we camped on Louie Lake, up the Pinantan road a mile from the holding pasture.

Sleeping on the cold ground with what bedroll we each had brought with us, in the first grey light of dawn we were in the saddle.

It was a hard drive. The road led through timbered country and a reluctant cow was easily lost. The lead cows knew where they were going, travelling too fast. The drag came slowly, unable to hurry because of the calves. The old Indian in charge of the lead failed to hold the pace down. He had been a great cowboy in his time but age had taken the edge off him.

We went through other groups of cattle, and there'd be a furious half hour sorting out the strays afterwards. Doug was in a constant state of urgency.

We reached the cow camp in early afternoon. We held the cattle in a large corral while we ate our lunch. After that we lit a fire, heated a couple of irons and started branding, castrating, marking, and vaccinating calves. I knew this job well and held my own "rastling" calves. All this done, we turned the herd onto the open range, loaded up the chuck wagon with camp outfit and grub, and returned to the ranch.

I was glad it was over. I'd been taught to handle cattle as easily as possible, only to be rough when necessary. It had been a point of pride to treat a horse with respect and keep the beef on the hoof, rather than run it off. This big-outfit way of doing it was entirely alien and I still suspect a bit unwise. At any rate I found it impossible to fit in. I will agree I was green and unhandy, but more from not understanding why we should all be riding around in a lather than lack of experience. So it goes. You learn it one way and find it done another.

After a couple of days off, haying began. I was given a good team and assigned to raking hay, alternately with operating a sweep. Haying was different in this country, much more efficient. After the hay was in long windrows, we gathered it with the sweep and took it directly to the stack. Fewer men could move much more hay than by the pitch fork method.

We had good weather. The North Thompson Valley at that point receives far less annual precipitation than the Cariboo and this factor certainly cuts down the cost of hay production. We did have some rain, but since the hay lay in windrows it was not costly to dry it and bring it in after the rain.

Doug had a side delivery rake which he used for rolling the windrows after a rain. This machine is designed for throwing a row of hay out to the side. It picks up about two mower swaths at a time and leaves them in a neat roll, especially useful for picking up with a bailer. Doug only used it for turning windrows made with a buck rake, which worked well enough provided the windrows hadn't been made too heavy to begin with. Otherwise the machine couldn't stand the work and a breakdown was inevitable.

I was unfortunate enough to be driving it one day when a cog broke. I could see it had been broken before and, I presumed, in much the same way.

Doug said: "Why can't you be careful with my equipment? You can't pull your weight in the saddle, now you're no good in the hayfield."

"Maybe the hay's too heavy."

"The blazes it is! I've been using this machine to turn hay for years."

There was no point in taking all this rough talk very seriously. The cog was welded in town and put back on the machine. I took it out to turn windrows and promptly the cog broke again.

Doug declared violently if you wanted it done right, you had to do it yourself or have one of your boys do it. He fixed it again and sent his son Jim out with the machine. Secretly, I wished him the best of luck. I was pleased to be standing nearby when he came back with the machine, the cog broken again in a new spot.

"Hay's too heavy for it," he declared. "The machine was never built for that job."

Doug didn't say anything to Jim, but he told me to go out and turn hay with a buck rake. I had the prudence to keep my mouth shut.

I had hired on with the understanding that Doug could use me for the roundup and the first crop of hay. Now that we neared the end of the crop I was happy I would be going.

More My Kind

I needed two things when I left the Palmer ranch: a job and a chance to earn back some vestige of self-confidence. The first I could do something about, the second only hope for.

Through the Old Man I'd met a man with a small cow outfit east of Kamloops on the old Vernon highway, Rupert Duck. He was talkative without being boastful, and to meet him in town he might have been a moderately successful businessman in any venture. He ranched to make his living and he wasn't busy playing wild West. I'd liked what I'd seen of him, and when I met him in town the very day I finished at Palmer's, I naturally asked him for work.

"I can use you," he said. "We're not done haying by a long way and you could help me with a little fall work. I won't need you in the winter though because Peter's home to stay now." Peter, his only son, my age, had also finished high school that spring and now would put all his time into the ranch.

"Winter's a long way off. I'll come out on the bus on Sunday evening."

"Fair enough. You got a bedroll?"

"I got a bedroll."

"See you Sunday."

I shared the bunkhouse with Charlie Perkins, a man of thirty-five or more whose family lived in one of the cabins on the range, and a chunky young lad of fourteen, fresh out of the city, willing enough but green as grass.

Charlie was a likeable fellow, a good working man but a drifter, a confirmed, irretrievable drifter. I laid it to his marriage more than anything; besides that, some men are made that way. But he and his wife didn't hit it off and, without fixing any blame, this was the root of his shiftlessness. He could have been a steady man for Rupert, but he'd come that spring and he went that fall.

I soon earned a place in the bunkhouse fraternity. Charlie and the boy weren't much company for each other and Charlie eagerly accepted me after establishing that I wasn't afraid to take on a bad horse, laying more store in guts than performance.

Too, I gave the boy a touch of friendship he needed badly. So recently alone on a crew, I knew his trouble and in small ways proffered him the kindness I had missed.

And I earned a place on the job again that I could hold with respect, most important of all. Our days began with the milking of a half-dozen cows, before breakfast. We hayed in the good weather, fixed fence or rode in the wet. We milked again in the evenings, tended our teams or saddle horses, and fed a few hogs, with skim milk and crushed grain.

An industrious routine, carried out in a friendly way, it respected boy and man. An error never drew contempt. Working with confidence, I knew what I did was appreciated, not only paid for at a hundred a month and my board.

The family was close: Dorothy, Rupert's wife, a strong-minded woman, Pamela, the oldest of the children, then in nursing training, followed by Peter, my age, and last of all Penelope, a bright child perhaps five years behind Peter.

The ranch house and outbuildings, the corrals, and the main hayfields lay in a warm valley several miles south of and several hundred feet above the South Thompson River. On Robin's Range, a grass and timbered hill country still higher and farther south, lay several more places, all part of the ranch. Hay and grain grew on these upper fields and surrounding them under open timber were the main ranges for the cow herd in the summer and fall. Under fence were two partly open, hard grass pastures where the beef would finish for market.

Talking to Rupert in the moments there were for it, I pieced together the history of Holmwood, as the ranch was known, and at the same time, because the two were largely synonymous, the history of the family in Canada.

The first of the Ducks to come out from England was old Jacob. Rupert always called him old Jacob and I got a picture of a work-hardened stalwart who'd been born with his whiskers already grown. He'd been drawn by the Cariboo gold rush, but he'd had the sense, after maybe four years on the creeks at Barkerville and panning a stake out of the gravel, to turn to the soil. He left the Cariboo and started what is now the Bostock ranch, a modest spread at Monte Creek, about the same distance from Kamloops as Holmwood but on the South Thompson. That was back in '66 or '67, as near as Rupert could figure it.

Then Rupert's father arrived in '83, much the same cut of a man I gathered, to work for old Jacob. He crossed the States on the old Union Pacific Railroad to San Francisco, coming up the coast by steamer. He came inland through the Fraser Canyon by Cariboo stage.

He worked for Jacob for a number of years, then for Bostock when Jacob sold the place to him. After that he rented a farm at Westwold, on the road from Kamloops to Vernon and the Okanagan Valley. There Rupert was born in '97, at a time when the biggest concern in the country thereabouts was probably the BX Ranch at Vernon, an outfit raising horses for the booming stagecoach business on the Cariboo road.

Rupert came to Holmwood at two years of age when his father bought the first half section there. In 1926 he turned the place, a thousand acres deeded, over to Rupert and Arthur, his other son. There'd been a great acreage under lease on the Range too, but that had been lost to settlers. Still, it was a fair ranch to build in twenty-six years and it had been done by plain hard work and thrift. Rupert recalled how, after the hay had been cut with horse mowers, the old man had sent the boys out with scythes to cut in the corners of the fences where the mower couldn't reach.

Rupert bought Art's share after the war and also bought back much of the homestead land on Robin's Range. Now he kept something over a hundred head of cattle, a number of sheep, and often a few hogs. He had a chicken house and milked enough cows to ship a can of cream a week. He did no one thing in a big way but always had something to sell.

Constantly alert to improve the ranch and farm operation, when the price of beef and other produce was high in the latter part of the forties, he invested the extra money in only enough machinery to economize his operation and not, as many did, in all the machinery he would have liked to own.

Much of the profit of those good years went into expanding the hay lands. When times toughened up in the early fifties and beef couldn't go out of the country because of an epidemic of hoof-and-mouth disease, making prices drop from lack of U.S. market competition, he held his own, falling back on what was selling, not hurt by what wasn't.

I struck up a friendship with Peter that has lasted us both through the years. A compatible fellow, he was different enough to be interesting, same enough to understand. An enthusiastic ballplayer, he went to town whenever he could for practices and to play for a team in Kamloops.

He had enjoyed belonging to a 4-H calf club and in consequence knew a great deal about a good beef carcass and how to achieve it, through breeding and feeding, that had escaped me. In fact, it was only shortly after I arrived there that he proposed to feed up another steer for showing in the Christmas fat stock sale in Kamloops and solicited our help one evening to bring in the chosen animal.

"Hey, you guys," he said, poking his head in the bunkhouse door. "You think you're cowboys, come and help me run in my steer."

We saddled some horses, going out with him where the young stock ranged, beyond the hayfields. We found the chosen one and brought him along with several others, planning to single him out and turn the others back at the corral.

The corral lay within a larger yard and as we neared the gate into the yard there was a chance to let the extras slip back, crowding the single steer through. This we did.

Charlie was closing the gate behind him while Peter and I turned away to drive the others back to the range when the crash of straining gate poles brought us up in our tracks.

We swung around to see the steer coming through full tilt to catch the others, Charlie by the gate astounded, and the gate itself wide open, the latch torn clean off. The steer had hit just as the latch was closing.

He ran like a mad animal. We soon had to give up the attempt to bring him in, resolving to try again another evening when, we hoped, he would calm down, be manageable.

This we did, two nights later. Now we brought the company all the way into the main corral, from which there could be no breaking out, before we turned them back. Then Charlie, Peter, and I went into the corral to halter him.

Peter brought the halter and I a lariat. Starting the steer running against the fence, from right to left, I swung the loop out, dropping it over his head, a little sloppy by the best standards but nonetheless I had him.

I took two turns on the snubbing post in the centre of the corral and started taking in the slack. Soon the steer was close to the post, no more than six feet of rope left.

"Time for that halter, Peter," Charlie suggested, and they moved in from either side, sliding the halter on. Then I saw the sign, sure as lightning before the thunder.

"Look out!" I cried. He caught Peter, not seriously, as, wide-eyed, ears straight out, suddenly he went on the rampage. I held the rope tight while Peter got away. The steer turned on me at the post. I dropped the rope, went for the fence.

172

I caught the top log, throwing myself upward. Safe, I reached down for Charlie, catching his arm, helping him but not soon enough. He winced with pain as the steer smashed his leg against the fence. He dropped on the other side, his leg badly bruised.

"Well, there's your steer, halter and all," I offered Peter when we gathered outside the fence to ponder the matter. "Just lead him into the barn."

"You're so helpful. As the saying goes, after you, my dear Alphonse."

I acknowledged there was no safe way to go near him. We consulted Rupert, who had come by then, along with the young boy, to see how we were doing. Somebody suggested that if we could get hold of the lariat and pass it between the gate and the latch post, then, tying other ropes to it, take a long lead into the barn and the box stall, we could open the gate and all we would have to do was take the slack out of the rope to have the steer into the stall. It all sounded very workable.

Peter went to the far side of the corral, making as if to enter. The steer thus distracted, I slipped quickly into the corral and came out with the lariat end, passing it through so that when the gate was opened later it would lead the steer out.

Then we tied ropes to it, taking a long lead into the barn, through the box-stall gate, and, finally, around the manger pole, a couple of wraps to hold him. I stood up on the manger pole with the rope, ready to take out the slack as it came to me.

Rupert put his head in the door. "You ready?"

"Sure am."

He shouted back to Peter. "Let him out!" Then he walked through the barn and out the other door.

Peter was fast on his feet. He let the steer out, then ran beyond his reach in the big yard. I held fast, bringing the beast up short at the end of the rope. As he rushed around in front of the barn I kept drawing in slack rope.

Finally we came to an impasse. I had the steer nearly to the barn door, but he'd come no farther. Rupert put his head through the small, ventilation opening in the other door to ask how I was doing. I explained the problem.

"Perhaps, if Peter thinks he's fast enough, he could run by the steer into the barn. The steer'll chase him, but I'll take up the rope. Tell him anyway and see what he says."

Rupert went to the yard fence and climbed up to shout this intelligence over to Peter. Peter was game and he made a dash for the door. The young boy thought he could make it, indeed he could, and he ran after him. The ranch collie followed on his heels and the steer stood dumbfounded while this veritable procession went flying by.

Then he went after it, right through the barn door. I gathered slack at a great pace, knowing well what hung on doing so.

Now Peter hadn't expected the boy to follow him and he heard the pounding behind him, long past the box-stall gate. He headed for that two-by-two opening in the far door.

Nor did the boy realize the dog was in the chase. The dog brushed his legs in the excitement a time or two and the boy, in sheer terror, eyed the hole in the door himself. It was going to be a tight squeeze.

"Look out!" I hollered, having stopped the steer and aiming to prevent Peter and the boy crushing each other in that hole. But it was the wrong thing to holler. It only added to the confusion and not until they were embracing each other and the dog in combat for that inadequate escape route, did they discover what really had taken place.

By this time the steer had charged into the box stall after me, safe on the manger pole, and it only remained to close the gate, to which Peter attended while catching his breath.

"Quite a run you had, Peter."

"Next time you get an idea like that, you keep it to yourself."

There was little hope in anyone's mind that his steer would become manageable for show purposes. Peter had a try at taming him, but within the month we turned him back on the range and it was too late to begin with another.

There was no doubt my stay at Holmwood was the best part of the summer. Nothing terribly exciting happened; we simply went about the task of ranching day by day, matter-of-factly, in dignity. We had more rain in August than there'd been in July, so in the gaps between haying we cut logs for a new corral fence, snaking them across the valley from the timber beyond the hayfields. Soon a spanking new corral replaced the old, and as Mrs. Duck said, the rain was bad for the hay but good for the ranch.

Mainly, of course, we made hay. Rupert gave me a horse sweep to drive and one old mare, one young gelding. Between myself and the old mare, we taught the young gelding his job, and day by day we pushed hay off the meadow onto the teeth of the hydraulic stacker which Peter ran from the big tractor, and the stacks piled up, one after the other. A little differently done perhaps, it was still my trade, the trade which had been my father's.

One would have thought I'd ask no more of life and in a way I guess I didn't. But somehow in the midst of decent folk and honest work, I grew restless. I was glad in a way it wasn't steady work, that in time I would go though I hadn't the least thought where. Still, something would fill the gap, the way it had the spring I left the Cariboo. But would it? Maybe the gap was down inside of me, in my nature, in my age. At seventeen, life confuses.

On A Notion

And in time the haying was over. Some fencing and riding followed. The crisp fall weather came; before long it would be feeding time. My work was over and so I left. Out of school five months, I'd been through two jobs already.

Well, what should I do? I had no answer to the question; I didn't even like to ask the question. I began to feel eternally dissatisfied, even in the work I loved so well. I wanted to go somewhere, I didn't know where. I wanted something, I didn't know what.

I took a notion to go to sea. The idea didn't drop out of the sky but not far from it. Long ago, before the ranch had absorbed my imagination completely, I had read stories of the sea and dreamed of being a sailor. Perhaps it was not surprising that in a fit of wanderlust I should salvage such an ambition from my childhood.

I knew a chap, Johnny Harper, who lived on the west side of the North Thompson River a few miles out of Kamloops, who'd been in the merchant marine, so I went to talk to him. A man of forty or more, he'd come away from the sea to care for an ailing parent and mind the place. He longed for his old life, I could tell by his talk, and he grew as enthused as myself, showing me fragments of faraway places, bits of colourful tapestry and figures carved from strange-smelling wood.

"Mind you," he acknowledged, "I've been away for a long time. I can't really say what your chances are. A healthy young fellow used to go out a deck hand and even come back something better if he looked sharp. Certainly there was always a job of some kind."

"I mean to try. I suppose there'll be something doing. I don't really mind what sort of a job, so long as it gets me around a bit. It would be grand to circle the globe."

"Just one thing," he cautioned. "Think twice before you go foreign flag. You might have a devil of a time getting back to Canada. There's always some fellow jumping ship or landing in jail, and a captain will pick up who he can to make up the crew but with no guarantee at all about bringing you back to your home port."

"I see. I suppose conditions vary too." Now we were getting down to things I hadn't thought about.

"Yes. Very much so. Another good reason for taking care about foreign ships. Standards on some are frightful. Poor pay and bad food. Sometimes no discipline and there's fighting among the men. You must be wary of all those things."

He talked on and of course my grand adventure gathered luster by the minute. It was hard to draw away when at last I had to go. He took my hand in parting. "I wish you luck and I wish I could be with you. It would be good to feel the sea again."

Back at the Old Man's place I assembled some gear, mainly a couple of changes of work clothes and the best of my dress clothing to wear in the city. The best of my dress clothing amounted to very little and was rather badly worn. I had no yen for clothes and spent practically no money on anything but work togs.

Just before I left, I chanced to meet a friend and distant cousin, Lally Coulthurst. She lived in Kamloops where her husband, Paddy, was in law. She was a Pease, and away back in England the Peases and the Frys were connected. She'd heard what I was up to.

"Now look, there's just one thing I want to tell you," she said. "You may find yourself up against it if things don't work out the way you plan. I want you to remember you have a cousin of sorts in Vancouver. Well, in Burnaby actually, but that's all part of Vancouver, just a little farther out from downtown. Anyway, you go and see him, or Jean, if he's not home. He works on a ship himself. An Imperial Oil tanker, up and down the coast."

"You mean Roger Pease."

"That's right."

"I've never met him."

"That doesn't matter. What are cousins for? Here, I'll give you his phone number. Just ring him up and tell him who you are." She fumbled about for paper and pencil and wrote down a telephone number, handing it to me. "There you are. Now don't lose it."

I tucked the slip of paper away in a corner of my wallet and I must say by the time I'd gone about the last of my errands before leaving Kamloops, I'd quite forgotten it.

I took a bus to Vancouver because it offered the cheapest fare. I had no doubt the sum of money with me, my summer's earnings and all I had in the world, was sufficient, but there was no point squandering it. Had I seen into the future I might have hopped a freight.

I took a room at three dollars and a half a day in a respectable but decidedly not posh hotel. It was on the edge of the wrong side of town, but then most of the shipping firms and hiring halls were to be found there. Anyway, I neither was nor could afford to be posh.

I had travelled through the night, arriving in the morning. Therefore, as soon as I had settled in the hotel and eaten breakfast at what seemed an appropriate café, I set at once to finding work. Not quite sure how to begin, I simply walked the sidewalks looking for the names of shipping firms on doorways.

All day I found two. At the first was a sign saying no hiring here and at the second I engaged in a fruitless conversation at a grubby little counter, in a grubby little office, with a grubby little man.

"What do you want?"

"I'm looking for work."

"What kind of work? What can you do?"

"Well I'd hoped to go to sea as a deck hand."

"Do you belong to the union?"

"No. I don't."

"We don't hire anyone who doesn't belong to the union."

"I see. Perhaps I could join the union?"

"I don't see how. You have to have a job to join the union."

"But …"

"Good day." He turned back to his desk. I stood a moment, then left abruptly, annoyed at the way I'd been treated, vexed at the problem of breaking into that tight little circle: no union membership, no job; no job, no union membership.

But it was just that tight little circle, I learned in the next few days, that was the sum of matters on the waterfront. A non-union man could only hire on when a union man couldn't be found to take a job. Then, so hired, he joined the union. Only in such a way did he break in. Just now there were union men out of work and so the jobs were closed to anyone else.

Nonetheless I held my chin up. I'd never been in a situation where if I kept trying I couldn't enjoy some success, so I kept trying. I couldn't be at it all the time of course, so I thought I would visit my brother who at that time was attending the University of British Columbia in another part of the city.

I hadn't an address so I went out to the campus and, knowing he was in second-year Agriculture, soon found in the agriculture building the lecture room he should be in at that particular moment. There I went to wait in the hallway outside the door until he would come out. It was late in the day, it should be his last lecture, and perhaps I could go home with him and thereby know where he bought his room and board.

He was among the last to come out. He stopped still, staring at me as if he couldn't believe his eyes.

"What in blazes," he exclaimed at last, "are you doing here?" For some unknown reason he seemed displeased.

"I came to Vancouver to look for work. I'm trying to go to sea. I thought I might as well visit you, seein' as I'm here." I hadn't seen Roger in a long time.

"You must be crazy. And you look seedy as a tramp. Those all the clothes you got?"

"Well, listen here," I protested, astonished. "These clothes are all right. Gee, they may be a little worn, but there ain't nothin' wrong with 'em."

"Ah, ya look like a bum. So you're gonna go to sea. Big deal. Why don't you smarten up and do something worthwhile?"

"Whadda ya mean? What's eatin' you, anyway? You got a bellyache or sumpin'?"

"Oh, you make me tired. You don't care for anybody's feelings but your own. Well go to sea or be a half-baked cowboy all your life. See who cares."

"You're makin' a lotta noise about it."

"Well, I don't give a hoot, but you sure don't care about Mum's feelings, quitting school and tramping around."

"I'm not tramping around. Anyway, I finished high school."

"What's that these days? You know she always wanted you to go to university."

"So I'd be somebody. Okay, I don't want to be anybody. And I don't like school. And I don't go much for you, either."

"Well, I gotta go to a lecture. I'll be late, yatterin' with you."

"I thought this'n would be your last for the day."

"No. Got one more. So long, brother. Come and see me again when I got more time."

"Fat chance of that." But my words were wasted. Already he was racing for his next lecture, leaving me standing there wondering what was wrong with his head, though in fact, of course, I knew.

Really, Roger meant only the best. The way I'd failed to get along with Mother, finally pulling stakes over it, and the way I'd cut off my education, genuinely distressed him. His outbreak was partly annoyance over these issues, partly disappointment. He really did care, enough that he wished I'd pull up my socks. By his set of values, my socks were away below my ankles.

Realizing these things, I mellowed, but not enough that I'd come to see him again for a jolly long time. But I did make a searching inspection of my appearance the next time I passed a full-length mirror on the sidewalk in front of a clothier's. He was right. I looked seedy as they make 'em.

The job hunting went on but to no more avail than before. Now I began looking for anything. I stopped daily at the National Employment Service, but there was no demand for labourers and that was all I could call myself. I realized too that I was going for the second and third time to some shipping offices. I had even given a tentative look at a few foreign flags, though I'd caught fragments of conversations in hiring halls that should have put me off that idea for good.

What it came down to was that Canada was going out of the shipping business. We had no more merchant marine. The unions blamed the shippers, saying they patronized foreign ships paying sweatshop wages, providing foul keep for their sailors. The companies blamed the unions, saying they had driven wages so high that competitive shipping rates couldn't pay a crew. What all this meant to me was my money was running out and I had no prospect of work at all.

Discouraged, I started putting off the daily round of useless enquiries, more often going down by the piers to watch the longshoremen at work. Or other times I would simply stand against a dock railing, the salty air of the Pacific blowing on my face, pushing away the odors of the waterfront. It was hard for an imaginative boy not to be carried away by the romance of it all, but I only need think of my wet feet, in shoes now coming apart from the constant walking on wet pavement, to be brought back to harsh reality.

One day I noticed a lean, older man doing much the same as I was, idling time away along the docks while the gulls screeched raucously about and ships' horns, somewhere out in the drizzling rain, blared mournfully of their coming and going. I realized I'd seen him somewhere before, perhaps on the street, maybe in a hiring hall.

He approached me when he saw I had lit a cigarette.

181

"Can you spare a smoke?"

"Makin's. Here, help yourself." I passed him the tobacco and papers. Funny, I thought. I'd expected him to smell of drink, like the panhandlers along the skid road. But then I saw he was dressed more neatly and, though plainly on his uppers, was clean. His face was shaven, a face I saw on closer inspection to be firm and well drawn, aging but distinct.

Skillfully, he made a cigarette, then handed back my pouch. "Thanks." He lit up and leaned over the rail.

I grew curious about him but wondered if I should speak. He himself didn't move away but neither did he make conversation.

At last I broke the ice. "You a seaman?"

He sighed. "Yes. Or maybe I was a seaman."

"There isn't much doing, is there?"

He drew heavily on the cigarette. I saw with surprise that his hands shook as he flicked a skiff of ash from the end of the smoke. He waited awhile before speaking, as though he wasn't quite sure what he wanted to say. In fact, I'd more or less concluded he didn't intend to reply, when he began.

"No, you might say that, all right, that there isn't much doing, matter of fact there isn't a damn thing doing." He paused, drawing on the cigarette again, peering out into the rain and the vague outlines of the inlet. "Give it a couple of years, maybe a little more, and there won't be a merchant ship anywhere under a Canadian flag. You want a job, you'll climb into a sweaty hole with a bunch of gibbering foreigners who don't give a damn how they live or what they get for it."

There seemed something wrong in what he said, but I preferred to feel guilty for him, rather than argue the matter. I had pretty strong feelings about slighting people who spoke a language other than English. It was incredible the way he sensed my disapproval.

"Don't get me wrong. I don't say everybody's got to be like us to be decent. What I'm getting at is that because those beggars'll work for damn near nothing and live like low-grade pigs, we can't get jobs any more. If they'd fight a bit, hold out for something halfways fit for a man, their bloody lines wouldn't be carrying all the cargo from here to hell and gone because nobody else can do it so cheap."

"Maybe they haven't much choice. Maybe they haven't a good union or maybe they're so darn glad to get any job they don't want a union."

"Probably some of both. I don't know, really."

"Has our own union got things too good for us? Is it true what the companies say: that they can't pay the union rates and stay in competition for cargo?"

He looked at me directly for the first time. "You don't belong to the union, do you?"

"No." I shook my head. "Hell, I don't even belong on the waterfront. I'm just a kid who thought he'd like to go to sea." Then in explanation: "I'm only seventeen. I just look older'n I am."

He went back to my question. "Yes, I think partly the union's to blame. Pushing wages up and demanding too much in living conditions. I tried to say that at a meeting one time. They had some hoods there, told me to shut up or I'd get thrown out. You've never been at a meeting, you wouldn't know what that's like."

We both felt we'd exhausted the subject, or perhaps the physical consequences of the conditions we discussed were too acutely upon us. In any event we fell silent and I drew out my tobacco. We both made another cigarette and lit up from the last one.

I was curious about my companion and nothing else would have explained the rude directness of my next question.

"Why aren't you down in the hiring hall with the others? Isn't that the best way to get work once you're in the union?" Shocked at myself, I started to apologize but he cut in.

"Oh, I've spent hours there. Time enough, if I had a chance at all. I get fed up with the place. Or I should say I get fed up with the men who hang around there."

"How is that?" I'd gone so far, I might as well pry the rest from him.

"The men who put to sea aren't the cut they used to be. Or I used to think they were, one or the other. Oh, there were muttonheads in every crew, there always will be. That's mankind for you. But in every crew there were a few decent blokes to pal up with, men who'd read a good book and brought a few with them or could play checkers or chess. I don't mean educated men but I mean decent men. Now, hell, girlie magazines and dirty jokes is the fare and like it or not it's all there is."

"I see."

"Some of them hang around that hiring hall with no intention of going out. They haven't worked for months, maybe years. They'll sit around there all day, then go sponge off the Salvation Army for meals and a place to flop. They don't want work, they've settled for charity."

He was intense and it was hard not to be swayed by him. Still, I wondered what a man did do when he hadn't had a chance to work for months and his benefits ran out. A single man couldn't get welfare relief. What was there, other than the Sally Ann?

"You really want to go to sea? Or was it just a notion?"

"A notion, but one I'd hate to part with if I could get anything to go on."

"I'd knock it off if I were you." Then he prepared to go. "Thanks for the smokes. I've got to go." He turned away.

"G'bye, captain."

He stopped with alarming quickness and spun on me. "What made you say that?"

"Nothing," I said hastily. "I don't know. Except you seem that way to me. Not sort of run of the mill. I'm sorry."

Then he smiled. "It's all right. I was a captain once. But it's not a story for a youngster who'd like to go to sea. So long." Then he was really gone and I turned my face back into the wind, absorbed by the mystery of a strange man, a mystery I'd likely never solve.

Over the next few days my situation grew critical. My money was running short. Already I ate only two meals, sometimes one, a day to make the funds stretch out. Watching out for a cheaper place to stay, I disliked the thought of moving into the drab and hateful little rooming houses along the skid road, in the really shabby stretch of town. There seemed no choice if I was to economize, but I put it off even yet, I dreaded the places so much.

I must have looked my plight. Once I went into a café I'd not been in before to eat the only meal of the day. I finished the main course I'd ordered, the least costly fare on the menu. The girl asked my choice of desserts, the pudding or the fruit.

"No thanks, miss. I'll skip it." I felt I must not add to my bill for such a luxury.

She went away to make up my slip, then came back again. "Are you sure you won't eat the dessert?"

"No, miss. I'm … I'm not really hungry." I sounded as casual as I could manage.

She looked directly at me, then away. "The dessert goes with the meal. It doesn't cost any more."

"Oh."

"The pudding or the fruit?"

"The pudding, thanks."

She fetched it and I avoided meeting her eyes. There were tears in mine.

Two more days went by, hopelessly. I trod steadfastly from place to place, any place there might be work, finding nothing. My drab appearance, worsening daily in the constant rain, did me no good, either. Far from going to visit Roger, I hoped now I might not accidentally meet him on the street. His horror would know no bounds. But there was little likelihood of that. He had no cause to frequent the streets of my fruitless quest.

I counted my money and checked out of the hotel. I trudged with my belongings many blocks into the grey and ugly places of the down and out, the destitute, the forgotten, the self-betrayed who respected nothing, not so much as their own persons. There I chose an ill-drawn sign bleakly saying "Rooms," over an open door leading to a flight of steps.

I stopped on the sidewalk to ease the hand which had been carrying the rope-bound box of my belongings, while I stared apprehensively into the dimness of the stair well. I was shocked by the sudden appearance of an elderly man coming shakily down the stairs, an attendant of some sort on either side to steady him, a hat partially shielding his face.

With a leap of my heart I saw who it was: my captain, the man at the dock rail. He looked to neither left nor right as he passed and I mightn't have been there. Only as my eyes followed him did I realize that an ambulance vehicle was parked against the curb, between a van and a large truck. The attendants helped him into it.

I grasped my box, heading for the door. I climbed the stairs, at the top of which I found a dingy office. A short, fat man answered my knock.

"I'd like a room."

"Okay. Sign the book. A dollar a day. Pay in advance."

He indicated a black book on a desk. I hurriedly scrawled my name in it and gave him three dollars. Three dollars for three days and two dollars left to eat with. Then I'd be done.

"The man who just left in the ambulance, what happened to him? Who was he?"

The fat man shrugged. "Some old guy. Been here a couple of weeks. Paid it all ahead when he came an' I never seen him after that. Woman in the room next to him come'n said somethin' about he was starvin' himself, so I called an ambulance. He was pretty weak, all right. Couldn't walk by his self."

The misery of it made me indignant. "Well, what do you do when you've run out of money and you can't get a job? What do you do?"

He shrugged again. "I dunno. Sally Ann never turned a man down, I guess."

"He was too proud for that."

"His tough luck, I guess. Take number nine, at the end of the hall on the right. You stay past three days, pay up ahead of time." He closed the door.

Three days went by. I had only a handful of change. I was desperate. I could not bear to turn to the Old Man, to send for fare to Kamloops, as ready as I knew he would be to help. I had set out so full of confidence, it would be unthinkable to turn back so soon.

I had only one other choice. I had been putting it out of my mind for a week. Now I reached for my wallet and searched out the slip of paper with the telephone number on it. As you said, Lally Coulthurst, what are cousins for? I would turn to Roger Pease. I couldn't do otherwise.

HARD TIMES

Roger and Jean Pease lived in a pleasant little tree-surrounded house off the tramline between Vancouver and New Westminster, in what is properly known as Burnaby. You could almost imagine, but for the frequent honk of the tram horn, that you weren't in the city at all. I came to think of their place as something of a retreat in a very alien world and, truly, it was an only port in my personal storm.

Jean met me in town and took me home, literally out of the rain. I felt self-conscious, hurrying along beside this striding little woman whose day was all one great rush, who had gathered me up like so much family and couldn't imagine why I hadn't phoned her the moment I had arrived in town.

"But I didn't think I should just land on you. I really thought I'd find work right away."

"Not as easy as all that in the big city. Come on, we'll miss the tram." And we ran in the rain for the great ugly tramcar that would hurtle along in the darkness, spilling out at a dozen stops the hurrying, worrying men and women whose days were in the city, whose nights were as far away from it as they could manage to run.

Jean worked in the office of the Art Gallery on Georgia Street. She spent an hour going, another coming back, some days more. I was appalled at the idea of two hours or more of every working day being wasted on a tramcar. Everyone faced the same problem to a greater or lesser extent, but to a boy who'd never known a bunkhouse more than three minutes' walk from the barn it was an awesome prospect.

Yet she seemed to manage. She rose before six to make breakfast and lunches for her two boys, Michael, about twelve, Tony, perhaps nine. Then off she went to work while off they went to school, and she was back in the evening to make them a dinner that apologized to no appetite, and they were keen and eager youngsters.

Roger was due home on leave in a matter of days and I set to job hunting again, hoping I might have a useful talk with him on his arrival. His ship, an Imperial Oil tanker, was even now working up the coast against the winter gales and would tie into Ioco before another week was up.

My hopes rose then with what seemed a stroke of luck. The National Employment Office sent me on a call from a newspaper publisher in Burnaby, the municipality in which I now lived. He wanted a man to sell newspaper subscriptions.

I found the plant and introduced myself to the manager.

"Had any experience selling?"

"No."

"I see. This is door-to-door. Straight commission. No sales, no wages. Sell lots, make lots. Got it?"

"I guess. Where do I sell?"

"Any house, any place. Better to stick to Burnaby though. It's a Burnaby paper. I'll give you some forms and some sample copies and you can go to it."

I had never liked door-to-door salesmen. They struck me as a breed that goes about persuading people to buy things they likely don't want or need and, chances are, could buy at their local store for the same price or less, any day they wanted. I was no more enamoured of being a salesman than I was of being pestered by one. I wasn't, in fact, cut out for one.

But I tried, of course. I had an obligation to myself and now to the Peases to do the best I might.

I knocked on a door. A massive woman answered, staring at me without expression.

"How do you do? I represent the Burnaby Courier. Would you like to buy a subscription? This is a very promising little newspaper and ..."

"Noospaper?"

"Yes. Newspaper. You know ... well, newspaper."

"Not so goot, my En-glis."

"Oh, I see. In that case, ma'am, you'd have no need of a newspaper. Awfully sorry to trouble you. 'By now." Away I went, relieved that the interview was over. Then I steeled myself for the next one, going over and over that bit about this is a very promising little newspaper.

I knocked on another door. An elderly gentleman answered.

"How do you do? I represent ..."

"Go away, young man. Can't you find anything more useful to do than bother people, trying to sell them stuff? Good day." The door closed, most firmly. I shrugged, made my way to another house. There a young woman answered, surrounded by toddlers. This time I got through my pitch, even spread out a sample copy of the *Courier*, which we inspected jointly.

"Well, I don't know," she said slowly. "I'd like to buy your paper, mister, but I got so much to pay for, with the kids and all, it sure piles up. My husband don't make too much and it seems we only just get by as it is."

I folded up the paper. "Ma'am, I don't believe you really need this paper at all. It was just if you wanted to have it. I'd never persuade you to buy it, if you weren't sure."

"I'd better not," she sighed, as if much of her life consisted of concluding she'd better not. I trod along my way.

So it went through the entire day. I returned the subscription forms and the newspapers, chalking it all up to experience. You can't do something you don't believe in.

Roger came home. He was hardly a man you'd spot as seagoing. Shorter than myself, slight, and dressed neatly in town clothes, you'd have put him down for an office man on his day off. I told him the story of my disappointments and he listened thoughtfully, making a cigarette.

"You've picked an unfortunate time," he said at last.

"An understatement."

He laughed. "True. It isn't likely to get any better, either."

Then more seriously: "As a matter of fact, this business about no more Canadian merchant marine isn't as far-fetched as it seems. You might find the situation no better, even in the summer months when the pressure for work of any kind is off."

"I don't want to give it up. Not yet. Maybe in another month I'll be good and sick of it, but I'd like to stick it out that long anyway."

"By all means. Only way you'll go away satisfied."

"In the meantime I'll still try to find anything I can lay my hands on to pay my way."

"Except selling newspapers?" I'd told him about that debacle.

"Except selling newspapers. Decidedly."

I had worked in a butcher shop after school in Williams Lake for several months one year, and on the strength of this experience I began calling at retail meat stores in the east end of Vancouver, the closest part of the city to where I now lived. After three days of constant tramping I caught a lead. A proprietor I spoke to had a friend with a small business in an outlying shopping district who wanted help in his store.

I took the address and found my way, identifying myself, saying who'd sent me.

"Yeah. Hermie called me." He was a little man, maybe thirty-five and I instantly disliked him. His face was narrow, his nose too pointed, his manner cunning. His shop was small, occupying a rented side in a groceteria establishment.

"He said you needed a helper."

There was a silence. Then: "Yeah. Well, Hermie didn't really get me right. I said I hoped I'd be able to put on some help, if business'd pick up. I'm not really ready to put anyone on for a while."

Oh my Lord! Was nothing to come my way? I turned about, looking out the window, vexed and distressed and not a little annoyed at the vagaries of fate.

I turned back. "Any use putting my name down? You could let me know."

He shrugged. "Could do." He reached for a paper and pencil. "You really up against it for work?"

"Yes. Never worse."

"Maybe I could give you a break. I don't really need you, but I could take you on to help you."

"You couldn't help me more."

"I can't pay you very much."

I sighed. I could hardly bargain. "I'd appreciate anything fair."

There was another pause. Then tentatively: "You might not think what I could pay was fair."

Hell, get it over with. "How much?"

"Fifteen dollars a week."

Prepared for something meagre, I registered nothing, I felt sure. But inside I despised the little cheat with all my venom. Fifteen dollars a week. Sixty a month and I board myself. It hadn't been so bad in cow country since the Depression.

"I'll take it. Start tomorrow?"

"First thing. Be here at eight. Hour for lunch. Close at six, seven on Saturdays."

I discovered what it was to work only to exist and, so working, only exist. I rose before six to be to work on time after the tram ride; I waited sometimes an hour after work to catch a tram for home. I gave Jean ten dollars of my weekly earnings, keeping just so much as would pay my tram fare and buy tobacco, and a pittance to put toward my fare back to Kamloops for which I knew I must now save.

Had there been more time to spend with Jean and Roger it would all have been bearable and the life in some measure rewarding. But as it was I saw them only fleetingly at the beginning and again at the end of a day spent going, working, returning, all in a dull state of drudgery. I began to see for the first time the hopelessness that must attend those who eke out their whole lives in subservience to a routine of motions meaningless to their own spirits, that they might eat, be clothed, have shelter. How superior the hay camp, the feed ground, the hard creative work in which one's own diligence played an essential part in the whole, useful function of a ranch. How superior to me, at any rate.

Inwardly I had only contempt for this conniving creature who held me in the palm of his hand at a child's pittance. I soon gathered he won favour with others no better than with me. He thought himself a dandy with the ladies. Many came to the shop, for his prices were better than the only other shop in the neighbourhood, but I soon learned it was more than my imagination that they disliked his familiarity.

Once, returning to work from the counter down the street where I bought coffee to accompany my sandwiches, I happened to follow two housewives, overhearing their conversation.

"I have to get a roast for Sunday. Are you going home now? Wait for me and I'll catch the bus with you."

"Do you buy from Lover Boy?"

"Only for his prices. Ugh! What a creep!"

"You said it. I'll wait outside. I don't mind it for my roast, but I'm not going to take it for yours."

A single man, he lived with his parents, I gathered, and at least two nights a week he went from work to a nightclub in the city. The next day he would tell me tales of his exploits with women there, none of which I believed. I wondered that he could afford it for I had some idea of the profit he could make on the turnover at the shop. Then I suspected he wasn't paying his parents for his keep, only graciously taking home cuts of meat which hadn't moved out of the counter during the week.

Near my tram stop there was another shop. Occasionally the owner would still be working there when I came after closing time to wait for my ride home. I didn't see any help, but I presumed that he let them off at a reasonable hour, only staying late himself to cut ahead for the following day.

One evening a tram went by loaded, as frequently one would, and, knowing I had half an hour before the next one, I went to the door of his shop and knocked. The chap came with a key and opened the door.

"Sorry," he said. "I'm closed."

"I know," I replied. "I wanted to talk to you." He looked puzzled and I explained: "I work at the shop over on Ninth."

"Oh yes. Come in. You work for the little guy there."

"That's right." I stepped in and he closed the door. He went back to his work while I sat on the counter, watching.

"Do you know him? The fellow I work for, I mean."

"No, not really. We all know each other in the trade, but not so I ever talk to him."

"How much should I get paid, working in his shop?"

"How experienced are you? Not very, or you wouldn't be asking that."

"I worked after school one winter in Williams Lake, up country. I can bone out and cut a little. I don't know much but I'm not useless. I have a hard time remembering prices."

"Doesn't he put the prices on his cuts?"

"Not always."

"Well. What does he pay you?"

"Fifteen dollars a week."

He all but dropped his saw. He stopped work to stare at me. "Straight goods? Fifteen a week?"

"'Sfact."

"That's terrible. We pay a completely inexperienced beginner at least thirty and then only until he's learned enough to pull his weight. How do you live on it?"

"I don't. If my cousin wasn't helping me, I'd never get by."

"You should quit."

"Don't dare. Nothing else doing that I can find."

He shook his head. "That's a hell of a bind to be in."

I laughed, sliding off the counter. "Oh, I don't know. It's been a good lesson. I'm going back where I came from and I'll never work in the city again, be sure of that."

"Don't blame you." He put away his tools and hung up his apron. Then we left his shop, he to go home, I to wait for the tram.

I made up my mind. I would have gone on had there been any hope of ultimately finding a ship. But working the hours I did, there was no time for standing in hiring halls, waiting for a miracle to happen. And I could not much longer accept the kindness of Roger and Jean, unable to pay them fairly for my board and room.

I worked a few more weeks. Then, my fare at last collected, I quit. I indulged in no recriminations, I simply quit.

I was not happy to go back, my venture come to naught. Still, it was with a great sense of relief that I thought of turning my back on the city. I said my thanks and goodbyes to Roger and Jean and caught the next bus out of town for the Interior.

Bull Sale

I was not long back in Kamloops before I confirmed what I'd supposed would be the case: the ranches needing only feeding crews and with men to spare for other jobs, there was no sudden prospect of employ-ment. Still I was determined to get by as best I could. Returning from defeat, I was in no mood to accept the Old Man's help any more than I could avoid. In an ugly frame of mind all around, I must have been a distressing number-two son.

Alex Bulman, a rancher with holdings near Kamloops, had a herd of cows to move from Westwold, forty miles east of the city, to a place on the Willow Ranch road, the back way into the Nicola country and some of British Columbia's biggest cow outfits. He asked me if I'd take on a couple of days of winter riding and of course I leaped at it.

It was cold, no two ways about that. A west wind, actually a deflected northerly blow, funnelled down the valleys, every cow in the country turning her tail to it. Into the teeth of this I drove his reluctant cattle for two steady days, holding over the night at the Duck Ranch at Holmwood, gaining a visit thereby.

Out of the saddle so long, I turned stiff as a board with the cold. I stumbled around uselessly whenever I dared get down from my horse. But what of it, the cold and stiffness? I was earning two days' pay and I'd come down to where two days' pay was nothing at which to sniff my humbled nose.

That done, I went on in my search. January faded. In February Safeway Stores, a retail chain organization, opened a new outlet in Kamloops with an expanded meat counter. I found work there, regularly at first but then on a part-time basis, usually the three last days in the week. The wages were just and in the three days I made more than Lover Boy had paid me for a week. My heart wasn't in it, but it was work and work of any kind I wanted.

In March the British Columbia Beef Cattle Growers held their annual Bull Sale and Fat Stock Show. There was an opening for the week of the show for a night watchman, experienced enough with livestock not to be nonplussed by the eventualities inherent in upwards of a hundred bulls all tethered together in one large barn. Fortunately, while the Old Man was secretary of the show, Ralph Devick, one of the principal salesmen for the Livestock Producers' Co-operative, was manager and I could therefore reasonably approach him for the job with no impropriety in my connections. He put me on, accepting my undertaking that notwithstanding the three days at the end of the week in which I would work both night and day, I would hold things together.

The barn, show ring, and offices of the Association were all housed together in one large building. In the barn itself were long, double rows of stalls, one on each wall and more face to face down the middle. Between every four or five stalls was an open space where an exhibitor could pile feed for his bulls and keep the usual collection of show ring gear: halters, ropes, brushes and so forth.

My task consisted mainly of safeguarding the building and the livestock against any intruder and watching the bulls for trouble. The Herefords were all tied by halters and the Aberdeen Angus by halters and nose ropes, but there was always the possibility of a bull breaking loose and setting the barn in an uproar. Apart from these security duties, I would sweep the offices and the elevated seats in the show ring and tend the furnace used to heat the ring and a tank that supplied hot water to the washing stalls where the bulls were scrubbed to be at their glossy best for the show. There was enough to do to keep awake and I was glad to be around a job in some way connected with beef on the hoof instead of on a cutting block in a retail market.

The first night passed without incident. I checked all the halter ropes when I came on at nine o'clock, satisfying myself they were secure, making doubly sure of the Aberdeen Angus. These scrappy little rascals were bellowing and stomping all the time and I'd as soon have ten Herefords loose and on the prod as one black Angus.

Then I set to sweeping the offices and the ring and cleaning the wash stalls. This saw me through to midnight. Thereafter I made a routine tour of the building and the outside corrals, where a number of animals in the fat stock classes were kept, every half to three quarters of an hour. Between tours I sat in the office reading back issues of *The Western Horseman* or the *Family Herald*. Toward morning I stoked the furnaces, and when Ralph Devick showed up at seven I had everything tiptop.

"How'd it go?"

"Quiet as lambs."

"Okay. See you tonight."

"You bet." With that I was off home for a sleep.

So it went for two more nights. The fourth night I had company, an unemployed cowboy who was marking time in Kamloops until spring riding would take him out on a ranch somewhere. He'd searched for other work to no avail and only his reputation for honesty kept him in room and meals. I knew him as one knows anyone in a small city in the same pickle, commiserating with each other over the lack of work. We called him Slim. He was over six feet and lean as a willow branch. I wondered his belt kept his trousers up.

It was good to have him there and I knew Devick wouldn't mind. He toured the outside stock while I swept up and afterwards we sat in the office drinking coffee, trading yarns between trips into the barn for inspection.

The night promised to be no different than any other until three in the morning when Slim stood up and yawned, stretching his long arms. "I'll take a walk through the barn for you. I'm getting sleepy."

"We just did, fifteen minutes ago."

"That all? Seems longer. Guess I'm tired, must be why."

"We'll stoke the furnace in a little while. Takes about two hours to get the water hot. Some of these fellows are still doing a little washing. Wonder they don't wash the hair right off their livestock."

Slim disappeared through the door. In seconds he came back, as wide awake as if he'd just got up.

"Come here quick. You got trouble, I think."

I thought of loose bulls and flew for the door.

"Sh! Don't make a noise."

Puzzled, I followed him. We went through the show ring to the door leading into the barn. There we stopped. Slim peered cautiously around.

"There," he said softly. "Look over there, on the east wall."

I did so. There, glancing furtively about, lurched the figure of a man, going from tackle box to tackle box, trying locks, searching under tarpaulins. He'd have entered the barn by one of the double doors for bringing in stock and feed.

"Call the police for me, Slim. I'll get hold of him."

"Maybe I better help you. We could call the police after."

"No. I think I can handle him and I don't want you to have to be involved. If I don't have him in the office by the time you get the call through you can come and give me a hand."

"Okay." With that he went to make the call.

I waited till the fellow had applied himself to another strong box, then sprinted into the barn. I was nearly to him when he looked up and saw me.

He scrambled up from the box, running into the clear way back of the stalls. He started for the south door.

I changed direction, to collide with him. We went down together in a heap on the straw of the barn floor. I rolled quickly, trying to grab him.

He was up but I caught his foot, brought him down again. I knew by now he was no size and if I could once take hold or sit on him, I had him. The reek of liquor told me he was at least partly drunk.

This time I was up by the time he reached his knees. I flew at him, spread-eagled, crushing him on the ground. A nearly full bottle of whiskey rolled away in the straw.

"You done, fella?"

He grunted. "Yeah. I quit. Lemme up."

"Come up easy." I moved cautiously off him, twisting an arm behind him while we both rose to our feet. Holding him hard with one hand, I reached for the whiskey bottle with the other.

"Let's go. The way I came. Through the door by the wash stalls."

He went easily, stumbling a little. How much was drunkenness and how much a deliberate intention to get me off my guard, I wondered. Anyway he tried to bolt at the exit near the office door. I all but dropped the whiskey bottle in the scuffle, but Slim had the door opened and I forced him through by sheer advantage of weight. In the office I let him go. He crumpled on a chair.

"You get the police?"

"They're coming."

I turned to the trespasser. "What were you up to?" Then I realized my question was foolish by the excessive obviousness of the answer.

Anyway he ignored it. He became suddenly agitated. "You called the cops?"

"Sure. We couldn't do much else."

I'd put the whiskey on a desk. He lunged for it. I grabbed it from him.

"Oh, please, mister, please. Gimme a drink. I gotta have a drink. Godammit, take pity on me. I gotta have it." The words poured from him in a wild, shameless appeal for the whiskey.

"No, dammit," I said, pushing away his imploring hands.

"Wait a minute, Al," Slim intervened. "Maybe it would be easier on him if we did let him have it. It won't make any difference and nobody'd be the wiser. The police'll take the whiskey anyway. He's a pitiful mess."

Looking at it that way, I could see Slim's point. But for the grace of God …

"Here, take it."

He tore the top from the bottle and took the liquor down in feverish gulps. When he'd had so much it seemed dangerous to let him take more, we wrenched the bottle away and forced him back on the chair.

"I've never seen a man crazy for it like that before," I said. It had been a disgusting and in some sense a frightening sight.

"What it's like to be an alchy, I guess."

Soon two policemen arrived. I related the incident exactly as it had happened. "Will I have to give evidence in court?" I was due on at the butcher shop in the morning for the weekend work and would have to give up precious wages.

"I don't think so. We'd have to go some to prove theft. After all, the whiskey could be his and he's got nothing else on him. We'll charge him on drunkenness, and we've got the evidence of that ourselves." Then they led him away, taking the whiskey with them.

I shrugged at Slim. "All in a night's work, eh? You think that whiskey was his or did it come out of an unlocked gear box in the barn?"

"Out of a gear box. That was Highland Cream. High-priced Scotch. Better'n I'd buy, much less that poor devil."

I reported the stolen whiskey to Devick in the morning. He felt there was little point in worrying about the loss, whosoever it was. I'd done my duty and the police were obligated to keep the evidence, what little remained of it. Silently I had misgivings now about having let him drink it, but at the time I had been regarding it as his own. But it mattered little. I changed my clothes in a back room off the Old Man's office and went up town for breakfast, then to put on a butcher's apron for the day.

That day went well enough and also the following night. Then the struggle against weariness began. It was Friday and time in the shop dragged terribly. I forced myself to my work and drank double quantities of coffee at the break. As soon as the shop closed I went to the barns to sleep as well as I might, slouched in an armchair in the Old Man's office which lay vacant for other purposes after six o'clock.

Ralph Devick stirred me at nine-thirty and I went through my work bit by bit, making it last so I couldn't sit in the office where the danger of falling asleep would face me. The hours of the morning dragged by and I realized the worst part of it all was the way time bore down on a man, making drudgery of everything he did.

Devick came in early enough that I had an hour's rest before going for breakfast and the last day in the shop. Still it would be a long day. On Saturdays we closed at eight in the evening and I was therefore robbed of a short sleep like the one the evening before.

But at least I was busy. We did as much trade on Saturdays as we did through all the earlier part of the week. Hopped up with coffee, I worked my way, minute by torturous minute, through to closing time and the short respite of the walk in the fresh air to the edge of town and the bull barns.

I set to the night's work at once, feeling I must do the sweeping early and then walk constantly about the building and the outside corrals to keep awake. Even the walking promised to be a burden, much less perform work. I finished the sweeping and other tasks by eleven, then began the long seven hours in which staying awake, even on my feet, became a sheer act of will, performed in a vague halfway world in which the snorting of the Angus bulls became an indispensable and constant alarm.

I gave up looking at my watch because it was intolerable to see, after an age of struggling against the urge to lie down on the baled straw and give in to sleep, that only five minutes, ten at the most, had gone by.

The bulls were restless. Someone had asked Devick to locate a good cow for milking and, finding one, he'd put her in the barn for the night in an empty stall. It was my luck that by midnight she had rapidly come into heat and every grain fed bull in the barn began raging in an agony of frustration. The Aberdeen Angus rattled their nose chains and banged their great heads on the manger boards in sheer fury. I resigned myself to this new burden, debating about but finally deciding against moving the cow out. I checked all the halter ropes again and, I thought, assured myself adequately of the security of the situation.

If only I could lie down, if even for five minutes, maybe ten. But I daren't. Perhaps if I sat, rested my legs. Damn those Angus bulls. Won't they quit? How can their noses stand the constant jerking on the ring? The straw bales look so inviting. just a moment or two, that would be all. Surely the bulls ...

No. Godammit! Quickly! Outside again. I'd drained the outside pipes earlier against the danger of frost. After all, March is March. Freeze one night, thaw the next. But I checked them again. It occupied me and the fresh air helped. Somehow five minutes went by, then ten, then fifteen. It will be morning, eventually. Morning always comes. When it is morning and I look back, it won't have been so long. But now it is ages.

I went back in the barn. The bulls, I thought, are quieter. No, they aren't, it's just me. I'm getting daft. I went into the office and sat on a chair. I'll sit on the very edge, I decided. If I go to sleep, I'll fall off, wake up. I looked at my watch. Three o'clock.

I didn't fall but I must have begun to. The time? How long asleep? But I wasn't really, or could I have? ... Twenty after three. Only twenty minutes. Lucky. Could have been an hour and twenty. Time to make a round. Won't sit down again afterwards. Keep walking. The bulls are getting worse. They're bellowing hard, practically screaming with rage.

I went through the ring, shaking my head, imagining at least that I felt fresher. I listened to the tick of my watch to be sure it hadn't stopped. Then I reached the door. By golly, they really were going at it. I had never heard that much commotion in the barn before.

Then I was truly awake, out of the half-way world of that night for the first time. There were four bulls loose in the east aisle, Herefords, thank Heaven.

I ran down the aisle and grabbed the first dangling halter shank I came to. Everywhere bulls were raging, hitting their shanks hard. I tried to think if I'd checked the ropes the night before, that century ago when I'd come to work. Only a poorly tied shank would come loose.

I tied the bull on the handiest stall post, although that still left him standing in the aisle. Better that than waste time getting him to an empty stall. I went for the next and tied him too, though he bounced at me twice, scaring blazes out of me, making it no easy matter to stand there in front of him clutching his halter rope.

The remaining two were fighting. I knew I must do something at once. Bulls still tied were exploding in their stalls. Damn wonder the cow didn't get bred, I thought. They must have started fighting before they reached her. Otherwise they'd all have been around her. As it was she was still two aisles away.

Then I wondered why I thought of that with two loose bulls still in front of me. Forcing myself, I rushed in and caught a halter shank. I ducked into an empty stall and scrambled over the partition, at the same time wrapping the shank around the partition post. In a moment I had it tied.

The remaining bull struck the one I'd just tied three times, hard, in the ribs and flank, before I caught his rope. I jerked at him, finally drawing him down the aisle. He snorted and bawled, lunging at me but not out-and-out attacking. I was scared to hell and I wanted to clear right out of there but I didn't. I saw an open stall and repeated the previous performance, only this time I shifted the shank to the manger board after I got him quieted down.

I wasn't done. I had yet to shift the other bulls into stalls. I didn't sweat about which stalls. The men who'd tied them shoddily could do that. But it all went well. After the last one was secure, I went to the office and drank the remains of a thermos of coffee, shaking horribly. Then I walked the barn for the rest of the night.

It was Sunday morning and I hadn't been in a bed since Wednesday. It was also the last night of the sale, so I went to the Old Man's house and slept all day, got up for a meal and went back to bed and slept all night.

Back into town on Monday, I took up the search for steady work again. Nothing came my way immediately, but in a couple of weeks the store took me on full time which was hunkydory till the day I could land a job with a pitch fork attached to it. I'd had my fill of working in town.

A few weeks later I met Slim at noon hour. He came in the grill where I was eating lunch. He'd landed a job in the Nicola country and was going out on the bus that afternoon.

"Good for you," I congratulated him. "Wish it was me. I get a job on a ranch again, I'll sure stay the devil outa town."

"I know what you mean. I'm going to get next winter's work lined up just as soon as I can."

We dawdled over our coffee, using up my last few minutes. "Say," he said suddenly. "You remember that little guy we caught in the barn when you were night watching at the bull sale? I saw him last week. He just got out of jail."

"That a fact? What'd he have to say?"

Slim thought a moment, though Slim was far from a pensive man. "I'll tell you something," he went on at last. "I feel sorry for that guy. I asked him what was the matter with him, why he didn't have more sense than to pull a stunt like that. He told me he didn't remember much about it. He'd got goofed up on wine earlier in the evening. He come up from Vancouver early in the fall, he said. Hasn't had a job anywhere for a couple of years. He got to selling dope, but he left the coast to try to get out of it. He says he's going back 'cause it's the only thing he can get to do. Guess he's no good for anything. No brains for paperwork and no muscle for labouring."

It was a long speech for Slim, and he stopped awhile. Then he added: "Makes you think, don't it?"

"Yes," I agreed. "It makes you think."

Dude Wrangler

The weeks crawled by in a monotonous round of butcher-shop routine. Light trade Monday, some trade Tuesday. Busy Wednesday morning, closed Wednesday afternoon. Busy again Thursday and try to be cut ahead for the weekend. Turmoil Friday and sheer pandemonium Saturday. Lay off Sunday and light trade Monday. Monday upon Monday.

It was in May that I met Pete Douthwaite in town. I had come to know him when I worked at Holmwood, for he and Rupert Duck were tillicums from away back. He had a small place up on the west side of the North Thompson River at McLure, several miles south of Louis Creek where I had crossed to the east side in my trek out of the Cariboo. Pete was trying to make a dude ranch out of a place that wasn't big enough or suitable for stock.

A slight man, not tall, Pete had a droopy eyelid that gave him a perpetual look of mischievous wickedness. He had both a temper and a sense of humour and sometimes one got in the way of the other, making it devilish hard to know how to take him.

But the sense of humour had the upper hand and I doubt if he ever missed an opportunity to make a joke. You hurt your foot, he laughed at your limp, made you laugh too.

Once he found himself sitting next to Brian Chance at a social gathering. Chance was the manager of the Douglas Lake Cattle Company in the Nicola country, an outfit running fifteen thousand head. Everyone knew Brian Chance, so Pete naturally said hello, how are things.

"Oh, very well, thank you. You'll have to forgive me, but I'm not sure I know your name." One of the most genuine gentlemen in western Canada, Chance was anxious not to offend.

"Douthwaite," Pete replied. "Pete Douthwaite. I have a place up the North Thompson River."

"Oh, I see." The wheels went around visibly as Chance tried hard to place him. He knew virtually every man in the territory who owned even a small place but Douthwaite rung no bells. "In cattle?" he asked at last.

"Yes," Pete replied, casually. "Matter of fact," he went on, "I doubled my herd last week."

"Oh?" Chance remained puzzled, no doubt wondering how a major purchase of cattle had taken place without his knowing it.

"Yep," Pete affirmed. "Both m'cows had calves."

"Both your cows … ? Oh, I see, I see. You had two cows and they both had … Hm. Very good. Very good indeed."

That was Pete, straight-faced as a Methodist minister. I thought him the most entertaining cuss I'd ever met, and I was glad to run into him in town.

"How things going with you, Pete?"

"Not bad, considering who I am and how I live. And you?"

"Oh, fair. I'm working. I'd like to get out of town though."

"Would you? I guess it would seem tame to a bona fide ranch-type boy like you, but I need a man for the summer. Do some haying and chase dudes if I get any business."

"You got hay, you got horses, you got a man. When do I start?"

"When can you start?"

"I'd like to give a week's notice. Say a week Monday?"

"Fine. How about money?"

I shrugged. "Goin' wages and my grub. What's goin' wages?"

"Hundred a month?"

"That's all anybody's paying I've heard of. Suits me, so long as you got a big plate where I can collect the rest of it."

So it was that two Sundays later found me standing by the dirt track that passed his place, bedroll over my shoulder, saddle against my hip. There in the trees across a tumbling stream sat the bunkhouse. To the north a hundred yards were the corrals, the barnyard, the barn itself. Beyond it the alfalfa field stretched to a stand of light aspen, backed by the dark green of a pine forest. Lord, it was good to be home!

Pete had his own house a hundred yards through the trees to the south. This was a farm cottage, expanding into a lodge by the addition of a large room on one end. Here, I found, we took our meals with Pete and his pretty wife, Nicki, we including Herbie, Pete's regular hired hand, a Brooklyn boy come west, a little older than I and darned near unintelligible at first because of the common-law cross of his Brooklynese with Pete's Cheshire English.

East of the house about five minutes' walk through the wood were the guest cabins, rustic units Pete and Herbie had built on the high bank just where it broke away to the river itself. In fact the entire place lay between mountain and river on a bench just so big as to hold its patchwork of hayfield, pasture, and tended woods around the buildings.

I soon fell into the pattern of the place: cows to milk before six, breakfast at six-thirty, on with the job around seven. Pete and Herbie continued their building while I irrigated a hay crop and made myself known to the twenty-odd horses which needed riding enough that they wouldn't do something unexpected one day with a dude aboard. The country rocky and shaley along the trails we rode, I always had a horse to shoe — last year's worn plates till he grew some hoof, new shoes when he had hoof enough to put them on.

The crop ready to cut, I went to haying and only interrupted Pete and Herbie when it came time to stack. Mind you, it was no great hayfield and I'd hardly started haying but I was done and spreading water around to grow another crop. Still, all this was my work: fencing now and again, haying, gentling down the horses. I was happy, happier than I'd been in a hell of a while, you come right down to it.

Then we had dudes, a party out from Vancouver who stayed about a week. We rode trail with them every day, sometimes high on the mountains for scenery, others to a lake for a barbecue, maybe to a stream for some fishing. Hardly a burdensome task, all a boy need do was remember that peoples' worth hung on other things besides whether they knew which side of a horse you climbed up from.

There were, too, tense moments, a natural consequence it seemed of city folks spending a week in the bush. Once in a while a horse would take his head on the trail and there'd be some talking to do to overcome an attack of nervousness. Or a gal would get her feet wet fording a small river and for a moment you expected her to quit the saddle and start swimming but she didn't.

We took the party fishing one afternoon, but the young lady didn't care to fish. While her brother waded off up the stream I found a clean bit of shade where we could pass the time. I tied up the horses and sat a decent distance from where she lay, so I could be sociable if she wanted to talk and keep my mouth shut if she didn't.

She chatted with me, lying on her back looking up through the trees at the sky, her elbows out and her hands folded beneath her head. I nodded and made exchanges as best I could though she was a sight too sophisticated for me to feel at ease with her. While we talked I watched her, she being powerful gentle on the eyes.

A snake, coiled unseen in the grass, suddenly raised his head not a foot from her bare throat. I froze. A goddamn rattler, I thought, fighting back the terror I felt for her. I daren't warn her. Move and she'd be hit.

But it couldn't be a rattler, not here. Or could it? They'd been seen down the river. She went on talking and I stared, motionless, never so useless in my life.

It was not a rattler. I concluded that and the relief was immense. But what to say, what to do?

She looked at me. "Don't you think so?"

Think what? I hadn't been listening. "Yes," I said, slowly. Vaguely too, I guess.

"You're not listening to me," she accused.

I started to protest but didn't finish. The snake moved, slithered across her throat.

She screamed, sat up, clutched beneath her chin. The snake was gone in the grass.

I jumped to her at once. "You're perfectly safe. And I'm awfully sorry. It was a grass snake. Harmless."

"A snake?" she cried, trembling.

"Yes, but only a grass snake. They can't hurt you."

"You saw it. That was why you ..."

"But I couldn't tell you. It would have been as bad or worse. I hoped it would go the other way but it didn't. Are you all right now?"

She had gathered herself together wonderfully. She laughed, a little nervously. "I'm fine. Grand experience. Just what I've always dreamed about." Then she lay back to search around for what she'd been saying when I'd first seen the snake and lost the conversation. Meanwhile I moved back once more to a proper distance. Rule number one, the cowboys don't sit too handy to the female guests.

The party left and we turned back to other tasks. Then one day an American, a middle-aged businessman, and his wife arrived. They'd seen the Whitewood Lodge sign and they wondered what Pete had to offer in the way of a real pack trip into the hills.

"The best," Pete assured them. "The best." He went on to describe Adler Lake, a little jewel of a tarn nestled in the pine trees up on the Bonaparte Plateau, full of eager rainbow trout and a good day's ride from the ranch. The cabin wasn't ready but we had canvas enough to take along and I could see, before Pete was done talking, that we had us some customers.

I ran in the horses while Pete gathered gear, putting together the packs. Herbie saddled a horse and struck out at once with a short crosscut saw and an axe to clear the trail of any deadfalls that might have come down since the last trip in.

The horses chosen, I strung them out, halter shank to tail hair, and led them up the road to the foot of the trail on Fish Trap

Creek, some four miles north of the ranch. There I staked them for the night and threw my bedroll under a tree, to sleep as best I might till daybreak when Pete would arrive with the packs, packsaddles, canvas, grub, gear, and guests.

The American and his wife were good scouts and we enjoyed them. He climbed out of the pickup all bundled against the chill of the dawn and hailed me as if I was his own long-lost stableboy.

"Say, how'd you sleep last night? You got them hosses ready? We got a mess o' saddles an' gear here, boy. Say, you better get yourself some coffee here while I tend them hosses for you."

Pete winked at me while he brought me sandwiches and a thermos of coffee from the truck, so I handed a halter shank to the eager traveller, let him take over. He tied that one and fetched the rest off their stake ropes while I ate my breakfast and took a briefing from Pete.

"We'll pack up and get out of here as soon as we can. I've the boxes made up and balanced so we shouldn't be long. We want to be at the Forestry cabin for lunch and into Adler in plenty of time to camp. I'll take the lead and entertain a bit and you crowd right along with the pack horses. We'll need to tighten the packs after the first climb but we should travel steady after that."

"Got you."

We packed up quickly, putting it all on three horses with ease, and better that than overload two. Then we mounted up our guests, taking care with their stirrup lengths, and struck out.

The trail climbed hard up the gulch of Fish Trap Creek. After a scrambling half hour it levelled out so we tightened the pack hitches. Then we dropped again, fording the fast running stream, only to climb once more on the opposite bank. We left the bush of the benchland behind, travelling now under a towering stand of mature pine.

The climb more gentle, we kept at it for another three hours. Then the country noticeably levelled out and I suddenly realized I'd been spilled back into my own territory, the great jack pine upland that stretches northward from the high bench above the

Thompson Rivers, through the Bridge Lake country, past the 100 Mile, past the Old Man's meadows, far into the Horsefly and country I hadn't seen or imagined, vast and magnificent. North of here, across this same plateau and through this same belt of timber I'd ridden the Mount Olie trail only two years before although it felt half a lifetime.

We crossed small streams but more often the bogs and swamps of the flatland. At noon we broke out on a small meadow with its lily-padded pond and an old Forestry cabin at the timber's edge. There we ate our lunch while the horses grazed on the wild sedge grass. On a smaller scale, it might have been the Blaze.

We gained no altitude now as we pushed on. Occasionally we'd drop into a gully to cross a slow-moving stream or plunge through a mudhole in the trail but the relief was out of it compared to the benchlands of the river valleys. Sometimes we'd break out into an opening to follow the edge of a meadow, then slip into the timber again at the end of it. Once a muledeer buck, standing aloof in the timber, watched us go by. Seeing the rest of the party had missed the sight, I kept the treasure to myself.

With time before dusk to make a camp, we came on Adler Lake. It was all Pete had claimed it to be, a beautiful little body of still water, the trees of an untramped forest crowding all about it. Every moment a fish rose, sending out waves of circular ripples. The American grew ecstatic, reminding me we had guests to care for, yanking me out of the reverie I'd fallen into along the trail.

Herbie had a fire going and having eaten all his sandwiches before noon, demanded quick access to the grub boxes.

I dropped him the lead halter shank. "Middle horse. Help yourself."

Pete took the American and his wife to the lake for some immediate fishing from a boat he'd packed in laboriously over the trail on his most trusted horse a year earlier, while I stripped the pack animals and saddle mounts, taking them along the shore to hobble them out. Herbie rustled a quick bite, then began sorting gear from the dumped loads, preparatory to making camp.

Returning, I helped him and soon we had a camp together. Later Pete came back with his guests, who'd taken turns in the small boat to catch a fine string of rainbow trout a few feet out from shore. We fried these up in bacon grease, serving them with hot rice well buttered from a bottleful in the grub box. Later we all lazed around the campfire, telling yarns and listening, but for us mostly listening because the American had a bagful of good ones and clearly he loved to spin them.

We passed two idyllic days. We were top-heavy with help from the necessity of a man clearing the trail ahead, and even without Herbie it would have been a wrangler's paradise. I alternated the horses between tethering and hobbling, keeping them hungry enough that they'd eat rather than travel. We all took turns at cooking.

Pete had the foresight to have brought a few pocket books in the pack, and with little hosting to do other than shove the boat out for his fisherman, he waded through the lot of them. Herbie and I merely lay about, each in his own thoughts, and mine, in all that heavy scent of pine and sedge along the water's edge, were nostalgically of my old home in a faraway forest of the same hue. How easily a long-forgotten smell will stir the memory of one's heart!

Then a stupid thing happened and, in youth, so irrevocable. It was the morning we packed up to leave.

Much had gone wrong, from cinders in the coffee to a pesky breeze that blew smoke in your face whichever side of the fire you hunkered on to fry the bacon. Somehow I made a breakfast fit to eat, but it was much too late with a day's ride ahead of us.

Pete took his guests for a last bit of fishing after breakfast while I went for the horses and Herbie began breaking camp. The horses had strayed a long way in spite of their hobbles and gathering them took ages longer than there was to spare for it.

Coming back to camp at last, I expected the packs would be ready with little left to do but rig the horses and get out. Such was not the case. Herbie's morning was as bad as mine and, grumpy as a bear, he had hardly begun balancing the pack boxes. Even the big tent provided for the guests had yet to be struck. All this, and we should have been on the trail an hour ago.

"This all you got done?"

"What's it look like? And what happened to you? Take you all day to unhobble a few horses?"

"The beggars were away off in the bush."

"I can just imagine."

We shut up then and fumbled about our tasks, frustrated by our own disorganization, wondering why the blazes it takes three hours sometimes to do forty-five minutes' work. After a while I wondered aloud where Pete was.

"Down at the lake chewin' the fat. Least he could do is help."

"Yeah," I agreed, responding readily to any place to put the blame but where it belonged. "You'd think he'd lend a hand, wouldn'ya?"

We went on construing the whole debacle of our late start to be Pete's fault, from a poor breakfast fire on up. We allowed the next thing we knew, he'd be sitting around reading pocket books while we did all the work.

Finally he did leave his guests at the lake to come to see how we were doing. By this time most of the pack boxes were ready, but the canvas and bedding had yet to be bundled for lashing on top of the packs.

Pete was visibly annoyed. "Away to one of our real early starts, I see. Godammit, I bring twice the manpower I need on a four-day trip and I still have to do half the work myself." He grabbed a pack box and fitted it on a saddle, then reached for another one. They were badly balanced and he cursed as he began juggling gear between them to even them up.

Incensed, I hitched the next two boxes on the horse nearest me. "You feel so bloody bad about it, I'll take my time soon's we get back to the ranch."

The second those words were out I'd have swallowed them but for choking on foolish pride. Twice I looked at Pete, his back turned to me, lashing a tent to pile on the pack he was making. Twice I tried to form the words to take it all back and twice I couldn't. Maybe without Herbie there I'd have done it but as it was I grew only more angry, hurt with myself.

Pete helped me lash my pack once I'd made it up. Handing the rope back and forth, we were unavoidably face to face. Pete grinned at me. "Nothing like a good scrap to start the day, eh?"

He couldn't have been more fair. There was the invitation, easily given, easily acceptable, to erase what I'd said. All it needed was a word from me. Yeah, I could say, casually, sorry about what I said. Didn't really mean it.

But the moment passed and I didn't say it. Turning away, I couldn't retrace. The opportunity gone, I was sorry I hadn't used it, but it was too late now. I went intently on with my work. Pete shrugged, went on with his.

Fortunately the guests missed all this, and sullen though I felt, I had the sense to keep it from them. We rode out at last, pushing the horses to make up time. Our stop at lunch was brief, and nearing dusk we scrambled down the last miles of the trail to the road at Fish Trap. There we threw rigging off the horses into the pickup truck and Pete took the guests on to the ranch, leaving Herbie and me to ride the last stretch, leading the spare mounts.

I didn't talk to Herbie about what had happened between myself and Pete. Back to the ranch after dark, I decided to forego supper at the lodge, going directly to the bunkhouse instead.

I got up with Herbie the next morning, the foolishness of yesterday strangely unreal but, I knew, hopelessly done. I debated about rolling my blankets at once, but then decided I'd leave that for the time being and help as usual with the milking. Anyway, I was fiercely hungry and like it or not I would have to show up for breakfast.

The meal was no different than ever except that I kept my silence save for essential courtesies. The guests remained in their cabin until much later and I was spared facing them in my terse mood. After breakfast I scoured the milk buckets, waiting for a chance to see Pete alone and settle my time with him, get it over with. I had no idea how I might get a ride back to Kamloops to seek other work, but that would have to sort itself out.

The guests came for breakfast and Pete remained in the lodge. I packed fuel for the kitchen stove and split more ahead in the woodshed while I waited. At last they settled their account and left, thanking us all for a good trip. I stifled my misery and managed a grin as I took the hand the American offered me.

"So long, Canada."

"So long, Mister. Have a good trip."

They were gone. Pete gave Herbie instructions for the day and Herbie went to carry them out. Then Pete turned to me.

"You could look the horses over for loose shoes and do any fixing you think they need. We ought to bring in the rest from the far pasture sometime, too, and ride them up a bit."

I looked at him in silence for some moments. "You're forgetting I quit," I said, at last.

Pete sighed. "You still stuck on that?"

"I don't say somethin' if I don't mean it."

"Look, boy, we're not angels, either of us. There're no wings sprouting out of your shirt, or mine. So we get grouchy now and again. So what? Somebody asks me what kind of a man you are, I'd say you turned out fine. And you've got nothing against me. Somebody asks you how was I to work for, what are you going to say?"

I looked away, ashamed. "You been good to me. I got no gripe."

"Well?"

"I don't know. Whatever you say."

"I say back to work."

"'Sfine with me. I'll get the horses straightened around. The big mare got a loose shoe, I know." I hurried away so he couldn't see how close I was to crying. Eighteen now, it would hardly do.

RIDE WHICH HORSE?

I stayed on with Pete nearly to the end of August. I finished a little more haying and worked on a couple of green horses to bring them to a standard fit for dudes. I made one more trip to Adler, not with guests, but with flooring for the cabin there, cut into four-foot lengths and packed in balanced bundles, suspended on each side of the packsaddles.

But at last there was no more for me to do. Business hadn't been what Pete had hoped it would, even for the first summer of opening for guests. There'd be work again the following season if I happened to want it, but for the winter I must look elsewhere. I gathered my gear and said goodbye to Nicki and Herbie. Then Pete drove me out to Kamloops.

On a notion — much of what I did was on a notion — I went to Williams Lake to visit with my mother. While there of course I kept an eye out for a job, passing word to those I knew that I was in the market for work. I stayed in a cabin I rented and visited my mother during her hours off from her job at the hospital, poking about my old haunts at other times.

Someone told me a man operating a frozen-food plant and meat shop wanted help. Half-heartedly I went to see him, not sure I wanted to work in a butchering job again but prepared to put in time at it perhaps until better might come along.

He was a little man with something oddly vague about him, a nervous weakness I thought, and I experienced an odd mixture at first meeting of pity and dislike. He might have been forty-five, probably no more, yet he gave the impression that life's decay was upon him. I said I had heard he wanted a butcher.

"Can you take over the cutting? I'm not really a butcher myself and I can't seem to keep help these days. I can run the business, but I need someone to handle this end of it."

I could see by his counter that his butchering was bad. "I can handle your cutting. How much can you pay?" I'd learned a lot in the time I'd worked for Safeway and had little doubt I could straighten his shop.

"Forty-five a week?"

"That'll do to start."

I soon sized matters up. His business was twofold. First, he rented lockers in the freezing plant to people who wished a place to freeze their own meats and vegetables. Second, he operated a fairly complete retail meat counter. My task was to cut for this counter and for customers bringing in their own beef or buying a beef at a savings from the establishment. It struck me as a good combination and should certainly make money.

The cooler, however, was in frightful shape, nothing in order. With stock not rotated, I found pieces of meat beginning to smell and sides, half butchered, left hanging where they'd never sell. Customers' halves were backed up on one rack and should have been butchered to be put in lockers days earlier.

But it was far from irreparable. I told my employer that if he would wait on the customers I would put the shop to rights at once. He agreed and I set to work. I put on a sale of ground beef and stew, carefully trimming and selling the older meat. Then I cleaned up the part sides that hung here and there, in between times catching up the locker cutting. By the end of the first week everything came to shipshape.

I also came to be wiser about my boss, the odd vagueness explained. He was an alcoholic with a bottle-a-day thirst. My contempt gave way even more to pity when I saw how hopelessly enmeshed he was by the craving for liquor. I even felt I must help him as best I could, at least put the operation of his meat counter and cooler on a proper paying basis. Mind you, it wouldn't be easy with him running to the back of the shop for a snort between customers.

During the second week I dropped the inventory of meat to where it belonged. By then I also had an idea of our volume and I therefore advised him what we would need to order from the wholesalers for delivery for the following week.

"Fine," he said. "I'll take care of that. Say, you're doing all right, aren't you. Got everything straightened around pretty quick."

"Well, I've done what I could. I think everything will go well enough now." I was embarrassed by the compliment, coming from him.

The next week came and by Tuesday night no meat had arrived on any of the freight trucks into town from the south. I wondered if perhaps we had an arrangement with one of the nearby ranchers. We must have more to go on by Thursday morning at the latest with the weekend trade coming up.

"When do you expect the meat in?" I asked him, as we tidied up the shop.

"The meat?"

"Yes. From the packers. We're going to be out of some cuts by noon tomorrow."

"Oh. Well, don't worry about that. I'll tend to that."

Wednesday passed. Thursday came but still no meat. I approached him again, as something had to be done at once. He was in the back. It was early morning, but even so he was half done a bottle of rye whiskey.

"What about meat? I've just turned away a customer for a rump roast." Our understanding that he would take the counter already was falling apart. More and more I was waiting on customers and cutting between times.

He nodded and signalled me to follow him into the cooler. This I did. Once inside he went to a fine carcass, already split in half, that had been brought in by a local rancher. He took the name tag off it. "There you are. Take that one."

I hesitated, certain I had understood this meat to be intended for the man's own locker. Then I concluded I must be wrong or that perhaps the boss had telephoned him and made arrangements to buy it. In any case, it must be in order to use it and I went to work at once, breaking the sides into cuts I could use in the counter that was now woefully short in all sections.

I worked hard that day, waiting on customers and cutting ahead for the weekend. Early in the afternoon I brought out to the front a customer's side of beef which I felt must reach his locker by that evening. It had been hanging a week longer than necessary now and I'd have no chance to work on it Friday or Saturday. I could perhaps have it done by closing time by cutting on it between customers.

By three o'clock, all but the trimmings, the meat that grinds into hamburger or is cut into stew, had reached the locker. Now the trimmings are a substantial quantity of meat, the difference, in fact, between profit and loss in the retail trade. I began cutting and grinding, ready to wrap for the freezer.

The boss had been watching and now that I reached this stage he told me not to put any more in the locker. "We'll sell all that by five o'clock," he said.

"But ..."

Then I knew. At first I'd thought he was merely mistaken about whose beef it was, but now I knew and I also understood clearly about the beef I'd broken that morning for the counter. I stood dumbfounded, lost momentarily as to what I must do.

As if sure of my complicity, the little man, whom I hated now, winked at me and walked into the back, no doubt for another swig at the old crock.

I slipped off my apron. Picking up a boning knife, I followed him into the back of the shop.

"I want my time," I said, evenly. I'd been around some for a boy my age but all this hanky-panky was new stuff to me and the knife in my hand trembled slightly against my best effort to prevent it.

"What do you mean?"

"My time. My pay. I'm quitting."

"You wouldn't quit me with the weekend business coming up, would you?" His manner had changed. He was imploring now and perhaps a little afraid.

"I'm quitting. You know why. You going to pull that stuff, you do it without me."

"You're jumping to conclusions."

"I don't think so. Come on, now. Pay me."

He gave me cash and I hurried away from his shop, immensely relieved. On Saturday I saw both the rancher whose beef I'd put in the counter and the man whose trimmings I'd been told to sell. I passed on what had happened, leaving it to them to decide how it should be settled. I offered to give evidence in court if this was their wish but neither chose that course, preferring to settle privately.

So I was out of a job, too often, I could see that. Mother saw the vacuum in my affairs and skillfully filled it. She persuaded me to go to university, to take up my schooling again. There was some money in an education insurance fund I could use.

I agreed, said I'd have a go. And I had a go. Even Roger's scepticism, which knew no bounds when he discovered me on the campus a few days later, was ill-founded, in that first year. I struggled in the only genuine effort at studying since tenth grade in high school. By Christmas I had overcome lost time, by term end in May I carried a high second-class average. Even I was prepared to believe in the possibility of a fine academic future.

I took work that summer in a sawmill, alien place of whining machinery and stinking diesel engines. Often I thought how much more I would enjoy the longer day working in a hayfield somewhere, yet for the sake of higher wages I stuck with fir bark and sawdust. I must have money to pay board and fees in the great North American tradition of working one's way through college.

I returned for the second year. Somehow the spirit of achievement and the high objectives of youth's ambition had let me down a little. I no longer thought of myself as a gowned and gloried scholar in tomorrow's halls of learning. The image had faded and dissolved. In its place was an oft felt hunger to be on my way again, to strap my rigging on some rancher's cow horse, to throw my bedroll where pay and board might take me.

I stuck it till Christmas but I knew then it would be useless to go on. I telephoned to Rupert Duck.

"This is Fry here. Alan Fry."

"Oh yes." His voice expressed surprise over the hundreds of miles of wire.

"I'm looking for work."

"I thought you were back in school."

"Was. Ain't no more. You got anything I could do?"

Luck was with me. "I need a man to feed cattle on Robin's Range in January."

"You got one. I'll be there."

"I hope you know what you're doing."

"See you. G'bye."

I reported for work at the ranch at Holmwood in the first days of the new year. Nineteen, coming twenty, I seemed no further ahead than the last time I'd been there.

"What do you plan on next?" Dorothy asked me. "Ballet?"

I could see what she meant. It was like picking your horse out of the corral in the morning. Any one of several would do but you had to settle on one. But that was my trouble. Which horse would I ride?

ICE ON THE SADDLE

 R upert had bought more hay land on
Robin's Range, old homestead ground,
and my job was to live on the range for the
rest of the winter to care for the cow herd,
feeding out the hay in daily sleigh loads
until some time in March when it would
all be gone.

I wouldn't have to batch, however. Rupert
arranged that I would board with
the Wickstroms, an old-settler couple living a mile through the
bush from the place where I would keep the cattle. This was a stride
ahead of stirring up my own grub every day and I felt duly grateful.

I took a team and sleigh up to the range, my few belongings
dumped on the rack, to move in. I would in fact bunk in a cabin
next door with an old Norwegian, Charlie Leeburg, but I'd take
my meals and generally do my living with the Wickstroms. I'd
keep my team in the barn there and travel daily to the cow herd.

The afternoon of that same day I opened a stack at the new feed
ground, spreading out a big load in a large circle on the clean,
untracked snow. Then early the following morning, before
daybreak, I rode down to the ranch on the mare I'd led up behind
the rack, to bring the cattle. Peter helped me and by midafternoon
the cows were strung out on the hay I'd put out, eating contentedly.
I was established.

I enjoyed the Wickstroms. Scandinavian settler stock, they'd
been homesteaded on the range since before the depression. Old

Wickstrom, like many of his countrymen, had been a good woodsman but a poor farmer. He'd built fine cabins and good barns but he hadn't made the land pay. Still, it mattered little. Old and close to bedridden now, he looked back on a life of adequacy if not plenty, working for Rupert's father in the summer time, hacking railroad ties with a broadaxe in the winters.

"Ay never got rich," he told me, his eyes twinkling. "But ay sure raised a damn fine bunch o' kids."

And that he did. I never was positive just how many but give or take a boy or girl, there were seven or more. They were all grown up now. One boy was lost in the war, while two served and came back.

One of these, Arnold, was the only son now home. Unmarried, he lived with the old folks when he wasn't away working in logging camps. A huge, blond-haired man, he was as strong as two of me. A congenial fellow too, he'd often feed cattle with me in trade for my helping him cut wood. We had plenty of forty below zero that winter and the big heater destroyed fir blocks by the cord.

Mrs. Wickstrom stayed active in defiance of her age. One of her married daughters stayed with her for part of that winter, but there was no question about whose kitchen it was. She'd offer to throw the lot of us out if we cluttered up her table with cards when she had a mind to put coffee on, and she bossed the old man about cheerfully, telling him he was more trouble to raise than all the kids together. He'd grin wickedly, sassing her back, and she'd slap him on top of his head with a heap more affection than heft.

Charlie Leeburg had the cabin immediately adjacent. He batched, preferring to live in his own disarray than conform to a woman's standards. Nonetheless he spent the greater part of each day visiting with the old Wickstrom, warily gauging his favour with Mrs. Wickstrom, leaving huffily when she'd had enough of him and threatened to throw his cap in the stove, an ancient headgear he wore indoors and out, forsaking it only at bedtime.

My work with the cattle never took me beyond noon, except for the days I might ride back to drift through the feeding cows to look for early calvers or signs of other trouble, and so I had my afternoons to spend most times in the Wickstrom cabin.

The three old people all had pensions and with the allowance left him from his, Wickstrom craved to play cards. Leeburg was equally devoted to the vagaries of chance and so the winter in some measure became one long poker game for small stakes, Arnold and I playing to lose as much as win or, if we won, distributing the proceeds back in the form of an occasional jug of good whiskey, a treat the old men loved as fondly as they did a handful of aces on a big pot.

The feeding went well. I left the Wickstrom place every morning after daybreak and by ten-thirty or eleven had the big load of hay out that would feed the cattle for the day. Then I'd take an axe to the beaver ponds in the creek by the meadow to open up the water holes, enough that no cow had to stand around on the ice too long waiting a chance to drink.

Some days I might cut a few rails to tighten up the stackyard fence and when I had to open a new stack, there'd be an extra hour shovelling snow from the top and breaking trail with the team to get at it.

I was pestered after a time by stray horses, unwanted beasts that drifted about the ranges of the cow country, hog-fat in the summer and fall, close to death by starvation in the winter and spring. I gathered somehow that the few head sponging on my particular feed ground had originated in the Nicola country, so I decided to push them back that way, off the Robin's Range road, down toward the Willow Ranch.

I waited for a break in the cold snap, finally choosing a day with a soft, south wind blowing. Done feeding as quickly as possible, I ate an early lunch, strapped my rigging on my saddle horse and gathered up the strays, seven in all, then pushed them off the feed ground onto the road west.

I set out by twelve o'clock at the latest. The horses travelled well and no cold wind to face, I prodded them along at a persistent trot, putting mile after mile behind me. I passed Barnhartsvale, the settlement halfway between Kamloops and Holmwood. Then I turned south toward the Nicola country. I figured to put the strays past a ranch that straddled the road, the fences of which would be a barrier to their return.

A few miles down that road, I felt the wind change. It wasn't much at first: only a slight shift from south to west and a few degrees chillier. Sheltered as I was by a north-and-south valley, the shift even cut the velocity of the wind as I detected it. I pushed on, determined to put in the two more hours that would see the strays where I wanted to leave them.

I came to the first fence crossing the road, passing through the gate. It would take half an hour to reach the next fence, beyond which I'd leave the horses. It was taking off a mitt to close the gate latch that told me the temperature had dropped. But up above the sky was overcast, not clear and brittle the way it would be if a severe plunge of the mercury were coming.

Reaching the next fence, I put the horses through. My feet cold, I dismounted, stomping around to warm them up. Then I mounted up again and as I started back, a fine snow began to fall, a sharp, wind-driven snow, cold weather snow, the very worst.

But it won't be so bad, I thought, as I hunched up in the saddle for warmth. This kind of a wind comes out of the west. I take it from the sheltered side to Barnhartsvale and from the back when I turn eastward onto the Range. No trouble at all.

No trouble at all except my feet were damn near frozen. What a miserable break after waiting all this time for a soft day! And how come so cold, with an overcast sky and a snowstorm? I had a vague idea of weather forces and pictured a meeting of moist Pacific air with a freezing arctic blast, stirring up a tempest in the sky, throwing snow and cold wind at a man, all in one serving.

The temperature continued to drop. It could be down to fifteen above, going for ten, going for zero, easy weather without a wind, the frozen counterpart of hell with one. The snow, a million driving needles of ice, kept coming. The wind rose, even in the valley. I could hear it moaning in the treetops on the slopes above.

It was dark long before I came to Barnhartsvale and the eastward turn, nine miles yet to go. But at last the wind would be on my back, pushing me along, not fighting me on my way. It would? Funny. The snow kept driving in my face. But why an east wind? What meteorological prank was this to play on a man whose feet were numb with the creeping cold?

I broke out onto the big bench where the road rises from the valley and spills a man onto the unbroken, open grassland. No tree to check it, no draw to cower in away from it, the howling gale and its jabbing needles of ice swept against a man, as pitiless as the fury above that spawned it.

My horse balked, turning to go back in the timber. I cursed, struck him with the spurs. He faced it then, head down, flying wisps of mane lashing back, feet stumbling through the sifting drifts.

I closed my eyes, daren't open them. When I did, to gather from evidence more certain than the unsteady stumbling of the horse beneath me that we still held the road, the biting ice stung the naked eyes, left them burning.

We pushed on. There was no road now, only a vague tree line to the south and an indefinite sky line somewhere to the north, scantily seen across the wind, a mitt raised uselessly to shield a man's face from the onslaught while he groped for bearings. The drifts deepening, the road got lost somewhere beneath the piling coat of white obstruction.

I've gone too far. Somewhere back there I should have turned toward the hill. Turn too soon, hit the barbed wire. Turn to late, miss the road where it climbs, a mile across the flat, into the timber. Oh Lord, if one could only reach the timber!

The feeling was going from my feet and my numbed senses weren't too far lost to know the danger of that. I must walk, to put the blood to going again. But first I must hit the timber, for I'd go nowhere, stumbling in all this drifted snow, leather chaps as stiff as boards. I turned south, making for the timber where the road should be, giving back ground I'd crossed and shouldn't have.

How dark the world could be on a foul night, despite the snow that swirled about everywhere.

I found the road again and after an age of blind riding, reached the timber. The wind dropped and mightn't have existed but for the howling in the treetops. I crawled thankfully down from the saddle, holding my weight by my hands as, gingerly, I experimented with the usefulness of my legs.

Soon I stumbled a step or two. Then I could walk, and I started out, up the road between the trees, knowing I must be thawed within the half-hour, for the blizzard could only hit me twice as hard when I would reach the top of the hill and the open again.

I wondered if I would reach the top. How painful the struggle to keep my feet moving in the deepening snow, higher and higher, footstep by reluctant footstep, pulling along a stubborn saddle horse whose only ambition seemed to be to find a sheltered place and quit.

Just before the top I mounted up, dismounted again at once. I took off a mitt and with my fingernails scratched at the ice that had formed on the saddle leather, which, seat warmed, had made water of the first snow to hit it. I removed the ice as best I could and once more mounted up. It was a cold seat but it was the only one and would damned well have to do.

The wind howled at the crest. Head down, I rode into it. Eyes closed again, I let the horse go, knowing he'd find his way now with a bank above and a fence below.

How many more miles, I wondered. Four? Maybe five? I thought it was seven from Barnhartsvale to the old Tuscon place. Was it two more to Wickstrom's corner? Three?

Now I'm by the Lee place. Must be two miles to the Tuscon. Oh, what's the use, trying to figure it out. Makes it no shorter.

I entered the timber and again I walked, tying a gunny sack from the back of the saddle over the seat. The sack had been there since last I carried a lunch. Wish I'd carried a lunch today. My numb fingers clawed feebly at the saddle strings, hardly as if they were mine, and I cursed them.

Two more open stretches to go. Wonder what time it is? Somewhere near the belt line of my trousers was a watch pocket with a watch in it. I didn't care enough to take off a mitt and fumble for a watch I likely couldn't see if I did get it out.

I mounted up, rode through the next stretch of open. Down again another time and up. After an age I reached the Wickstrom turnoff. Then it was only a mile, now a half, a quarter, a hundred yards. Was home ever so welcome? I couldn't remember when.

My horse in the barn, I stumbled to the cabin. Inside, the heat dazed me. I fell on a chair, stretching out my legs so Arnold could get the chaps off, then the boots. The felt insoles were frozen to the bottom of the boots.

"You didn't have much time left, Al. You nearly froze your feet."

I nodded. "The weather played a switch on me, didn't it?"

"Sure did. We've been thinking about you out in that blizzard, wondering how you were making out."

Soon I climbed outside a big plate of hot stew and warmed up. Then I went to Charlie's cabin to turn in. It was nearly midnight.

A week later the stray horses were back on my feed ground. I let them stay. What's a few extra feeds of hay a day to a big outfit? Why practically nothing, that's what. The devil with it.

WOOD TICKS

The cold weather held on doggedly but there was no shortage of feed. The colder the day, the more hay I'd put out, knowing when it was done I'd take the cattle to the home ranch where better feed awaited them. How different from that merciless winter before the Old Man sold out!

March approaching, I watched the cattle more closely. Half a dozen cows showed signs of calving. Then one morning with a cold northwester blowing, I found a new calf, off in the spruce thickets, an anxious cow standing by.

I shook my head. "Well, old girl, you've done it now, haven't you? I put you in a shed, it'll be tough on your calf when he comes out later. I don't put you in a shed, your calf'll maybe freeze to the ground where he lies."

The old white-faced cow stared at me, then at her calf and lowed softly. I shrugged and left them. Better he makes it where he is, if he can. Gets any colder, I thought, I'll get him into someplace to break the wind a little better than a spruce swamp.

It was the end of February. I had ten days' hay left. I hoped the cold would break before I moved. I rode down to the ranch one afternoon and told Rupert to expect me.

"Fine," he declared. "You'll be here in time to let Peter and me go to the bull sale."

I thought of the bull sale two years ago and smiled. At the pace I'd seen it then, I wouldn't mind missing it now. "I'll need a sleigh driver," I said, getting back to the business at hand.

"Okay. I won't send Peter up, though. You get anyone you can up there for the day and I'll settle with him when you come down. Arnold might be interested."

"Fine."

The day came that I put out the last of the hay. Arnold was disinclined to drive team, but a young immigrant Scotsman putting in the winter in a cabin a couple of miles down the road was glad of the few dollars he'd make. I arranged to meet him the next day on the feed ground, immediately after daybreak.

The temperature dropped and the wind increased. I wondered if I would ever know what it was to ride in warm saddle leather again. Two small calves in the herd now, I must put them on the rack for they'd never travel afoot.

The lariat so much stiff cable, I unbent it, swinging it out in an awkward loop. Only by herding the calves into snow over their bellies did I rope them. I bedded them with hay on the sleigh and, the team and sleigh in the lead, we started out, the cattle stringing along behind in the broken trail.

An eventless drive, I spent more time walking to keep warm than riding. A cow couldn't go anywhere, suppose she had the notion, for everywhere the snow was up to her flanks. We simply trudged along, team in the lead, herd next, cowboy last. By early afternoon we reached Holmwood, turning the cattle onto hay Rupert had put out for them in the morning, freeing two stiff calves to their anxious mothers. We went to the ranch house to eat and after settling with Rupert my Scotsman rode home on the saddle horse he'd led down behind the sleigh rack.

The weather changed in time for the bull sale. March went and by early April there was no snow left, the promise of an early green grass everywhere. The calves came, more new ones daily, until at last a whole new crop of beef makers sprinted around the meadow.

The grass began and we quit feeding. After a while we gathered the cows and calves for branding, then turned the herd out on open range near the ranch. We dehorned the yearling stock, keeping them in the field close to home to be sure they all quit bleeding properly. Between times we worked on a new barn roof and readied machinery for spring plowing and planting.

Rupert rode down to the range on the breaks of the South Thompson River one day and came back reporting grass enough to take the cattle there, all but the steers that would go on Robin's Range to the Tuscon place to finish.

So Peter and I gathered the yearlings with the cows and calves, pushing them down the road then through the light timber toward the river range. It was the first hot weather we'd had and a fine dust rose behind the cattle as we hazed them along the wagon tracks between the scattered trees.

A yearling began giving me trouble. Twice he'd drifted off and stood in a thicket. Twice I'd brought him back. Now he was at it again and he seemed sluggish about responding when I went for him in the patch of brush he'd chosen.

"Hey, Peter. There's somethin' wrong with this yearling. I think he's sick."

"He's sick or you're sick? Can'tcha cowboy a little yearling like that 'thout trouble?" We were forever joshing each other.

"No, real goods. This animal's groggy. Somethin' wrong."

We moved in on both sides of him and saw the trouble at once, a cluster of engorged ticks, fat balls the size of marbles, nested in the hide at the base of the horns.

"Ticks," Peter observed. "Ugh."

"My sentiments, exactly. Guess we got to take him back to the ranch, huh?"

"Yes, but he'll never travel. I'll have to go back for the pickup and we'll load him in. We can get the pickup in here."

"Okay. I'll wait. The cattle will move on by themselves now, won't they? Can't be more'n a mile to where we'd leave 'em."

"About that. You better stay here. This fella gets off in the woods, we'll never find him."

Peter went back and I waited until, much later, he arrived with the pickup. I unrolled my lariat but I couldn't haze the groggy beast into the open to get a throw at him.

Finally Peter took the rope. On foot, he lunged wildly after the sick animal, scaring him from the thicket and in another jump flipping the rope on him.

"See how it's done?"

"Yeah," I agreed. "I see. I been wrong all this time. Thought I was supposed to sit on a horse."

He handed me the rope and soon I had the animal to the pickup. We threw him and loaded him, tying his feet securely. Then Peter drove to the ranch to unload him in the barnyard and pluck ticks, while I followed up the cattle to be sure they reached the piece of range on which we wanted them.

What we'd found was bad news to Rupert. The wood tick, occasionally seen in the Cariboo, is often a dreaded menace on the spring ranges of the dry belt: the Kamloops, Nicola, and Okanagan country.

It is in the first warm days that the hibernating tick comes to life, climbing on nearby vegetation to drop on any animal that brushes by. Then the little parasite crawls to the vulnerable spots: the base of the horns, the flank, the whirl on the backbone at the top of the shoulders. The head buries through the hide into the flesh and the sucking goes on until the tick, engorged to the size of your thumbnail, drops away.

An animal might gather a few dozen ticks in the first warm days of spring. Chances are, he'll bear the parasite and outside of losing a little weight, be none the worse for it. But some years more than others the tick inflicts a paralysis and the grief for the rancher begins. By the time he knows he has tick trouble he might be short a half-dozen young stock, the age class particularly vulnerable.

The beast we brought in was visibly low, but the ticks once

removed, he gained ground quickly. It remained only to keep him around a few days, then turn him out once more.

But the safety of the other yearling stock was a horse of another gait. Rupert had been planning to put both Peter and me to work plowing and discing for a crop of grain and some new hay. That had to be changed.

"Alan, you'll have to start riding, every day for a while. Take two ropes with you and if you find any dopey animals, get them down and pick the ticks. We can't truck them all back here."

Every morning after breakfast then I tied a lunch to my saddle and went to ride the bush range between the ranch and the breaks of the river, a typical benchland, dry, gulch-cut and covered by a mixture of sparse pine and open grass.

The weather stayed fine, ideal, Rupert commented ruefully, for ticks. I counted the animals I saw each day to form some idea of what might be missing but more and more I began to see it was a hit and miss operation, with a lot of pure chance to it. A yearling could go down in a brushy draw somewhere and we'd be lucky if we ever saw his bones.

I watched for stock and I watched for tracks, well aware that if I saved one animal I'd pay my wages, justifying the days spent in the saddle instead of on a plow. One hot afternoon I came to puzzling signs in the dry earth near a thicket of second growth pine.

There'd been a struggle of sorts. Cloven hoof tracks, more scratched into the ground than imprinted, lay in a disarray that bespoke no direction. I dismounted but mounted up again at once for the pattern made less sense the closer I got to it.

I looked for more tracks of the same nature. There were some closer to the thicket, the ground fouled in the same way. I followed these up and saw more. Then I was riding quickly through the thicket, following the trail of a struggling beast, as fast as my eyes could pick it up.

I didn't lose the tracks again, for the signs of struggle marked every foot of the way, through the thicket, across a clearing, into another thicket, out again beyond. There lay the yearling, dead I felt sure till I saw he wasn't bloated. I dropped down at once and walked up to him.

The air grew foul with the smell, yet a rising flank assured me the beast lived. I saw the cluster of ticks at once, in sickening abundance, buried back of the horn base.

With a gloved hand I reached for his head, raising it to try to detect consciousness. I dropped it, revolted. White maggots crawled about where the moist mouth lay against the ground. I fought against vomiting, turning away until I could steel myself against the sight.

What must I do? Should I pluck the ticks now, go for the truck later? He'd only live if we gave him the best of care, maybe not then. But time lost fetching the truck might leave the crucial carrier of paralysis just long enough to kill.

I looked at the disgusting cluster of ticks and it was hard not to leave the plucking till later, especially with the revolting stench of decay coming from a still live carcass. But how alive? I spotted more ticks between the flank and the underbelly.

I cursed and spat and drew off a glove. I hunkered down beside him at his back, a chap covered knee against him, and began. One by one, the tight skinned, fully engorged ticks came out. I dug a hole with the heel of my riding boot and put them in it, grinding them all down when the hole was full, then starting another.

In half an hour I had off all the ticks I could readily find but I declined to roll him over, partly at revulsion, mostly not wanting to wrench him around too much. There'd be enough of that when we'd load him on the pickup.

I mounted up and rode for the ranch, pulling in there an hour later with a badly lathered horse. Rupert saw me coming and knowing I knew better than to lather a horse for nothing, came to the barn door to meet me.

"What's up?"

"Yearling down. Gobs of ticks. Goddamn flies been layin' on him while he's still alive. Maggots crawlin' in his mouth." Rupert made a wry face. "Put your horse in. I'll fetch Peter and you can go for him right away. Can you get the truck to him?"

"Cut a tree or two, we can. I followed him through some thickets but when he went down he was in open pine again."

I put my horse in, loosening the cinch but leaving the saddle on. Peter arrived before long and we jumped into the pickup, heading down the road at once. On the way I gave him the messy details.

All was as I had left it. We had to cut four or five small trees to drive the pickup next the yearling, but with a scrape or two we made it. He'd lost a lot of weight and loading him was no more a task than had he been a heavy fall calf.

"Think he'll live?" I asked, once we had him loaded. The smell of his mouth and nostrils forced us away as soon as we'd done.

"Doubt it. He's starting to rot already."

We took him to the ranch, unloading him in the small corral. There we set to plucking off the last of the ticks and washing around his mouth and nostrils with a disinfectant solution Peter's mother prepared for us.

A while later a car drove into the yard and two young men came over to the corral. They were employees of the entomological laboratory at Kamloops, operated by the Federal Government. Rupert was with us, watching us work on his nearly dead beef maker, and he greeted the new arrivals. He'd telephoned them that he had an animal in bad shape from ticks, and because much of their research at the lab was devoted to fighting this little parasite, they'd lost no time coming.

"Any idea how long he's been down?" one asked.

"Can't be sure," Rupert replied. "We turned the young stock down toward the river over a week ago and we brought one animal in then that was dopey with ticks. This fellow must have been loaded up at the same time, but he showed no sign of it or the boys would have noticed him."

"Maybe the early part of this week?"

"Probably." Rupert turned to me. "Tracks tell you much?"

"No," I replied. "Only that they weren't today's. Ground as dry as that, last week's tracks look like yesterday's. Course the maggots mean he was lying there several days at least."

One of the men brought a hypodermic syringe and thrust a giant needle beneath the skin of the beast, forcing into him a large quantity of a white fluid.

"That'll cure him?" I asked, doubtfully.

He shrugged. "Maybe, maybe not. We know very little about how the tick does its damage. We know nothing certain about antidotes, though we have a few hints about what we should try."

"He gets better, then that guk is the clear berries, huh?"

"Could be. Also maybe you got the offending tick off in time and this didn't do anything for him."

I could see where this scientific business had a lot of hunch and guesswork in it, at the start at least, but I saw its worth just the same. If these fellows could come up with something, it would be God-sent on the spring ranges of the dry country.

With nothing to do now for the yearling but wait, I went back to riding again the following morning. For several days I found nothing but healthy animals, building fat on their haunches with the new shoots of bunch grass.

Then one morning I came on an animal in the early stages of the staggers. I'd seen him the day before and he'd been fine. I unrolled a lariat, wondering just how much strength he'd lost and wishing to heck I'd had more practice with a rope, seeing as I was all by myself out here on the open range and a crittur to tie up and pick ticks off.

I opened out a loop, coming up behind him to start him running. Too dopey, he wouldn't run. Therefore I couldn't rope him running, to throw him on a tight rope. There'd have to be other, less magnificent means than that.

I dropped the loop on his head and took a couple of turns on the saddle horn, then struck off, dragging him to the nearest stout tree. I slipped down to the ground and moved the rope quickly to the tree, tying it securely. It's a sick animal, I thought, that would let me get away with that.

Mounted up again, I unrolled the other rope. Behind the animal, I hazed him to move him a little, tossed the loop in front of his hind legs, let him get both feet in the loop, then tightened up.

I stretched him out backwards and he fell over sideways with a thump. I jumped down and dashed for his head, squatting on him before he could rise up. Then I took the rope my horse had slackened off by this time and lashed his feet. That done, I picked ticks.

He carried a fair load but not so many as the first two. In perhaps twenty minutes I had him clean and before I was done he was struggling against the ropes with unbelievable vigour. I thought of what Rupert had told me, that I must watch out for an animal after the ticks are off, for his recovery from the dopiness of the early paralysis is sometimes instantaneous once he's clean of the parasites.

I undid the neck rope and fetched my horse. Then I loosened the rope from his feet, turning at once to the stirrup and piling aboard. The steer scrambled to his feet, stared wildly about, then trotted off across the flat. I rolled up my ropes. So much for him.

The plague was widespread, we heard by the grapevine. Scores of animals were down in the Nicola country and nearly always yearlings. Perhaps it was that the shaggy hair of the young stock made a better host of him, or perhaps all the stock got dosed up with the horrid little beggars, but only the yearlings weren't big enough to take it and went down. Still, I never saw a calf in trouble, but the way their mothers licked the little red-and-white rascals clean all the time, there was an explanation for that.

There was danger, too, to man. Every evening after work I stripped down and searched my own hide, more than once picking off a tick looking for a place to bury in. Rare though it was, children had been paralyzed and made ill — and, even more rare, killed — after playing in the sagebrush in the first warm days of spring.

Mind you, I doubt if a cowman will ever be slain by the little crittur. Once you've seen the bloated back end of the tick sticking out of the hair of a cow beast you grow so conscious of crawling things that you react at once to the least tickle on your skin anywhere: you scurry under your clothing after the eight-footed rascal no matter where he is, or you are. It can be a mighty disconcerting experience for all hands at the supper table if you divine, just before dessert, that there's a tick in your trousers.

Miraculously, the beast we'd brought in near death survived and came to his feet. His mouth and nose cleaned up and soon he was eating all we fed him. Hard though it was to believe, it would only be a matter of a week or two and he'd go back on the range. The pattern of recovery from the tick was as sudden and inexplicable as the affliction.

I went on with the daily riding, but the signs of trouble diminished. Once more I came on an animal down but knew his succumbing was recent. I'd ridden the same patch of ground the day before and he'd not been there.

I dropped down beside him with a lariat. Seeing he was quiet, I debated about tying him, then decided I should. After all, I'd feel foolish if, a few ticks left to pick, he got to his feet and made to hell out of there.

His feet bound, I plucked ticks, a disgusting task I'd finally grown fair-to-middling proficient at doing. Now I carried a small bottle of coal oil in my shirt pocket to kill the little horrors, for I'd found crushing with my heel only burst the engorged ones, leaving the small, flat, hard ones to crawl away and start over again. Now when I collected a heel-hole full, I doused them with coal oil. It killed them outright.

The last ticks off, I brought my horse handy and stood him with the reins up on the saddle horn. Then I quickly untied the rope and prodded my patient in the backbone with my toe.

He scrambled up and on the way I got a look at a mean glint in his eyeball. I suddenly realized I'd been foolish and spun for my horse, going for the saddle without the formality of a foot in the stirrup.

The old horse jumped sideways to dodge the charge of the steer and I clung for my life, knowing there'd be no place to hide at ground level. Then the yearling ran off at the gallop for he had no quarrel with my horse and I gathered up my rope. That was the last animal we found down that season and I never did ask Rupert if the yearling count was short on the feed ground next winter.

The ticks over, we turned to other tasks. We plowed and worked the rich, brown earth. We sowed grain and new fields for hay. In a few short days the age-old magic worked and the fresh green of a new crop was everywhere on the ranch.

We rebuilt a mile or more of fence on the range and finished the new roof on the barn. The two-year-old steers, taken to the finishing pastures a month ago now, became sleek and firm, rounding out into high-grade beef. On occasional trips to the range, we'd seen them there, grazing in grass to their knees. In the summer ahead, they'd lay on poundage daily. It was good to see them thus for here in large measure was the object of all our labours: good, marketable beef for the dinner tables of the nation.

Then, in my life, times changed again. Pete Douthwaite, whose business at his guest ranch hadn't turned out as well as it should, had been in the army at a captain's rank for the winter. The Korean campaign, creating a shortage of officers, had brought such men as Pete to serve again, even if only for a short time.

Nicki, his pretty wife, had been staying with Dorothy Duck while Pete was away and on his return they both remained for a visit before returning to their own place on the North Thompson. In conversation he told us about a newly devised officer-training scheme being run by the army to fill the junior commissioned ranks. I thought no more of it, then.

But the old, unsettled feelings returned. Distant fields turned green, the ones at hand seemed to wane. There was no place more like home than where I was; inexplicably I yearned to leave. I wondered what you had to have beside senior matriculation to enter the Officer Candidate School. I wondered if I might sell myself to the examining board. Wonder turned to resolution.

I joined the Canadian Army Active Force on the nineteenth day of June, 1951, two months beyond my twentieth birthday.

SOLDIER

Appearing before an examining board at the Jericho Beach manning depot in Vancouver, I qualified, was sworn in, and with several other fellows from the west coast, boarded a train on a government warrant, heading east for Ontario.

The course required a year. On completion one would take the King's Commission, to serve a three-year hitch as a junior subaltern. The first two months were to be spent in assessment and basic training at the O.C.S. headquarters in Camp Borden, sixty miles north of Toronto. The weeding out would be done here, the successful few going on to corps schools throughout the nation.

The badge of rank for the two months at O.C.S. headquarters was a white flash on the epaulet, where the second lieutenant wears his lonely star. On posting to corps school we'd wear the badge of rank of a second lieutenant, although this was changed the following year, a flash to be worn under the star until we actually received the commission.

We arrived at Camp Borden on a sunny morning in the first day or two of July. An odd mixture of young men, of every background and place in life, in only hours we were thrown together in the toughest basic training course the army had run., if I am to believe a regimental sergeant major I spoke to afterwards, since men prepared in the raw weather of northern Scotland for the D-day landing.

The aims were several: to provide basic training in the short space of two months along traditional infantry lines; to weed out the unsuitable material, applying psychological pressure on top of an overloaded physical program, waiting to see who would break up; finally, to provide some instruction in proper mess conduct and the military concept of a gentleman's refinement. This gave away the feeling of the brass that here was a desperate means of making junior officers and a damned shame it had to be turned to.

It was a tough two months. We leaped out of bed at daybreak to prepare frantically for an inspection of quarters. We marched off to breakfast and back again. We made a last check, standing by our beds at attention for the benefit of the inspecting officer. We paraded for another inspection on the square.

We drilled and went to lectures. We crawled through mud and sand. We took apart a Bren gun and put it together again. We were told how to use a knife and fork at table.

We dashed back to quarters after the evening meal to wash, scrub, iron, and polish. At ten o'clock the lights went out, supervised. At ten-thirty they came on again, unsupervised, so we could finish our multitude of tasks, a fact well known and pointedly ignored by our instructors. After five hours sleep at the most, sometimes none, we'd start all over again.

In the middle of an excruciating struggle through a roll of barbed wire or across a slimy creek bottom one would be required to give intelligent answers about yesterday's lecture material.

One would be required to memorize a message, having it repeated no more than twice. At some unknown moment, in a minute or two, or a day or two, one would be called to attention and asked for it. One never had the blasted thing.

"You forgot it? YOU FORGOT IT? What the devil do you mean, you forgot it! You, sir, are the most miserable, godforsaken excuse for a soldier ever inflicted on the Canadian Army! Corporal, he says he forgot it. Sir! Get out of here, sir! ON THE DOUBLE!"

A program was executed with overwhelming success to convince every candidate that he personally was the last dog in the pack and any day now it was off to manning depot, back on civvy street where he belonged.

To lend credence to this implication of doom, a formidable number of candidates were sent back, from the first to last week of the course, to be mustered out in ignominy, with the most possible notice each time. One class was so decimated under this system that out of a hundred starters, not twenty finished the final week.

Insult was piled upon injury, to see who'd blow up. We crawled for two days through hot sand and slimy mud. We slept in holes in the ground, ate cold food. We were hounded at, hollered at, pushed, and abused until the heart was out of us.

The third weekend we got a pass. I went to Barrie, a small town near Borden, and found what a task it was to secure a hotel room while wearing a uniform. After being refused at several desks, I carefully watched, unseen, and saw civilians given a room not ten minutes after I had been told there were none.

I confronted the room clerk with what I had seen. "All I want," I told him, "is a place to sleep where some ugly nut with sergeant's stripes isn't going to yard me out in the middle of the night to grovel around in the mud. I've only an overnight pass."

He gave me a registration card and a key. "Okay, here you are. But just so you understand, I'll tell you something. This hotel would be out of business in a year if we started letting rooms to servicemen. We tried it. All we got was drunken parties that drove away the rest of our guests. A couple of months ago we gave a room to a captain, thinking it would be all right, a guy of his rank. We had to do a complete redecoration of the room after he checked out, and we had to ask him to check out. There must have been a dozen of them rowdying up there all night and we got six bucks out of it, one double room with bath." He had a point.

After a month on course we received a three-day pass. It came in time. With many on the breaking point, it was an opportunity to rest and to rake up a little extra courage with which to hang on.

To those from the east it was home to family and friends. To those from the far west, of course, it meant Toronto or perhaps

Montreal and amuse ourselves as best we might. I put in with several more to hire a taxi to Toronto. It cost no more than bus fare if we didn't mind crowding. We assured the driver that such a privation was peanuts alongside the indignities forced on us in the past four weeks.

I took a single room at the Ford Hotel — privacy I tell you, that was the thing — the popular stopping place for servicemen. Those I came with went their ways, after we told the driver to pick us up on the Monday afternoon following as we had to be in camp by that evening. We agreed to rendezvous in the lobby of my hotel.

With half my cohorts in the town there was no avoiding them, but in all truth I'd seen enough of those faces and that khaki to want to be alone for at least one evening. I toured the bars, taking a drink with a buddy but persistently refusing to join a party. At half past eleven, no later, I went to my room, showered, and absorbed the luxury of a full size bed. I slept until late the following morning.

I had my breakfast in the hotel and read a morning paper, something I had not done for weeks. We listened to the radio in the mess every noon for the news of Korea, but there was never time for the leisurely reading that a newspaper is intended for.

Then I walked about, debating what I should do for the next three days, coming to no conclusion. A little lonely, the strangeness of the city enclosing me, I realized I knew no one within thousands of miles save the odd mixture of men in the same uniform as myself.

Tiring of the aimless walking, I stopped at a lunch counter for a sandwich and milk. At perhaps one o'clock I returned to my hotel.

On my way to the room I spied a classmate down the corridor. He hailed me. An amusing fellow, he had a room with another cadet several doors down. I went with him to his room where he poured me a colossal drink of the best in whiskey. I could see I'd have to make it last, for he held no faith in empty glasses and would fill it up again when it was empty. I thought the glow of a stiff drink would be appropriate, but I didn't want to leave his room in a condition which would prevent me from arriving safely at my own.

Another cohort sat on the bed, without his trousers, exposing a pair of regulation shorts. These are an unglamorous garment of thin cotton designed in such a way as to do none of the things which a man's shorts should do. For the sake of regimentation we had to wear them, though we thought it a terrible sacrifice to be called upon to make, even in duty to our country.

"Where," I asked, "did your trousers go? You ought to wear 'em. They aren't up to much, I'll admit, but they're a step ahead of those, ugh, shorts."

He explained that he had sent them out an hour ago with one of the party to a press-while-you-wait establishment down the street. When the fellow failed to return after a little while, another was sent after him. This was a good explanation, and we all had another drink by which fashion we established a headstart over the two somewhere out in the town in charge of a pair of khaki pants.

An hour went by and still no trousers. The whiskey was going fast. I began to look for an opportunity to leave before the party grew any wetter. Finally we detached a third man after the pants, there being men to spare as more had arrived.

Then someone explained for the first time that the trousers were a matter of some urgency. Everyone was about to go to Queen Street to take the ferry to the Royal Canadian Yacht Club, there to be entertained by Miss Shirley Mann, charming daughter of Major General Mann, then retired.

I said I thought that was fine. "I would like to suggest, however, if it wouldn't be out of the way to make a suggestion, that if you're going to go on your party you'd better do something about George's trousers and look sharp about it."

One who seemed to be in charge of arrangements — I must confess it is all rather hazy now — made a telephone call, then informed me that I too was coming to Miss Mann's party.

This shocked me. While my experience had prepared me for many things, the prospect of being proper as old billy-ho at the Yacht Club made me a little desperate, a rather plain cowboy a long, long way from the saddle. I hid what was left of my drink. Afraid of something sober, I had no intention of facing it lit up.

Then, just as we were about to send a fourth volunteer on the trouser mission, the mysterious garment appeared, accompanied by all three bearers. They made some lame excuse, but it was clear the fear of drought had struck them and they had been fortifying themselves against it in the bars. Fortunately, and I wonder why to this day, no one was unmanageable or unpresentable. We straightened our ties and went on our way.

Miss Mann was wonderful, pretty to look at, entertaining to talk to. Kind and quick to smile, she put you at your ease the moment she said hello. She attached to no one but saw to it that each one had a good time. She knew an absolute regiment of young ladies and called on them to make even numbers. She tried to ensure that anyone attending her get-together was a gentleman, but if one turned out otherwise she could deal with him. Bless the girl. I owe her much.

"I have a friend for you," she explained to me as we returned on the ferry after a sort of evening luncheon at the club. She said it as though she had arranged the creation of someone for my personal benefit, as though she knew her solely because someday I would come along and need a companion. "We're all going up to my place for the rest of the evening and on the way you'll join our Sylvia Thomson. She'll take her car. Now isn't that fine?" Of course it was fine. It was wonderful. I couldn't think what I'd done to deserve it. From being alone to being thought about had happened so quickly it was still difficult to believe in it.

Red-Gold Hair

We drove up a quiet street in an older part of the town where we found Miss Thomson, a pretty person with red-gold hair, a face finely cut, warm in her greeting but sophisticated enough to keep something back, something to stir a man and make him seek it out.

She possessed an ancient Austin car which, like the one hoss shay in the last days of its service, was waiting for precisely the right moment to disintegrate into its component parts. I was invited to step in, which I did, then propped up the window with my swagger stick.

"Now you mustn't let anything fall on the floor."

"No?" I looked down. Through a hole below me I could see the street whizzing by. "I see," I agreed. "One mustn't."

I don't claim to recall much about the evening. I wasn't tanked or anything like that, mind you, though I admit to a few small drinks. It seems I made something of an ecstatic ass of myself over a bit of music from Carmen, laying my soul out in an almost maudlin attempt at sensibility.

Why does a man, even in the green of his youth, do a thing like that? Striving to look a veritable emotional sophisticate, one comes off a Philistine at best, a damned fool more likely. Sylvia was singularly unimpressed. But she was Sylvia, no longer Miss Thomson, and by evening's end I had a promise that the following day we would go to the art gallery together, it being Sunday in Toronto.

I suppose one might as well out with it. There would be no purpose in beating about to arrive at it circuitously, for it happened with just such an unsuspected suddenness. There in the strangeness of that great Ontario city, far from the wilds of the Cariboo and the cow country that spawned me, I fell in love — hopelessly, irretrievably in love — never to be quite out of it again.

I daren't speak a word of it of course, so overcome by all her grace and that gentle aloofness with which her womanly skills protected her. We were together the greater part of the day. We walked and talked. We went to the gallery, wandering through its rooms and hallways. Why, I didn't so much as hold her hand.

It came time to part. I couldn't see her on the following day and before evening I must be back to camp. Painfully, I wanted to see her again.

"If I survive the course, I'll have a few days' leave. I could come down."

"Well, of course we think Toronto is *the* place, but there's much more of Ontario you would like to see."

"No, I think I'd like to come here again. I'll be going artillery and that means Shilo. I won't have a chance to come back until my annual leave."

"But you'd want to go home then."

How could she be so dense? But of course she wasn't really. "I'll see," I said, miffed a little at her adamant inability to get the point. Still she allowed me a warm goodbye and I rode the long trip to camp with all my thoughts about her.

We might not have been away, if anything pushed harder than ever. Devilish means were employed to test our ingenuity. A tent after the fashion of a magician's puzzle was laid out on the ground. You had to raise it, directing three soldiers to do the work, soldiers who had been instructed to be stupid. They knew exactly how to put the tent together and if you gave an order which would lead to its erection, they would deliberately misconstrue your words, bringing the whole business crashing to the ground.

Or you might be taken to a ravine where there were lengths of rope and an old frame structure, weighing two hundred pounds or more, that had braced some equipment in shipment.

"This happens to be a very valuable radar device. The success of this entire campaign depends on getting it across this gulley. Here are the ropes at your disposal. Here are the men you must direct to do the work."

It looked like a lead-pipe cinch. I had no qualms at all, come my turn. "Oh, yes," the instructor chap added at that point, "yonder gulley is a mile and a half deep. Not a gulley really. More like the Grand Canyon." That so? Jolly glad someone mentioned it. I was about to send a man to his death in the bottom of the Grand Canyon.

One could be too ingenious. In an old gravel pit sat an abandoned building. Fifty yards away was a road. One was placed in the building with three soldiers, one of whom was said to be badly shot up and must be moved, if at all, on a stretcher. To help, you do have a stretcher.

The building is your prison, unguarded, but the sentry comes by on the road, shooting you dead as a mackerel if you're caught outside. In the far end there is a vault. This turns out on enquiry to be a furnace in which you, along with your handful of loyal soldiers, are to be cremated at the going down of the sun. Horrible fate, that.

Waiting my turn, I sneaked over for a look at the layout. I saw that the sentry made a fixed tour. He went the same distance down the road each round, in the same interval of time. Once walking away, he didn't turn back until the appointed place. I timed his tour by counting and tucked the information away for reference.

I have no idea why there wasn't someone at the top of the bank preventing this sort of thing. The game had to be on the honour system if it was to be difficult and there's no honour in love and war.

My name called, I went down and of course I had the men out of that make-believe incinerator in nothing flat. There was a terrible row.

"You didn't think your way out of that! You blundered your way out of it! Why didn't you do some figuring instead of just bolting out, taking a chance on it?"

I could see I was getting a goose egg for this performance anyway so I might as well out with it. "I did figure it out while the last cadet was doing his stint."

"You what?"

"I watched from up top while Connoly was going through."

"Oh, my God!" Felt sorry for the fellow, actually. He was downright put out.

There were more tiring hours on the parade square. There were evening lectures. We wrote exams, some scheduled, some unannounced. We had mess dinners to be sure we could eat without rolling peas down the old highway on a knife blade. Finally of course we drilled for the graduation parade at which we would receive our new badge of rank.

To make it clear these practices were no guarantee, a few more chaps got the old heave-ho. Going back to manning depot for discharge was always preceded by a formal visit to the Personnel Selection Officer of the school. We made up a parody of an old spiritual:

> I looked over Borden and what did I see
> Acomin' for to carry me home,
> The P.S.O. acomin' after me,
> Acomin' for to carry me home.

There were more verses but I have forgotten them. We divided into sections in a barrack-room choir and sang this nonsense with a beautifully serious harmonizing effect. It was wonderful.

Eventually we were told, with reservations to permit an about-face, that those still present might invite friends to the parade and the dance to be held in the OCS mess. Those who could, telephoned family and friends. Those far from home nearly all had come to know some young lady and those who hadn't, set about doing so with an almost improper single-mindedness, a matter in which the chaps from the East were often a help.

Nervously, I called to Toronto, almost hanging up as I heard Sylvia coming to the telephone at the other end.

"Hello."

"Hello. That you, Sylvia?"

"Yes."

"Oh." A pause. "How are you?"

"Very well, thank you. And you?"

"I'm okay. I guess." A longer pause. "Sylvia?"

"Yes?"

"There's a sort of dance thing here for the graduation."

"That's nice."

"Most of the fellas ... I mean everybody ..." Oh, bother! "Look, would you like to come? With me, I mean."

"Thank you very much. I'd love to."

Well, what do you know. That was easy. Now, only one more problem.

"Sylvia?"

"Yes?"

"I can't very well come down to bring you up. I thought maybe if you could come to Barrie ..."

"Don't worry about that. Shirley Mann is going up and I'll go with her. We'll stay in Barrie together and you can call for me there."

And that I did. It was a magnificent evening. The senior officers wore blues while we had our summer serge pressed to a knife's edge. There was all sorts of laughing over the past eight weeks and forgiving in our hearts the officers whose very souls we had learned to curse in silent, daily hatred.

It was strange after those weeks of sweat and disappointment, of swearing under a broiling sun against the burden of the training, to be at ease in a roomful of clean uniforms and unbelievably elegant creatures, fragrant and beautifully gowned. With an almost terrifying suddenness it was over. I took Sylvia back to her hotel, myself to return to camp, more stricken than ever by this twenty years of youth and loveliness.

I went down to Toronto then for a short leave. The National Exhibition was on, and there I spent most of my days, waiting for the precious evenings when I could be with Sylvia. I met her parents, fine and worth-while people in whom you could see at once the genuine goodness they had given her. Mr. Thomson, a stern appearing man but kind, must surely have wondered about this young fellow from away out West with a more than apparent interest in his daughter.

Then I had to leave, boarding a train for Shilo, Manitoba, the artillery corps school from where I would write letters to Sylvia and with what was left of my attention from that, learn to fire a field piece.

I used to think there was no more to it than shoving some cordite behind a projectile and touching her off. This was soon dispelled. We were back in school in earnest, learning to apply logarithms, graphs, tables of all kinds, weather information, and map data to old Betsy to make her hit the target.

We received a devastating pronouncement in November. No second lieutenants were to serve in Korea and no cadets from O.C.S. could expect promotion beyond that level in the first three-year hitch after receiving the commission. This was official. Through one of our number whose father worked in the upper echelons of defence, we heard, and I use the precise words that came to us, there is a certain class of officers for whom promotion is not desirable. It took no imagination to show us where we sat.

This was a bad blow. We had all joined up for action. Most had enquired and been assured that within three years of being commissioned we would see action if Canadian troops were on a front anywhere in the world. Now we faced six months of corps training and three years of holding establishments on Canadian soil.

I knew not what to think, nor do. I spoke with a man from the preceding class, and he had decided to refuse the commission. We couldn't be compelled to serve past the one-year training period, unless we accepted the commission and signed for three years. This seemed rash, but there was no other answer except mark time in holding establishments, which my friend was not prepared to do. I had seen enough peacetime soldiering to know I didn't want to go on with it indefinitely. It was all an awkward quandary.

Once more, in fact, I was at that tiresome problem: what should I do with my life? I had thought of permanent force. To bear arms in defence of your country is in every way honourable. In war I should never hesitate. But did I want to settle for it in a troubled peace?

Someday, too, I would take a wife. I daren't hope about Sylvia, but at some vague time in the future one expects to marry. The family life of a professional soldier can be disconcerting. To see much of them at all, a man must keep his wife and children in a nearby town or have a house in the married quarters available within the garrisons. The first is costly and difficult. You have to rent. You are gouged by the landlords, who understand your plight as well as you do.

Using married quarters is a poor plan. In Shilo the townsite was described in correspondence as a moral problem. It was put off limits to single soldiers. The wives of men who had been away on duty for many months, even a year or two, were clearly partly responsible. While I should never marry a woman of that kind, I wouldn't want to oblige one I did to live in such a community. There were, of course, fine people, families of good soldiers and citizens, living there. Unfortunately, there were many of the others as well.

On enlistment, permanent soldiering wasn't a serious thought and I could decide about it at the end of the first three-year term. Now, with the adventure thrown out of it, whether to stay hinged on whether one wanted to go permanent force. Nor was there any assurance one could go permanent.

If permanent force was not a worthy objective, was there any point left in the three-year hitch? My friend had decided not and was going to refuse the commission. He so informed the authorities, who set about puzzling what you do in such a case. I bided my time.

In December several of us were posted to an independent battery at Fort Osborne Barracks in Winnipeg. We were attached for training, but still officially were part of the school. Shortly after posting, the opportunity came to take our four weeks' annual leave, so I lost no time collecting all the pay I had coming, then going down to Toronto.

How wonderful to see Sylvia again but, equally, how dismal a venture. I screwed up the courage to put my feelings on the table, as it were, and, kindly though she treated me, she hadn't the words I wanted so much to hear.

I would have returned to Winnipeg at once, but she asked me earnestly to stay. Couldn't I see how genuinely she liked me and how pleasant it would be to visit together until my leave was up? I relented but only to discover how painfully inadequate a requital liking is for love.

I hadn't enough funds to stay out my entire leave, but stay it I would, so I sought a solution to the money problem. I had civvies with me and the Christmas rush was on. Christmas means turkeys. Turkeys? I could clean turkeys. I called on Loblaw's, a retail chain organization, and soon had work to earn some extra dollars — menial, maybe, but work nonetheless. My battery CO was a proper stuffed shirt about what was appropriate to an officer in the Canadian Army, and I reflected, standing there, aproned, flinging turkey guts at a box on the floor, what a hell of a state of affairs this would have been from *his* point of view.

The Christmas of 1951, then, I spent with the Thomsons in their pleasant old house on Summerhill Gardens in Toronto.

Before the new year I left that city and I left Sylvia, sad but reconciled, resolving to take up the philosophy of the chap who wrote the song: "If I can't be near the girl that I love, I'll love the girl that I'm near."

I turned to the other problem. Would I stay in the army or leave it? The old restlessness was on me again. Where does the trail lead? I must seek it. I dreamed of the hayfields of Holmwood and the timbered wilderness of my old home in the Cariboo, suddenly loathe to stay in the regimentation of army life. A little disappointed with myself, perhaps, I made the decision, knowing sooner or later it would have to be made.

I asked to be paraded before the CO and said I would not receive the commission, that I wished to be discharged. Wheels turned, albeit slowly. In May I went to the manning depot at Jericho Beach in Vancouver. There I was discharged.

EIGHT DOLLARS IN THE STACK
AND ALL THE CAYUSES YOU WANT

I t was one of the last days before I left Vancouver that I walked along Georgia Street west of the Granville Street inter-section, thinking of Sylvia, happily now, and I saw a little wooden horse in a window, perhaps five inches tall and very neatly carved. It was months since I had written her, and though she insisted on parting that we should write for friendship's sake, I had no intention of ever doing so again. Of course she couldn't write to me, for I left her no address.

Purely on a whim, I stepped into the shop. It was a clothing and dry goods store, in a Highland theme. Tartans all over the counters, one could almost smell the heather. A salesman approached me.

"Could I help you?"

"You could if you would sell me that little statuette of a horse in the window."

The salesman smiled. "Oh, that isn't for sale. It's one of the decorations we use in our window displays."

I certainly wasn't going to press the matter. "I see," I said. Then, in explanation: "I was going to send it to a girl I used to know."

I turned to go and he stopped me, the touch of romance too much for him. "Look, we can get something else to do in its place. You take it."

"That's very good of you, but it isn't that important to me. I wouldn't put you to any trouble."

"Oh, no trouble at all. In fact, I insist. You must have it to send to her." So I took it, packaged it up, and sent it to her. I'm sure it was by habit, not intention, that I put a return address on the parcel. Nonetheless I did, and promptly a letter reached me from Sylvia, telling me her news, scolding me roundly. Amused and pleased, I wrote, and from then on the letters came and went.

I left Vancouver for Kamloops. I visited with the Old Man a few days, then went on to Lac la Hache. There I stayed at my mother's house, visiting with her when she came down from her job at the hospital in Williams Lake.

I had it in mind to go on to Kitimat, in northwestern British Columbia, where the Aluminum Company of Canada was then building its huge smelters. Visiting about at Lac la Hache, I met a fellow I knew, but not well, who had a sawmill a few miles off the highway. He needed a man in the mill and asked me if I was busy. I told him the plain truth and he chided me to take the job. I never did go to Kitimat.

I bought a truck with some money left to me in a trust fund and augmented my wages by hauling sawdust from the mill, where I could have it for the taking, to people on the highway at Lac la Hache proper who used sawdust-burning stoves and furnaces.

I worked at the mill and sold my loads of sawdust until early July. The weather was wet and by the end of June the mill was closed most days, the ground so sodden timber couldn't be brought out over the logging roads. Spreading the wages for the time one worked over the time one didn't, there was no money in working in a sawmill.

In early July I was driving past the 115 Mile House, one of the old gold-rush stopping places on the Cariboo road, when Bordy Felker, the occupant then, hailed me down. Bordy ran the Lazy R cattle ranch and had been the principal buyer of the Old Man's land. A gruff mixture of Scots and German, he had sweated his way out of poverty to a half-million-dollar cow outfit by sheer labour, grit, and thrifty living. He had done it in the last era in which one could, figuratively speaking, build a ranch out of a sack of beans and a cow, but it had been at the expense of his every waking hour.

I stopped, glad to talk with him. The wet weather had been doing him no good. With over fourteen hundred tons of hay to harvest, some under contract, much under his own supervision, I could see where he had room for some legitimate troubles.

"What the hell," he demanded, right off, "are you workin' in that sawmill for anyway? Damn near nobody left in the country that knows how to put up hay and, by God, you waste your time in a sawmill. I don't know what's the matter with you anyway. Any tramp can work in a sawmill. You got any brains, you'd take a contract and put up the Anthony."

The Anthony meadow was a place he owned on the Eagle Lake road about eight miles from the highway, about halfway to the meadows we used to own and to Spout Lake. It was good for a little over a hundred tons of hay.

"The weather the way it is, I'd be crazy to buy your grief. Keep your confounded hay. Why, if I contract the Anthony it'll start raining tomorrow and it won't quit till snowfly."

He looked at me long and hard. He declared in the most decorative collection of four-letter words I have ever heard that if it kept on raining I wasn't going to work in a sawmill either and I might as well be waiting in the rain to put up hay as go back to a smelly old lumber pile. He must have known how close to my heart was his talk. Stray as I might, I was a ranch hand away down deep.

He suspected I was weakening. "I'll give you eight dollars a ton in the stack. You can have two good teams and all the cayuses you want."

I made some quick calculations in my head. "All right," I agreed. "I'll do it."

"You better get started. Time's wastin'."

"You know where I might hire some decent help?" I didn't want to be all summer at it, so I would need a couple of men.

"Don't bother me with your troubles, I got enough of my own." I was in business.

I knew one man, John Hodges, whom I might hire and who'd be the salvation of the whole scheme if I could get him. The Old Man had found him hiking up the Cariboo road in the Depression. He'd brought him to the ranch, where Mother fed him up, and, except for the war, he'd been in and out of Lac la Hache ever since. He was never thought to be a crackerjack of a man, but he was dependable and could do more in a hayfield than most men would give him credit.

He was in Alberta and about due to itch for home, I thought, so I sent him a wire. Then, while I waited for him to show up, I rustled a camp outfit and moved to the Anthony meadow cabin. The weather brightened, so I mowed and raked a little hay for a start. When I went to the road to pick up more gear there was John, measuring out guy-line rope with Bordy.

"You made it," I observed, glad to see him.

"Sure. You didn't think I'd leave you in a jam like this alone, did you?" Good old John, he served me well.

We went to work. I didn't want to be all summer, so I tried to find more crew. We kept cutting, raking, and shocking hay while I tried by various means to pick up additional help. With a good run of weather and a couple of hands I could clean up in three weeks, and there was more hay to contract.

Once I brought into camp a couple of the kind of men you should never hire, men you know are out-and-out tramps but you take them in hopes. Neither of them had a possession in the world outside of a rugged-looking bedroll. One had an abundance of shirts which he wore all at once. Indeed, you were never sure how many, for you couldn't see the bottom one.

I detailed this one to mow hay on a cleared sidehill next to the meadow, while John and I set about raising the stacking poles. In less than half an hour the big tramp was back to the stackyard.

"I ain't mowin' hay there," he complained. "There's a gulch on that sidehill'd swallow a mower."

It was a put-up excuse and I surged with anger when I saw the man so clearly. Into camp for a couple of meals and a day's pay, this was a gimmick by which to quit or be fired.

"Take your team to the barn and wait at the cabin. I'm going to the road tonight and I'll take you out." So I took him out and when I returned to the cabin I counted my shirts, on a hunch. I was missing the best of my army issue.

The other fellow stayed a few days and did an honest job of his work while he lasted. He was honest about himself, too. A bum, he admitted his only ambition was to take his few dollars to a beer parlour and, while it lasted, get drunk and be somebody. I took him out and paid him off.

I had to finish up that pile of hay with only John to help me. I telephoned Rupert Duck knowing he would be done haying, asking if I could rent a horse-driven hay sweep. He said, sure, keep it in good condition and give me ten dollars when you bring it back.

I fetched it on my truck, and we gathered the hay then into sweep loads, dumping them all around the stackyards. We topped them with pitchforks to hold out the rain until we had all the hay gathered and could start stacking.

Then John stacked while I pushed the hay at him. With it all so close I could keep him rushed, even setting my own slings.

"You think you like to hay, John?"

"C'mon, shov'er up here! I'm sick of this meadow and all its hay. I want to get out before snowfly!"

We worked like devils. John cooked breakfast while I wrangled horses. Then we slaved with hardly a break, stopping only for a short meal at noon. Darkness alone made us lay down the tools. Day after day we pecked away at that mountain of hay, the two of us against over a hundred tons.

We moved the poles to the final stack. Then one day we gathered the last of the hay into a sweep load and pushed it up where it belonged.

I sat on the sweep, through at last, watching while John put the finishing touches to the top of the stack. "You going to stay up there for the winter?" I shouted at him.

"Not by a darned sight! Grab that cable!" He threw his fork down so the handle, not the tines, hit the ground first. I could see how he wanted to come down and I jumped from the sweep just in time to grab the derrick cable as he flung himself onto the empty slings, which were still at the edge of the stack from dumping the last load. The cable whined in the pulley, dragging me along the ground as I sought to hold him from coming too fast, maybe breaking a leg.

"Holy cats!" I exploded. "You were sure in a hurry to get offa that stack!"

"You bet! Think I was homesteading up there?"

It was good to be done. The hay measured up well and I had over nine hundred dollars coming. I paid John off and settled some other debts. Not ten days after we finished the first snow came and, while it didn't stay, it showed me how close we were to being caught with hay on the ground.

I was wondering what to do next, knowing I didn't want to go into a sawmill again, when Bordy solved the problem. "You can stay in the cabin and build some fence for me. I'll give you four hundred dollars a mile for five-rail Russel fence and I'll supply the wire."

I took the contract. There was just over a mile to build and I set to splitting rails and stakes. I worked alone, happy to have a cabin to call my own and a job to do over which I was boss, however insignificant it might be to others. I was beginning to find a strange contentment I had never known before. I puzzled on it at times, for surely nothing very great was to come from putting up hay and building fence on contract but mostly I just accepted that, inexplicably, I was free from the old inward yearnings and it was good to be free.

Living where I did, the Wrights were my neighbours on one side and the Hamiltons on the other. In the years I had been away Burt Wright had died. Now Mrs. Wright with her three boys, Stanley, Willie, and David, was running their place, but it was old times again in every way to stop by their table on the trip to the road. And a weekend frequently found me out at Spout Lake, puttering around at something for Buster, life enriched again by Millie's tenderness.

Gussy Haller had sold his place to live at Kamloops but he still visited Lac la Hache regularly, sometimes coming up for the summer to work. He stopped by the Anthony one day not long after I had finished the fence, while I was just plain living, debating what to do next.

"Gussy! How're you?" I was fond of this old rascal, truly I was.

"Oh, no so bad!"

Gussy was just along in time, though he didn't know that. I set about explaining. A few days back I had been out hunting deer because my supply of venison, my principal diet, was running low. I hadn't shot a deer, but on my way home not three hundred yards from the cabin I noticed a hole in the slope of a small rise of ground.

Curious, I dropped on my knees, putting my face in the hole, waiting for my eyes to grow used to the dark so I could see. Then I saw. I excused myself hurriedly, backing off. I'd been face-to-face with a bear, deep in the sleep of hibernation.

With little daylight left I decided against a bear war on the spot. In hibernation this calf killer would stay put till spring. I would return.

I did return, three days later. I brought John Calam, a schoolteacher chap from the settlement at the highway, who was keen to share a little excitement.

I had no idea what it would take to wake my bear. We did the soft-shoe shuffle on the roof of the den and shouted halloo there down the porthole but to no avail.

I knelt at the opening, peering in. Again I could make out the face of a bear, two eyes and a black snout, though I must not have paid much mind to the size of the beast. "I'm going to shoot, John. We'll drag him out afterwards."

I brought the rifle level, touching off the round. The sound reverberated from the pit, echoing through the forest.

With a frantic bolt a large cub rushed from the den. I shot again quickly, killing him.

Then the truth sunk home. I had been face to face with a cub, but the distinction of size had made no impression. Now there was of necessity a full-grown female inside, due out any minute to tear the hide clear off me.

"Get back, John. Right back, quickly." I had another round in the chamber, the bolt home, the safety off. Step by step, I moved away, not daring to turn my back, anxious to give myself room for shooting in that split second when life itself would depend on one well-placed shot.

But that climactic moment, anticipated by nerves that were seething to act in it, never came. Puzzled, I moved closer, telling John to ready his rifle, not to be afraid to shoot. I listened at the opening, hearing an occasional grunt and then no more.

"I can't understand it," I admitted to John. "Surely a bear couldn't sleep through like that with its den partner shot right beside it. But I have heard a hibernating bear is like a drunk man to wake."

"What do you propose to do?"

I thought a moment. "We'll skin the cub for the rug. I'll come back tomorrow and if she's left the den there's enough snow to track her. If she hasn't, I'll get her out somehow."

This is where Gussy came along, and though he'd killed a mess of bear in his time, he was delighted at yet another chase. We soon made off to the den.

All was as I had left it. There were no tracks in the patches of snow about, so one could only conclude she was still in the den. We investigated this hypothesis. Gussy picked up a stick, poking around in the den with a thoughtful look on his face while I stood ready with my rifle. Finally he withdrew the stick.

"She's dead," he declared.

"The devil you say!" I hadn't thought of that. When I wounded the cub on the first shot, had I also fatally wounded her?

"You killed her when you shot the first time and hurt the cub."

I absorbed this, then took the stick to verify it but soon concluded I couldn't tell a live bear from a dead one and quit poking about. "What," I asked, "do you reckon we should do?"

"You take this rope and crawl in the hole. You tie it on her leg and I'll pull you back out, then we'll pull her out."

"We'll do that, huh?"

"Sure!" he said enthusiastically, handing me the rope with a twinkle in his eye. I hesitated briefly, then, closing my mind as best I could to the possibility of error, dropped to the ground, proceeding into the den.

All was darkness and bear stink. There was little room to move around and I reflected what a tight squeeze it would be if the old devil out there hanging onto my legs was wrong. Then he gave me a shove with wicked delight, squealing with laughter.

"What you doing down there?" I searched around for my voice, then swore at him, disengaging myself from a bear rug. I found a foreleg, fastened the rope, and shouted to Gussy to pull me out. He did so, with difficulty, weak with delight.

Then we pulled her out and sat on the ground, enjoying our joke, taking a breather.

"What are you doing next summer?" I asked, out of the blue.

"Oh, I don't know," he replied. "Work somewhere for a few dollars I guess."

"Come work for me. I'll contract the Anthony again and the Milk Ranch as well. Maggie can cook and we'll have a devil of a good time."

"Okay," he said. "I will." I was glad of that sudden pact. After all, home is with one's people and they were my people, close as my own blood.

MAKE HAY WHEN THE SUN SHINES

 I went into the winter on the fence contract for Felker; I came out of it on a contract for Mrs. Wright, re-fencing a spring pasture a few miles east of the Eagle Lake road. The cabin at the Anthony was still my home, for I'd already completed my arrangements with Felker to hay both the Anthony and the Milk Ranch that summer.

Come fall, the haying over, I could contract more fence for him at the McKinley meadows, out in the bush on the south side of the broad Lac la Hache valley. In fact, there was work ahead as far as a man wanted to look for it.

It was a beautiful spring. Breakup came early and green grass followed hard on the last of it. Cattle turned gratefully away from the feed grounds and often I'd see a band of mule deer feeding in the fields across the Eagle Lake road from my cabin at the Anthony. Once a bear got to mucking around outside my cabin, nearly catching the dishwater in the morning when, quite unaware, I flung open the door to heave it out in an abandoned but mighty swish. He fled, all black, furry bundle of him, and I was too much at peace with the world to fetch my rifle and give chase. He never returned.

Days off, I visited Spout. The woods around my cabin turned ablaze with a million wild flowers. I'd gather an armful and take them to Millie. She'd put them in the lodge at Spout and set another place at the table. Then I'd make a little wood or do some other small chore for Buster before returning to my work.

265

I passed by Wright's place each day on the way to their fence, and many an evening meal found me sitting in their circle. It is hard to think of a better life than one spent in hard work, good health, enduring friendships, and a comfortable home in a little tracked forest.

But there is another way. One day, unexpectedly, Sylvia entered my life again. She had come west with her mother for a trip, me the last thought in her mind, in fact not in her mind at all. In Vancouver, she was puzzling what part of the province she should choose to see. Mrs. Thomson had to return at once, Sylvia had the summer. As it has now been told to me, she wondered out loud if I might be any help to her in finding a place to stay.

As quickly as the thought came to her, she put it out of mind. It would be too much trouble. Still, Mrs. Thomson suggested, there would be no harm in writing. She hesitated, not wanting to ask the favour. Then she penned a note. How odd our fate: but for a chance meeting, but for a wooden horse, but for a moment of indecision, how much would never have happened!

Her letter came. I replied at once: come to Lac la Hache and I would recommend the finest place to stay. I thought no more of it than that, certainly not to press again an old suit. Soon she wrote she was coming and I met her at the station.

How strange in the early light of a summer dawn to feel an old love stir, a love one had quite forgotten. But I held her hand only the briefest moment. I had no right, no claim to the least bit more than that. But I had strongly to remind myself of what seemed the inexorability of that fact when she rode with me in the truck cab to the Lac la Hache Guest Ranch, where I had reserved a room for her until I would take her to stay at Spout Lake.

A day or two later I took her to Buster and Millie, and, since the truth will out, I will say that I made a pact with Millie that she would persuade Sylvia to stay if she showed any signs of wanting to move. But luck had turned my way. Millie and Sylvia struck up a lasting friendship. Seeing there was a shortage of help at the lodge, Sylvia changed her status from paying guest to second cook and bottle washer, staying the rest of the summer.

Gussy and Maggie came to hay, bringing Verne with them — a fine stroke of luck, for he was a strapping man now and having him on the crew solved the help problem neatly. Good weather to work in, we soon stacked the Milk Ranch, moving then back to the Anthony, only half so far to Spout Lake.

I spent every spare moment in Buster's camp. If it rained, I'd shrug my shoulders with a what-do-you-know-we-can't-hay-in-this-weather and shove off up the road. Gussy would care for the camp and the horses, sometimes going out with his carbine to put our meat supply in order. I would rush back the moment the rain quit and furiously we would hay again. Without Gussy to attest otherwise, however, one might justly conclude that I didn't hay at all that summer.

Maybe a man seeks a woman's heart with more vantage on his own ground, or perhaps there was magic in the wild flowers of the woods we explored on a Sunday afternoon.

But how different my cause from the hopeless uncertainty of two years before! How usefully the moon spread out over the surface of Spout in an evening when, her work done, we had moments together, moments of sureness, moments to be multiplied.

It was a rough, old, bone-dry jacket, made of canvas, and I'd thrown it on in my haste to leave the Anthony when the rain had stopped us haying. Now I wished I'd had more forethought, had taken something soft and reasonable for the purpose. But no mind. There on the shore of Spout in the moonlight, her hair more enchanting in red and gold than I'd ever seen it, I must chance it.

She objected mildly to being pressed against the garment. "It's all rough." But the objection was entirely verbal.

"If I asked you to marry me, what would you say?"

"Don't ask me yet."

"I haven't. I asked you what you'd say if I did."

"I wouldn't say no."

My heart sang. We spoke no more and soon I took her back to the lodge, for, the sky clearing, I must get back to the Anthony in hope of haying in the morning.

I drove back down the Eagle Lake road and somewhere near the height of land I stopped the truck. I stepped out to look at the sky again, more professionally now. There was no cloud bank in the west, the hated sign of an invading storm centre.

I stretched, sleepily, for it was late and driving along the twisting, bumpy track of this, the road of my boyhood, made me weary. Oddly, I had stopped just at the one place from which, through the mature pine that fringed an old burn, one could see the flat expanse of the Morton meadow. Noting this, I smiled to myself and thought happily of two boys and their Old Man, of crew and horses and a herd of long-gone cattle.

Then I looked at the sky once more before I stepped into the truck to start the motor and disrupt the silence of the night. And I thought of Sylvia.

I'll make hay tomorrow, I promised myself. Just see if I don't.

Afterword
The Milk Ranch Area Today

Unlike many modern thoroughfares that have savaged their heritage in the interest of wider lanes and more blacktop, today's Cariboo Highway (Highway 97) remains lined by clusters of weathered derelicts and restored buildings that pay homage to yesteryear.

Turning north off the Trans-Canada Highway and heading up Highway 97, travellers gain a sense of the regional history at such places as Hat Creek Ranch and Clinton's Old Cemetery. The charm of the Cariboo is embodied at the 108 Ranch, which sits between the Cariboo Wagon Road and the tranquil waters of 108 Mile Lake, north of 100 Mile House.

Now open to the public, these buildings are part of the 108 Heritage Site.

In the 1860s an alternate trail to the goldfields veered northeast of the Cariboo Wagon Road toward Horsefly. It was later replaced by an improved road angling out of Lac la Hache at 115 Mile. Along this road in the 1930s lay Julian Fry's Milk Ranch.

Although 40 years have passed since *The Ranch on the Cariboo* was first published and it was 60 summers ago that young Alan Fry surrendered the family herd to a stranger north of Lac la Hache along the Cariboo Road, there remain many relics of that era.

First and foremost, the Frys' "big house" has survived. Today, a country antique dealer invites visitors into the home's main rooms.

The road beyond the main house is now paved up to the junction with Timothy Lake Road, but cattle still graze at the roadside, en route to Rail Lake and the meadows beyond. Beyond Spout Lake, more cattle than cars now use the backroads that track west only to intersect the maze of logging roads that intrudes more and more on the ranches of yesteryear.

Brothers Alan and Roger Fry in front of the extension added to the original house in about 1934. Photo on right shows the entrance as it is today with antique dealer Bernice Karlsson in the doorway.

The "big house" of today is accessible to the public most days of the week as Browse Around Antiques.

Cattle pens north of Lac la Hache along the route Alan Fry steered the family herd in 1942.

271

This ranchland at the junction with Timothy Lake Road is west of the road to Spout Lake (upper right in the background).

Historic farmlands north of Spout Lake off the Eagle Lake Road.

Grazing lands north of Alfie Meadow are dissected by fence rails over a foot in diameter.

The Felker family's ranchlands along Highway 97 near 118 Mile House on Lac la Hache are being restored as a Cariboo heritage site.

OTHER CARIBOO-CHILCOTIN FAVOURITES

5.5 x 8.5   192 pp
1-895811-59-7
$17.95

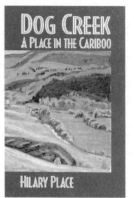

5.5 x 8.5   256 pp
1-895811-70-8
$18.95

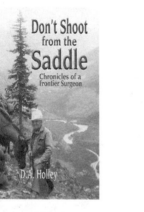

5.5 x 8.5   192 pp
1-894384-08-3
$16.95

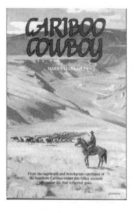

5.5 x 8.5   192 pp
1-895811-08-2
$16.95

CARIBOO CLASSICS
FROM ELDON LEE AND IRENE STANGOE

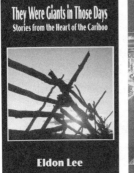

5.5 x 8.5   160 pp
1-895811-97-X
$16.95

5.5 x 8.5   192 pp
1-895811-43-0
$16.95

5.5 x 8.5   128 pp
1-895811-21-X
$11.95

5.5 x 8.5   160 pp
1-895811-99-6
$14.95

5.5 x 8.5   128 pp
1-895811-12-0
$12.95

5.5 x 8.5   160 pp
1-895811-25-2
$14.95

For other Heritage titles visit www.heritagehouse.ca

Author Bio

Alan Fry was born on the family ranch near Lac la Hache. At age twelve, he started working every school break on the ranch or, occasionally, in the sawmill. By sixteen he had earned his keep on various ranches in the Kamloops area.

Alan left ranching to complete a year at the University of Briitsh Columbia, and then joined the Canadian Army Active Force. While at Camp Borden, Ontario, he met and married Sylvia Thomson of Toronto. He returned to ranching in 1952, but two years later joined the Department of Indian Affairs.

He spent twenty years with Indian Affairs, and served as district superintendent in Kamloops, Vernon, Cranbrook, Hazelton, Prince Rupert, Whitehorse, Alert Bay, and Campbell River. He and Sylvia had two daughters, Margery and Lydia, before Sylvia died at age 39 in 1970. Alan left Indian Affairs and settled in the Yukon in 1974.

In 1980, he married Eileen Frankish. Alan and Eileen share eight grandchildren and divide their time between their home in Whitehorse and a cottage at Lake Leberge.

Alan is the author of seven books, including *How a People Die* (1970), *Come a Long Journey* (1971), *The Revenge of Annie Charlie* (1973) and *The Burden of Adrian Knowle* (1974). *The Ranch on the Cariboo* was first published in 1962.

Back cover photos (clockwise from bottom left): Cattle grazing in bushland, a homestead along the road to Spout Lake, Julian Fry's original log home, tranquil setting at 108 Mile Heritage site and Russell fence similar to that built by Alan Fry as a youth.